TRUMPETS FROM THE TOWER

BRILL'S STUDIES IN INTELLECTUAL HISTORY

PUBLISHED FOR THE SIR THOMAS BROWNE INSTITUTE
UNIVERSITY OF LEIDEN

TRUMPETS FROM THE TOWER

English Puritan Printing in the Netherlands
1600-1640

BY

KEITH L. SPRUNGER

E.J. BRILL
LEIDEN · NEW YORK · KÖLN
1994

The paper in this book meets the guidelines for permanence and durability of the Committee on Production Guidelines for Book Longevity of the Council on Library Resources.

BV
2369.5
.N4
S77
1994

Library of Congress Cataloging-in-Publication Data

94-076867
CIP

Die Deutsche Bibliothek – CIP-Einheitsaufnahme

Sprunger, Keith L.:
Trumpets from the tower : English puritan printing in the
Netherlands 1600 - 1640 / by Keith L. Sprunger. – Leiden ; New
York ; Köln : Brill, 1994
 (Brill's studies in intellectual history : Vol. 46)
 ISBN 90-04-09935-2
NE: GT

ISSN   0920-8607
ISBN   90 04 09935 2

PRINTED IN THE NETHERLANDS

To

My students,

past and present,

at Bethel College

CONTENTS

INDEXES

PREFACE

My interest in two topics merged in this book, English Puritan religion and the history of printing. The Puritan brotherhood combined a dedication for writing books and an effective program for getting them printed. My goal was to follow up on both of these aspects of Puritanism, the ideological and the technological, and to show how they reinforced one another. Hugh Broughton, Puritan controversialist extraordinary, reverenced the Bible as the "booke of all bookes." A Bible well printed, he urged, "is the glory of all Books"—all else "being bables in respect of it". However, that one book inspired the myriad of other Puritan books and, consequently, printing was, or ought to be, "for the truth of Religion". Broughton was one of the Puritans in Dutch exile; writing and getting his books printed were some of his chief activities. A unique phase of the history of Puritan printing and publishing occurred in the Netherlands. Without the restraints of English and Scottish censorship and controls, Puritan printing activities can be clearly observed.

The emphasis of the book is on Puritan, English-language printing done in two Dutch cities, Amsterdam and Leiden. The two cities, as far as Puritans were concerned, were the main centers of printing, and they functioned nearly as one printing-publishing unit. Puritans in the two cities frequently acted in concert, and when circumstances demanded or printing obstacles arose in one city, the printing would be quickly shifted to the printing houses in the other. Puritan printing and publishing in the Netherlands was part of a larger cause, not for its own sake; therefore, it is necessary to trace the relationship between Dutch printing and Puritan activities in Britain. I have asked a series of questions: Who were the authors? The printers? The publishers? The financial backers? The book distributors? What did Dutch printing mean to Puritanism as a whole?

The books produced in the Netherlands helped to galvanize and sustain the Puritan movements of Britain, the Netherlands, and America. The liberated printers and authors came out with books which raised a great commotion. Pastor John Paget of Amsterdam, cantankerous but astute, well understood what was going on when he likened the published book to a trumpet: The books spoke "as with sound of Trumpet from an high pinacle of the Printers Tower, and blowen abroad into many Countries".

The story picks up in 1600, about when Separatist Puritans began their own printing activity in Amsterdam; we end at 1640, the outbreak of revolution in England. Although the focus is on Amsterdam and Leiden, Puritan printing extended into many other cities (consider especially Rotterdam, Delft, Dordrecht, The Hague, and Middelburg), but these must await further study.

The question always arises: What do you mean by Puritanism? In this book I refer to English Calvinist dissent against established Anglican religion. This dissent, in addition to doctrine, often included opposition to church order and liturgy. Puritanism is a broad term including both Separatists and non-Separatists, Presbyterians, Congregationalists or Independents, and Baptists. The intellectual, theological currents of Puritanism also helped to inspire offshoots such as English Anabaptism and Quakerism. Not all persons of Puritan persuasion were visible nonconformists; many persons influenced by the doctrines of Puritan theology functioned within the Church of England (doctrinal Puritans).

Researching and writing a book leaves the author with a full ledger of "scholarly debts" to individuals and institutions which helped along the way. Grants from the ZWO (Netherlands Organization for the Advancement of Pure Research), the American Philosophical Society, the Huntington Library, and the Bethel College faculty development fund are gratefully acknowledged. During my 1983-84 sabbatical year, in the fall semester I was associated with the Sir Thomas Browne Institute at the University of Leiden, and this was a particularly valuable experience. I especially wish to thank the following associates of the Institute, both faculty and students, for their scholarly help: J.A. van Dorsten, director, now deceased, J. van den Berg, C.W. Schoneveld, P.G. Hoftijzer, T.S.J.G. Bögels, and J.C.M. Henselmans.

Libraries and archives are the "stuff" of the history of Puritan printing, and I thank every librarian and archivist who assisted my research. I am pleased to acknowledge the assistance of the directors and staff of the following. In the Netherlands: The Koninklijke Bibliotheek of The Hague; the Algemeen Rijksarchief, The Hague; the university libraries of Amsterdam and Leiden and of the Vrije Universiteit; at the University of Amsterdam, the Doopsgezinde Bibliotheek; the Gemeente Archieven of Amsterdam, Leiden, Rotterdam, and Delft; and the Rotterdam Gemeente Bibliotheek (the Remonstrant Collection). In England: the British Library, the Public Record Office, the Bodleian Library, Cambridge University Library, Dr. Williams's Library; and St. Bride's Printing Library. In Scotland: National Library of Scotland. In the United States: The Huntington Library, the Folger Shakespeare Library, Union Theological Seminary Library, New York, the Houghton Library, Harvard, the Library of Congress, Chicago Theological Seminary Library, University of Illinois Library, the University of Kansas Library, and certainly, at Bethel College, Dale R. Schrag, director, and the staffs of the College Library and the Mennonite Library and Archives.

Scholarly friends have also helped and offered encouragement and advice many times. I am especially grateful to P.G. Hoftijzer, editor for the Sir Thomas Browne Institute, Michael E. Moody (General Dynamics Corporation), and J. van den Berg for reading the manuscript and offering valuable suggestions. In addition to those mentioned above, I give special thanks to: R. Breugelmans, Keeper of Western Printed Books at the University of Leiden; S.L. Verheus and P. Visser of the Mennonite Library, University of Amsterdam; J. van der Haar, historian and bibliographer, for information and a visit of his personal library; P.J. Koopman, University of Amsterdam, for discussion about printer's marks and bibliography. Jeremy D. Bangs, Conservator of the Pilgrim Documents Center, Leiden, now of Plimouth Plantation, offered a great deal of help and light regarding the archives of Leiden. Also, thanks to Paul R. Sellin, UCLA; Peter Van Wingen, Library of Congress; Bonnie King for expert typing; and Allison Lemons for suggestions on translation. Above all, my thanks and love to my wife Aldine, who shared at every step of the way as we explored and searched for those "trumpets" (books) of the printer's tower.

Bethel College
North Newton, Kansas   Keith L. Sprunger

ABBREVIATIONS

AJ	*Amstelodamum Jaarboek.*
ARA	Algemeen Rijksarchief, The Hague.
BL	*Biografisch lexicon voor de geschiedenis van het Neder-landse Protestantisme*, 3 vols., Kampen: J.H. Kok, 1978-88.
BM	British Museum (British Library), London.
Bod.	Bodleian Library, Oxford.
BP	Boswell Papers, Add. MSS. 6394, 6395, British Library.
Briels, *ZB*	J.G.C.A. Briels, *Zuidnederlandse boekdrukkers en boekverkopers in de Republiek der Verenigde Neder-landen omstreeks 1570-1630*, Nieuwkoop: B. de Graaf, 1974.
Brook, *Puritans*	Benjamin Brook, *The Lives of the Puritans*, 3 vols., London, 1813.
Browne, *Congrega-tionalism*	John Browne, *History of Congregationalism and Memorials of the Churches in Norfolk and Suffolk*, London, 1877.
Burrage, *EED*	Champlin Burrage, *The Early English Dissenters in the Light of Recent Research*, 2 vols., Cambridge: Cambridge Univ. Press, 1912.
BWPGN	*Biographisch woordenboek van protestantsche godgeleer-den in Nederland*, 5 vols., The Hague: Nijhoff, 1919-56.
CSPD	*Calendar of State Papers Domestic.*
Carleton, *Letters*	Sir Dudley Carleton, *Letters from and to Sir Dudley Carleton*, London, 1757.
CR	Consistory Register.
Dexter and Dexter, *England and Holland*	Henry Martyn Dexter and Morton Dexter, *The England and Holland of the Pilgrims*, Boston: Houghton Mifflin, 1905.
DNB	*Dictionary of National Biography.*

DNR	*Documentatieblad Nadere Reformatie.*
DWL	Doctor Williams's Library, London.
ERC	English Reformed Church.
GA	Gemeente Archief (municipal archive).
Greaves and Zaller, *BD*	Richard L. Greaves and Robert Zaller (eds.), *Biographical Dictionary of British Radicals in the Seventeenth Century*, 3 vols., Brighton: The Harvester Press, 1982-84.
Gruys and De Wolf	J.A. Gruys and C. de Wolf, *Thesaurus 1473-1800, Nederlandse boekdrukkers en boekverkopers*, Nieuwkoop: De Graaf, 1989.
Harris and Jones (ed. Breugelmans)	*The Pilgrim Press...by Rendel Harris & Stephen K. Jones*, partial reprint with new contributions, Ed. by R. Breugelmans, Nieuwkoop: De Graaf Publishers, 1987.
HMC	Historical Manuscripts Commission.
Hoop Scheffer, "De Brownisten"	J.G. de Hoop Scheffer, "De Brownisten te Amsterdam gedurende den eersten tijd na hunne vestiging", *Verslagen en Mededeelingen van de Koninklijk Academie van Wetenschappen, Afd. Letterkunde*, 2^e reeks, 10 (1881), pp. 203-80, 302-99.
Hessels, *ELBA*	J.H. Hessels, *Ecclesiae Londino-Batavae Archivum*, 3 vols., Cambridge, 1887.
Hoftijzer, *Engelse boekverkopers*	P.G. Hoftijzer, *Engelse boekverkopers bij de beurs: De geschiedenis van de Amsterdamse boekhandels Bruyning en Swart, 1637-1724*, Amsterdam & Maarssen: APA-Holland University Press, 1987.
Johnson (1951)	A.F. Johnson, "The Exiled English Church at Amsterdam and its Press", *The Library*, 5th ser., 5 (1951), pp. 219-42.
Johnson (1954)	A.F. Johnson, "J.F. Stam, Amsterdam, and English Bibles", *The Library*, 5th ser., 9 (1954), pp. 185-93.
Johnson (1955)	A.F. Johnson, "Willem Christiaans, Leyden, and His English Books", *The Library*, 5th ser., 10 (1955), 121-23.
Kn.	Items from W.P.C. Knuttel, *Catalogus van de pamfletten-verzameling berustende in de Koninklijke Bibliotheek*, 9 vols., 's-Gravenhage, 1889-1920.

Kleerkooper and Van Stockum	M.M. Kleerkooper and W.P. van Stockum Jr., *De boekhandel te Amsterdam voornamelijk in de 17e eeuw*. 2 vols., 's-Gravenhage: Nijhoff, 1914-16.
Laud, *Works*	William Laud, *The Works*, 7 vols., Oxford, 1847-60.
Leiden Univ., *Album*	*Album Studiosorum Academiae Lugduno Batavae, MDLXXV-MDCCLXXV*, The Hague, 1875.
McKerrow	R.B. McKerrow, *A Dictionary of Printers and Booksellers in England, Scotland and Ireland, and of Foreign Printers of English Books 1557-1640*, London: The Bibliographical Society, 1968.
NAK	*Nederlands Archief voor Kerkgeschiedenis*.
NHK	Nederlandse Hervormde Kerk.
NNBW	*Nieuw Nederlandsch Biografisch Woordenboek*, 10 vols., eds. P.C. Molhuysen and P.J. Blok, Leiden, 1911-37.
NA	Notarial Archive.
PC *Acts*	*Acts of the Privy Council* (1613-1631), London, 1921-64.
Plomer (1641-67)	Henry Plomer, *A Dictionary of the Booksellers and Printers Who Were at Work in England, Scotland and Ireland from 1641-1667*, London: The Bibliographical Society, 1968.
PRO	Public Record Office, London.
Quick, "Icones"	John Quick, "Icones Sacrae Anglicanae", MS 38.34-35 (DWL).
RA	Rechterlijk Archief.
Res.	Resolutiën, Resolutions.
Sayle	C.E. Sayle, *Early English Printed Books in the University Library Cambridge (1475 to 1640)*, 4 vols., Cambridge: Cambridge Univ. Press, 1900-07.
Shaaber	Matthias A. Shaaber, *Check-list of Works of British Authors Printed Abroad, in Languages Other Than English, to 1641*, New York: The Bibliographical Society, 1975.
Simoni	Anna E.C. Simoni, *Catalogue of Books from the Low Countries 1601-1621 in the British Library*, London: The British Library, 1990.

STC	*Short-Title Catalogue of Books Printed in England, Scotland, & Ireland and of English Books Printed Abroad, 1475-1640,* Ed. A.W. Pollard and G.R. Redgrave; 2nd ed. by W.A. Jackson, F.S. Ferguson, and K.F. Pantzer. 2 vols., London: The Bibliographical Society, 1976-86.
Tiele	P.A. Tiele, *Bibliotheek van Nederlandsche pamfletten,* 3 vols., Amsterdam: Frederik Muller, 1858-61.
Van Eeghen, *AB*	I.H. van Eeghen, *De Amsterdamse boekhandel 1680-1725,* 5 vols., Amsterdam: Scheltema & Holkema, 1960-67; vol. 5, N. Israel, 1978.
Wing	D.G. Wing, *Short-title Catalogue of Books Printed in England, Scotland, Ireland, Wales, and British America and of English Books Printed in Other Countries 1641-1700,* 3 vols., New York, 1945 (2nd ed. revised, 1972-88).
Winwood, *Memorials*	Ralph Winwood, *Memorials of Affairs of State,* 3 vols., London, 1725.

CHAPTER 1

PURITANS AND THE PRINTING PRESS

Puritans, renowned as precise people of English religion, were disciples of the *Word*. "In the beginning was the Word", they read in the Bible, and the Word was the eternal God. Then in the sweep of sacred history, the "Word was made flesh" in Jesus Christ, teaching and preaching among us. In due time, faithful witnesses recorded in writing the messages of the Old and New Testaments. Righteous men and women produced commentaries and devotional books to aid the church. Finally, in the latter days, God's precious gift of printing powerfully multiplied the spread of the Gospel word. The printing press, to the eyes of faith, was not a machine of human invention, but a link in God's providential governance of the world. Puritans could never imagine history proceeding by chance. God is in control, "and we know that all things work together for good to them that love God".[1]

The printing press was one of these "good things" from the hand of God. As children of the Protestant Reformation, Puritans claimed this promise. They asserted that God surely had intervened in past times for the sake of Protestantism and that one of His instruments for setting the stage for reformation was the invention of printing. Many historical studies emphasize the close connection between Protestantism and printing. Across the centuries, history moved from an "oral culture" (the spoken word), to a "scribal or writing culture" (the written word), to a "print culture" (the printed word). Protestants and printing in the era of the printed word traveled together and energized one another. The Protestant Reformers skillfully utilized the printing press in the advancement of their cause. "Printing and Protestantism seem to go together naturally", Elizabeth Eisenstein has stated.[2]

---

[1] Biblical texts from John 1 and Romans 8.

[2] Elizabeth L. Eisenstein, *The Printing Press As an Agent of Change*, 2 vols. (Cambridge: Cambridge Univ. Press, 1982), especially pp. 43-44 and 306; A.G. Dickens and John Tonkin, *The Reformation in Historical Thought* (Cambridge, MA: Harvard

At the dawn of Reformation, Martin Luther turned to the printing press and the mass-produced book. As Luther's reforming activities speeded along, he gave God the glory for every victory. His God was indeed a mighty warrior and fortress. "It is wonderful", proclaimed Luther, "how at this moment in history all the arts have come to the light...like the art of book printing, God's highest and extremest act of grace, whereby the business of the Gospel is driven forward".[3] The author of many books, Luther had frequent dealings and frustrations with printers; many failed their high calling. Some printers grabbed for intolerable profits, and others settled for producing trivial work.[4] Luther hoped that the printer would be as spiritually devoted as he himself, not trivial and money hungry. The technological invention became a very significant factor in the history of the Reformation.[5] Examples of Protestant printers at the service of Protestant religion could be found in many Reformation areas. At Geneva the printing industry was one of the most important economic enterprises.[6]

The English Reformation shared in this book-inspired reform of religion. From its early days, King Henry VIII and his chief assistant Thomas Cromwell made effective use of the printed Bible and other books for rallying the English nation behind the break with Rome. For the practical politician, printing was a useful tool for the "management" of religion.[7] From the standpoint of faith, printing was a gift from the heavenlies. As the English monarchs moved toward Protestantism, printing carried the Reformation message to the people. The exception, of course, was Queen Mary, who followed a contrary

---

Univ. Press, 1985), p. 307, which refers to the topic of printing in the Reformation as "highly important".

[3] Luther's *Colloquia oder Tischreden*, in *Sämmtliche Schriften* (St. Louis: Concordia, n.d.), 22: 1658. In the Weimar edition (1912, rpt. 1967), sec 1:1038, 2:2772, 4:4697. M.H. Black, "The Printed Bible", *Cambridge History of the Bible*, vol. III, *The West from the Reformation to the Present Day*, ed. S.L. Greenslade (Cambridge: Cambridge Univ. Press, 1963), p. 432.

[4] *Luther's Works* (Philadelphia: Fortress Press, 1958-86), 48:18 and 54:141.

[5] Eisenstein, *Printing Press*, p. 378; H.D.L. Vervliet, "Gutenberg or Diderot?", *Quaerendo*, 8 (Winter 1978), p. 14.

[6] E. William Monter, *Calvin's Geneva* (New York: John Wiley & Sons, 1967), pp. 176-83. See also Miriam Chrisman, *Lay Culture, Learned Culture: Books and Social Change in Strasbourg 1480-1599* (New Haven: Yale Univ. Press, 1982), chap. 1.

[7] Arthur Slavin in *Print and Culture in the Renaissance: Essays on the Advent of Printing in Europe*, ed. Gerald P. Tyson and Sylvia S. Wagonheim (Newark: Univ. of Delaware Press, 1986), p. 100.

policy of anti-Protestantism. Her regime, however, showed a little less enthusiasm for the use of printing in any shape or form.[8] King James I proclaimed that he advanced the nation and the church "by my daily actions as by my printed books".[9]

The Church of England, under its political and spiritual lords, ministered Protestantism to the people with Bible and Prayer Book.[10] The Puritan side of the church, however, was not satisfied. By Puritan standards, the English church did not measure up to the command-ments of God or to the model Reformed churches of the Continent. Until England would be cleansed of popish-tainted ceremonies and the lordly prelacy, there was "but *a halfe-Reformation*".[11] The Separatist Puritans went further still and declared that the English church was antichristian and no church at all.

In the face of Puritanical and Catholic agitation, the authorities of church and state adopted the policies common to all European coun-tries of the "typographic age". They controlled printing presses and applied rigorous censorship. "Naughty printed books" must be repressed.[12] Dissenting opinions, whether Puritan, Catholic, or of whatever sect, were thwarted. Those who control the books of Eng-land would control the future direction, and Puritans did not much approve of the direction.

Puritans said: Papists, Spaniards, and crypto-Catholic bishops were at work to subjugate the books and spirit of England. Thomas Scott, a Puritan pastor in 1620, imagined a book plot emanating from the Spanish ambassador Gondomar. In Scott's pseudo history, he supposed that Gondomar, on behalf of Roman Catholics, could plot to monop-olize the books and libraries of England. This would disarm Protestants

---

[8] J.W. Martin, "The Marian Regime's Failure to Understand the Importance of Printing", *Huntington Library Quarterly*, 44 (1981), pp. 231-47.

[9] Kenneth Fincham and Peter Lake, "The Ecclesiastical Policy of King James I", *Journal of British Studies*, 24 (April 1985), p. 170.

[10] John N. Wall, Jr., "The Reformation in England and the Typographical Revolution", in *Print and Culture*, chap. 10.

[11] Henry Burton, *A Replie to a Relation, of the Conference between William Laude and Mr. Fisher*, STC 4154 (n.p., 1640), p. 262; G.J. Cuming, *A History of Anglican Liturgy*, 2nd ed. (London: The Macmillan Press, 1982), pp. 98-99.

[12] Proclamation of Henry VIII, in Colin Clair, *A History of Printing in Britain* (New York: Oxford Univ. Press, 1966), p. 107; Frederic A. Youngs Jr., "The Tudor Government and Dissident Religious Books", in *The Dissenting Tradition: Essays for Leland H. Carlson*, ed. C. Robert Cole and Michael E. Moody (Athens: Ohio Univ. Press, 1975), pp. 167-90.

intellectually and leave them impotent. If Gondomar should succeed in getting control of great libraries, like those of Isaac Casaubon and Sir Robert Cotton, and smaller ones as they became available for sale, Catholicism would prosper. "The most choice and singular pieces might be gleaned and gathered up by a Catholique hand". Scott vividly imagined Gondomar scheming, "I have made it a principall part of my imployment, to buy all the manuscripts and other ancient and rare Authours out of the hands of the Heretiques".[13] Scott was not the first to raise such an alarm. Earlier, John Foxe had reported that Catholic priests and friars "heaped up all Books that could be gotten, into their own Libraries" and then hoarded them.[14] Beware the evil spirits who monopolize books!

Printing explained by philosophy and history

The one great book, the Bible, was at the heart of Puritan theology. The preachers must preach the Word, and Christian believers must be attentive and obedient to it. Henoch Clapham (fl. 1595-1614), preacher at Amsterdam and London, neatly summarized a theology of the book: "The *Word* whereabout the Minister is to be imployed, is that Booke called *Bible* (of the Greeke word *Biblos*, a Booke) as being the peculiar Booke aduanced above all".[15] To serve the cause of that essential, divine Book godly writers produced other books of exposition and doctrine. Thus, the power of the divine Book became the power behind many books.

On the human level, books were clearly necessary for the functioning of national and church life. They linked the individual scholar to the heritage of the past and in the present day to an international fellowship of scholars. Many authors included a maxim or two about the value of books. For example, each book is a mirror or "index" of mind and actions, "an image of your mind, and a Discovery of that which may be looked for at your hands".[16] Thomas Brightman

---

[13] Thomas Scott, *Vox Populi*, STC 22100.6 (n.p., 1620), sig. Dlr. The *DNB* refers to Scott's writing as fabricated, "purported" history.

[14] John Foxe, *Acts and Monuments*, 9th ed., 3 vols. (London, 1684) I, 804.

[15] Henoch Clapham, *A Chronological Discourse*, STC 5336 (London, 1609), sig. F3v.

[16] *A True, Modest, and Just Defence*, STC 6469 (n.p., 1618), Epist. Ded.; Samuel R. Gardiner, ed., *Documents Relating to the Proceedings against William Prynne in 1634 and 1637*, in Camden Society, N.S., 18 (1877), p. 2.

(1562-1607), who delved into vast apocalyptic topics, declared that written books are the best authentic recorders of facts; books preserve knowledge, "being a faithfull helper of the memory". Without these, memory is fallible, and knowledge eventually would "eyther be utterly extinguished, or at the least wise corrupted".[17]

All of these opinions could apply nearly equally to hand-made manuscript books and to printed books. Puritan scholars of the early typographic age recognized that printing made a great leap forward by adding speed and effectiveness to the spreading of the message, far beyond what could be accomplished from any one pulpit or scriptorium. To print and publish meant becoming a public voice. A printed book is "a publique writing, proclaymed as it were uppon the house top", observed John Smyth of Amsterdam (c. 1570-1612).[18] John Paget (d. 1638), also of Amsterdam, imagined the published book as a blazing trumpet.[19] In the language of the time, "publication" meant to declare some news publicly and widely. Publish glad tidings. Printing a book was by far the best means of publication. The published book goes forward "to salute and pilgrimage the World".[20]

Erudite Puritans could give a more philosophical analysis of printing through the doctrine called *Technologia* or *Technometria*. The terms were used interchangeably. Technologia is a diagram of knowledge. The "Learned Doctor" William Ames (1576-1633) in his treatises of *technometria*, which blended philosophy and theology, provided a clearly defined place for "printing" and the "book". *Technometria* is the science of defining and delineating the arts according to their nature and use. It had its roots in the philosophy of Pierre de la Ramée (Peter Ramus, 1515-72), the favorite philosopher of Puritans, and even earlier in the classical lore of Greece and Rome. Ramus himself in his day had showed great appreciation for the art of printing as an aid to communication and progress.[21] According to Ramus and Ames, the task of *technometria* is to look at knowledge as a whole and

---

[17] Thomas Brightman, *A Revelation of the Apocalyps*, STC 3754 (Amsterdam, 1611), p. 161.

[18] John Smyth, *Paralleles, Censvres, Observations*, STC 22877 (n.p., 1609), sig. A2.

[19] John Paget, *An Answer to the Unjust Complaints of William Best*, STC 19097 (Amsterdam, 1635), preface.

[20] John Reynolds, *The Triumphs of Gods Revenge*, STC 20944 (London, 1635), book II, dedication.

[21] Vervliet, "Gutenberg or Diderot?", p. 16; Walter J. Ong, *Ramus: Method, and the Decay of Dialogue* (Cambridge, MA: Harvard Univ. Press, 1958), pp. 307-14.

then to define the boundaries of each and every art. When grouped together the arts are called *encyclopedia*. Using *technometria*, one took each one of the arts and spelled out its particular nature and use, however without losing sight of the overall pattern. The exposition proceeded by way of dichotomies [see chart].[22]

Art (knowledge emanating from God and directed toward good action) is divided into two parts, "its nature" and "its use". A book is a form of art, explained Ames. By its nature, "art can also be called a teaching (*doctrina*) insofar as it is taught; a discipline insofar as it is learned; a faculty insofar as it facilitates acting; a book or a system insofar as it is formed by pen or type in many letters composed among themselves and once inscribed in a book or on bark" (thesis 7, under the area of "idea").[23]

Printing, in turn, finds its rightful place in the second part of the dichotomy, under applied art or use. The use of the arts is through "faculty", and printing is one of the lower faculties, a mechanical art, within the province of grammar, associated with book making and librarianship. Printing, or typography, then "has to do with writing letters in customary characters by type. From typography arises *libraria*, bookmanship, which either puts together those things that have been transcribed by type (this belongs to bookbinders), or preserves those things that have been stored away within the bookbinders' covers (this belongs to librarians)."[24] Since the arts ultimately have their origin in the mind of God, a book reflects a divine order of things, and the printer's calling, although "less dignified" than the intellectual callings, is beneficial to society and pleasing to God. A similar Puritan Ramist treatment on the philosophy of books and printing was produced by the technometrist Alexander Richardson in his *The Logicians School-Master* (1629 and 1657). Techometria was the first philosophical step in rightly understanding books and printing.

Through the study of history, Puritans learned further to appreciate printing. The master historian of Puritans was John Foxe (1517-1577). By highlighting the role of printing in his *Acts and Monuments* (1563 and many editions thereafter), he provided the historical framework for

---

[22] K.L. Sprunger, *The Learned Doctor William Ames* (Urbana: Univ. of Illinois Press, 1972), chap. 6. The illustrated chart is a simplified version of the chart in Ames' *Opera*, vol. V.

[23] Ames, *Technometria* (1633), in Lee W. Gibbs, ed. and trans., *William Ames: Technometry* (Philadelphia: Univ. of Pennsylvania Press, 1979), p. 94.

[24] Ames, *Technometry*, thesis 139, p. 120.

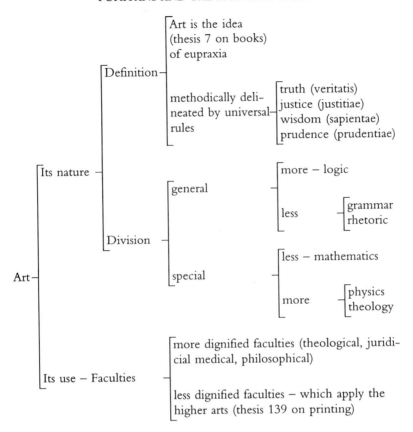

the proper Protestant appreciation of this invention. Moreover, Foxe was not only the writer of books, but himself was involved in the printing operations. He worked off and on as a compositor; and, while his books were in press, he had regular work at least once a week in the office of John Day of London. That was "our printing treadmill". The alliance between Christian author and Christian printer was well illustrated in the Foxe-Day connection: "Wherein as we haue much to prayse God for such good bookes left to the Church, and also for such Printers in preseruing by their industrie and charges such bookes from perishing".[25]

---

[25] C.L. Oastler, *John Day, the Elizabethan Printer* (Oxford: Oxford Bibliographical Society, 1975), p. 26.

Foxe was as much theologian as historian. His *Acts and Monuments*, commonly known as *The Book of Martyrs*, acknowledged God's powerful sovereign actions as the moving force in human history. Those who withstood God were enemies of Him and of His church; indeed they were persecutors and murderers. One was with God or against God. Foxe by faith discerned a providential scheme of Christian history that proceeded through five ages, beginning with Christ. The fifth age, the age of Reformation, ran from the year 1300 to the time of Queen Elizabeth. In this fifth age of history, Foxe emphasized the importance of Wycliffe, Protestantism, and among other factors, the inventions of gunpowder and the printing press.[26] He himself lived in this fifth age.

Foxe's history of the "latter 300 yeares", the fifth age, contained a spirited essay on printing, "The Benefit and Invention of Printing". He placed printing chronologically at the year 1450, just before the fall of Constantinople. The other technological wonder of the age, guns and gun powder, interested Foxe very little. Unlike the printing press, gunpowder had small potential for doing good. Like all good events, the invention of printing was a "divine and miraculous" gift from God. In the spirit of his forerunner Luther, who also sanctified printing, Foxe believed that God caused the invention of printing for the purpose of greater communication with mankind. Printing was one of those rare and extraordinary gifts, like the Pentecost gift of tongues. In olden times God spake through the miracle of many tongues to all peoples; now the Holy Ghost speaks "in innumerable sorts of Books". Regarding printing, "without all doubt God himself was the ordainer and disposer thereof".[27] With what result?

Foxe identified primarily three blessed fruits of printing: (1) The advancement of learning, enlightenment, and truth (2) The reduced cost of books, so that many more people can afford to read, and (3) The speedy dissemination of knowledge. Because of these benefits to the Gospel, the art of printing can surely be a ministry of books.

Underlying Foxe's appreciation of printing was a powerful love of Protestantism and a loathing of Catholicism. Printing's enlightenment

---

[26] V. Norskov Olsen, *John Foxe and the Elizabethan Church* (Berkeley: Univ. of California Press, 1973), pp. 69-71; Rosemary O'Day, *The Debate on the English Reformation* (London: Methuen, 1986), pp. 16-30.

[27] The essay on "The Benefit and Invention of Printing" comes in section VI, 5th age, "Pertaining to the Last 300 Years", *Acts and Monuments* (1684), I, 803-804. In the Townsend-Cattley ed. (1837), this appears in III, 718-22.

and truth was the doctrine of Protestantism, and Foxe's enemy of truth was the Catholic church. Because printing and Protestantism were so much in step, Foxe deduced that the Catholic church must hate printing and books. Obviously, the Pope survived only by keeping people in ignorance and darkness. When heroic voices like Hus and Jerome of Prague rose up, the old church persecuted them, the better to entangle and tyrannize the world ("either the Pope is Antichrist, or else that Antichrist is near Cousin to the Pope"). In the fifteenth century, at the moment of extreme need—papal persecutions everywhere—God called forth printing, His "secret operation", whereby He "began to work for his Church, not with Sword and Target to subdue his exalted adversary, but with Printing, Writing and Reading to convince darkness by light, error by truth, ignorance by learning". With so many printing presses now in existence, The Pope can never again hope to monopolize the flow of information, even through outward repression. Though "tongues dare not speak, yet the hearts of Men daily (no doubt) be instructed through the benefit of Printing".[28] When people freely have access to the doctrines of truth, Foxe confidently assumed, they will flee from Popish superstitions.

"God hath opened the Press to preach." Foxe gave several historical examples. "When *Erasmus* wrote, and *Frobenius* Printed, what a blow thereby was given to all Friars and Monks in the World." Then came "the Pen of *Luther*", and his truth would never cease.[29] In Luther's Germany, the books went to the people in their own language, "that all people may see and read upon them; and so upon the sight of the Books, they lightly follow the true light of Gods word". This Protestant light came bravely to "whole Cities and Countries".[30] With the printing press in action, the Pope's days are surely numbered, because every printing press is a battering ram, or a blockhouse, against "the high Castle of St. Angel". Foxe prophesied: "Either the Pope must abolish Knowledge and Printing, or Printing at length will root him out". Popes and priests are ever the enemies of printing, for their power depends upon "lack of knowledge and ignorance of simple Christians".[31] Foxe's historical writing was infused with confident visions of victory and a wonderful new age.

---

[28] Ibid.
[29] Ibid.
[30] Foxe, II, 333.
[31] Ibid., I, 804.

The central theme of Foxe's essay on printing was the advancement of Protestantism because of the printing press. Other advantages of printing were also sure to follow. Printed books were cheaper to produce and more available. In former times hand-copied books were so expensive "that few could attain to the Buying, fewer to the Reading and Studying thereof; which Books now by the means of this Art, are made easie unto all Men". Foxe recalled how one English-man, Nicolas Bulward, in the reign of Henry VI had paid the fabulous price of four marks and forty pence for one New Testament, but now that same amount would buy forty books.[32] Another blessing of printing was that authors could write and disseminate their writings much swifter than in olden times, to the wholesome benefit of man-kind.

> The Press in one day will do in Printing
> That none in one year can do in writing.

In short, printing books leads to more reading, "so Reading brought Learning, Learning shewed Light, by the brightness whereof blind Ignorance was suppressed, Error detected, and finally Gods Glory with Truth of his Word advanced". On this splendid note, Foxe ended his discourse on printing. "And thus much for the worthy commendation of Printing."[33] Foxe's Christian paean in praise of printing fore-shadows the future prophets of progress like Condorcet, who, in their more secular ways, saw printing as a historical turning point for the better.

At many other points in the *Acts and Monuments*, Foxe pointed out some excellent effects of printing, nearly always with a slap at the Papists. In England the popish prelates opposed printing and, consequently, reformation. In the reign of King Henry VIII, Foxe highlighted William Tyndale and Thomas Cromwell as keen English-men who understood the true connection between printing and reform. Although opposed in their good works, both persevered. Tyndale was forced abroad into exile, but from the far and near places of the Continent, he sent back books. His books "being compiled, published, and sent over into *England*, it cannot be spoken what a door of light they opened to the eyes of the whole *English* Nation, which before were many years shut up in darkness". Did the English

---

[32] Ibid., I, 755, 804.
[33] Ibid., I, 804.

receive the printed word with gladness? Most honest English people welcomed the Biblical word, but the English bishops, like popish prelates everywhere, resisted the books. "Darkness hateth light".[34]

The English Reformation at last triumphed with the royal support of Henry VIII and Edward VI. Then came another dark chapter. Queen Mary in 1553 made a desperate try to re-impose the Catholic religion upon the nation. With her tyrannous reign came fires, banishments, and new proclamations against books. The Marian persecutions provided Foxe with many of his most vivid martyr stories. Again and again, faithful Christians suffered horribly for the sake of loving and reading the English Bible and other godly books. Popish books of "manifest Idolatry" contended with Protestant books.[35]

Finally, in 1558 came the accession of Queen Elizabeth, the English Deborah, and Foxe's chronicle of persecutions ceased. Almost immediately after its publication, Foxe's book established itself as the authoritative historical interpretation of the English Protestant church. The Puritan group of the English church thoroughly approved of Foxe's combination of theology, history, anti-Catholicism, and English patriotism. Whether Foxe himself should be identified as a Puritan or more generally as an "English Protestant" is a matter of debate. Regardless, nearly every Puritan praised Foxe as a brother in convictions; he was their indispensable historian, except on the most recent events. There was one important addition, however, one more chapter which Puritans of succeeding generations must add to Foxe's history—the chapter of recent Anglican persecutions. With the reign of Queen Elizabeth (1558-1603) Foxe assumed the end of English martyrdom and the victory of the English Reformation. Many Puritans saw it in a very different way.

Puritans often complained that the Church of England, as reconstructed by Elizabeth, was only partially reformed and that the new Anglican prelates, like Catholic prelates of previous times, continued to persecute and murder sincere nonconformists. For Puritans of uncompromising views, the bloody age of martyrdoms never ceased. Puritan books were as much banned as before, and the prelates of Elizabeth, James I, and Charles I hindered many Puritan activities. Puritan writers insisted that they must tell this story. Henry Ainsworth, the Separatist leader, prayed "that God will one day rayse up another

---

[34] Ibid., II, 302-303.
[35] Ibid., III, 226.

Iohn Fox" to write an updated book "of his later martyrs, for the view of posterity".[36]

The message that Anglican persecutions had replaced and perpetuated Catholic persecutions runs steadily through many Puritan writings. An early, albeit subtle, version of this Puritanized account of history occurred in Thomas Cartwright's *Confvtation of the Rhemists Translation* (written in the 1580s, printed in 1618). Following in the footsteps of master Foxe, Cartwright explained that the Catholic church for selfish reasons did not allow the Bible and other pious books to come into the hands of common people. Bishops and inquisitors withheld the Scriptures, persecuted common people who read them, and caused a "night of ignorance". Nevertheless, the Bible is the most necessary book, containing "milke" and "strong meates" in every book, chapter, and almost every verse. In former times controlled by the Catholic church, readers were rare, and few could personally "reade, reason, dispute, turne and tosse the Scriptures". In newer times, the printing press was in action and the ordinary people could read, "easie meanes...to disperse the copies into the hands of every man". Everyone should learn to read, Cartwright stressed, every age, every sex, and every degree. The printed Bible is "easily and lightly obtained" by tailors, smiths, artificers, and women "through the benefit of Printing".[37] Then, after penning these hopeful words, Cartwright had his own book suppressed by the "Protestant" bishops.

Cartwright's challenge in writing was to refute and demolish the Catholic doctrines. In so doing, he experienced the Puritan dilemma of presenting a critique of Catholic ceremonialism based on the Bible and Protestant simplicity and finding that these very criticisms applied almost equally well to Anglican ceremonialism. Was the enemy Rome or Canterbury? Without explicitly attacking the established Church of England, Cartwright's implication was all too clear—"distastful passages, (shooting at Rome, but glancing at Canterbury)".[38] Seeing the double message, Archbishop Whitgift in 1586 stopped the printing of the book, which consequently lay unpublished for a generation. Except for a small part in 1602 at Edinburgh, the full book did not

---

[36] Reported by John Paget, *An Arrow against the Separation*, STC 19098 (Amsterdam, 1618), p. 253.

[37] Thomas Cartwright, *A Confvtation of the Rhemists Translation*, STC 4709 (n.p., 1618), Preface to the Reader.

[38] Thomas Fuller, *Church History*, 3rd. ed., ed. James Nichols (London, 1842), III, 70.

appear until 1618, when it came forth from William Brewster and Thomas Brewer at the secret "Pilgrim Press" at Leiden.

The same kind of Puritan interpretation was woven into numerous books printed in Puritan print shops. The "Pilgrim Press" produced several books, in addition to Cartwright's *Confvtation*, with an explicit statement about the blessings of Protestant printing presses. Among these books celebrating printing was a new edition in 1617 of Thomas Whetenhall's *Discourse of the Abuses*, originally done in 1606 by Jones' secret press. Whetenhall was an "ancient Christian Gentleman", self-appointed to administer a sharp rebuke to the ceremonious prelates of the Church of England. Of particular interest here is his historical sketch of the role of printing in Christian history, which he praised as one of God's three preparatory works leading to the Reformation. The first two preparatory works were Hus'reforms and the little sparks of the Gospel surviving in Bohemia. "Whereunto the third preparatiue was the admirable gift of God, and the blessed art of PRINTING." In His own wisdom, God kept the art of printing secret for a long time and finally revealed it at the moment in history when it would do the most good. Luther and Zwingli used both preaching and printing as Protestant weapons. Through printing "of innumerable books" the light of the Gospel spread everywhere. The Reformation succeeded "by *Preaching* and *Printing*".[39]

Another "Pilgrim Press" book, the anonymous *True Modest and Just Defence* (Leiden, 1618), formerly languished for fourteen years, unable to find a licensed English publisher. The only recourse was to go to the overseas printery at Leiden. The preface described an unceasing combat between the English Saints and Antichrist, i.e. between Puritan Christians and Anglican bishops. Much of the struggle was a battle of books, but in earthly terms, unless God intervenes, it was an *Impar Congressus*, an unequal struggle. The prelates controlled the printing presses, stationers, booksellers, and even "lothsome prisons at their command, wherein they shut us up". Nonconforming Puritan authors suffered.[40]

The anonymous *Certaine Arguments and Motives* (Amsterdam, 1634 and 1635), also hailed printing, in the spirit of Foxe, as a timely work of God. "*Printing* by the blessing of God hath beene a speciall meanes

---

[39] Thomas Whetenhall, *A Discovrse of the Abuses*, STC 25333 (n.p., 1617), "To The Reader" and pp. 73-75.

[40] *True, Modest, and Just Defence*, To the Reader, sig. A3v.

of spreading and divulging the Gospell in the Christian world in these latter times." And yet, this *"rare mystery, and most noble and famous* Art" is in danger in England from lordly bishops who censor and repress books; "the *Archbishops* and *Lord Bishops* of England are the maine hinderers of the free passage of the Gospel". They are wretches and vipers.[41] In book after book, one can hear a bitter Puritanical voice, adamantly anti-Catholic and strident against the Church of England's strict control of books and printing.

Commissioned by god for a ministry of printing

God had given Protestant Christians a great commission for preaching and printing. There were also great obstacles. To accomplish the Gospel ministry of books, many willing hands were required: Authors, printers, financial backers, publishers, booksellers, shippers to transport (and sometimes smuggle) books, and readers with open hearts. At the center of this network, of course, was the wonderful printing machine. Working together, with the machine, they were sufficient for "Plotting, Contriving, Composinge, Printing, Publishing, and Spreading of the book".[42] In the famous Martin Marprelate enterprise, at least twenty-three different persons collaborated in the printing and distribution of the books.[43] Clusters of Puritan brotherhoods in many areas were successful in producing and handling books which "passe underhand from man to man amongst them". These Puritan networks at the time were famously known: the "light brotherhood of *Non*-conformity"; the Cataline Conspiracy of books; "(*Cataline*-like) firebrands".[44] Stephen Foster's description is the "Caroline Underground" of "conventicling and clandestine publishing".[45] One of

---

[41] *Certaine Argvments and Motives*, STC 739 (n.p., 1634), pp. 3, 17-19; 2nd ed., STC 739.5 (n.p., 1635), pp. 3, 19-21.

[42] "Speech of Sir Robert Heath", in the Alexander Leighton case, Star Chamber, June 4, 1630, ed. Samuel R. Gardiner, *Camden Miscellany*, N.S., 14 (1875), p. 2.

[43] Leland H. Carlson, *Martin Marprelate, Gentleman* (San Marino: Huntington Library, 1981), p. 21.

[44] Peter Studley, *The Looking-Glasse of Schisme*, STC 23403 (London, 1634), pp. 257-58, 282; Patrick Scot, *Vox Vera*, STC 21863 (London, 1625), p. 35; Scot, *A Table-Booke for Princes*, STC 21860 (London, 1621) p. 157.

[45] Stephen Foster, *Notes from the Caroline Underground* (Hamden: Archon Books, 1978), p. xii.

their printed books of a few hundred copies, if well managed, was "more then enough" to nourish (or "poyson") an entire kingdom.[46]

The language of religion was applicable to writing and printing. The *pen* is a "consecrated" instrument, and in the hands of a devout author would be directed toward instruction, charity, the profit of the soul, and to the favor of heaven.[47] The *printer* should yield himself to God and be inspired "by the Lords leave".[48] The *printing press*, if used righteously, will advance the "glorious kingdom of Jesus Christ".[49] In spite of obstacles laid down by political and ecclesiastical authorities, Puritanism maintained itself quite vigorously for many decades; and certainly one of the large reasons for this sustained strength was its supply of books. In an age when the printing entrepreneur, reportedly, was backsliding into lukewarm religion and self-interest, Puritanism seemed to attract the loyalty of sufficient London printers, or printers overseas, willing to print Puritan books, often at some risk to their careers and fortunes. In the sixteenth century, this corps of Puritan printers included such stalwarts as John Day, Robert Waldegrave, Thomas Vautrollier, and the entire secretive "Martin Marprelate" group. "How praiseworthy" are such printers, said John Foxe.[50] In the seventeenth century Puritans gained very good service from John Bellamy, Michael Sparke, Matthew Simmons, Benjamin Allen, and Livewell Chapman, to mention just a few.[51] When the need for putting out a book was great, a printer, either in London or abroad, could almost always be found.

The printer's words of service to God often were at variance with the careless workmanship and errors contained in the printed books. Every book had its page of errata, where the printers begged pardon for the faults. "*Humanum est errare*", they said; we are doing the best we can.[52] Many authors complained that the quality of workmanship was

---

[46] Leighton Case, *Camden Miscellany*, p. 2.

[47] Reynolds, *Triumphs of Gods Revenge*, STC 20944, Author's Re-Advertisement, sig. A6v.

[48] Foxe, *Acts and Monuments*, II, 306.

[49] John Canne on his work of printing; see Champlin Burrage, "Was John Canne a Baptist?", *Transactions of the Baptist Historical Society*, 3 (1913), p. 230.

[50] O'Day, *Debate*, p. 26.

[51] Leona Rostenberg, *Literary, Political, Scientific, Religious & Legal Publishing, Printing, and Bookselling in England, 1551-1700: Twelve Studies* (New York: Burt Franklin, 1965), I, 97-129, 161-202, 203-36.

[52] H.S. Bennett, *English Books & Readers 1603-1640* (Cambridge: Cambridge Univ. Press, 1970), p. 208.

too low. The printer was a businessman with an investment to protect;
thus, a religiously inspired printer or bookseller was hard-pressed to balance his two convictions of service to God and profits. Was it enough
to simply gain a profit? Of course not. Nonconformists of conscience
pointed to certain despicable printers and booksellers who had poor
workmanship and would print anything for a price, "such lukewarme
gospellers and trades-men, that care not by what sordid meanes, and
superstitious filthinesse they enrich themselues".[53] Michael Sparke, one
of the printing zealots, knew another printer, a shame to the trade, who
would work for anyone who could pay, "if the *Devill* himself".[54]

On the other side of church opinion, Bishop Laud also complained
mightily about poor printing. He summoned several printers before
the High Commission to answer for careless printing errors. In 1631
Robert Barker had to come to court for his "Wicked Bible", which
contained the grievous misprinting of the Seventh Commandment
("Thou shalt committ adultry") and for using poor paper. Laud
scolded Bible printers, whatever their religious ideology, for desiring
"gaine, gaine, gaine, nothing els". Their sincere goal should be "to
benefitt the people".[55] Chrisman's study of sixteenth-century printing
at Strasbourg at first described the high commitment of the early
Reformation printers, followed in later years by the waning of printing
zeal.[56] The Strasbourg situation, by Laud's testimony and Puritan
complaints, repeated itself in other Protestant areas, including England.

Authors who went to Amsterdam for their printing found good
facilities available, if one paid the bill; but these were hardly sanctified
presses. The Dutch printers gladly produced books for Catholics,
Protestants, or Jews. As in England, printing was a business that had to
pay its own way. The Dutch printer "sets more store by his own good
than by the general good...".[57] Whether the Puritan book was any

---

[53] *Boanerges. Or the Hvmble Supplication of the Ministers of Scotland*, STC 3171.3
(Edinburgh, 1624), p. 30.

[54] Michael Sparke, *A Second Beacon Fired by Scintilla*, Wing S4818BA (London,
1652), pp. 7-8.

[55] S.R. Gardiner, ed., *Reports of Cases in Courts of Star Chamber and High Commission*, in Camden Society, N.S., 39 (1886), pp. 296-97, 305. A. S. Herbert, *Historical Catalogue of Printed Editions of the English Bible 1525-1961* (London: British and Foreign Bible Society, 1968), p. 162, referring to STC 2296 (Exod. 20:14).

[56] Chrisman, *Lay Culture, Learned Culture*, p. 30.

[57] David W. Davies, *The World of the Elseviers 1580-1712* (The Hague: Nijhoff,
1954), p. 139, referring to Willem Janszoon Blaeu.

the better or worse for coming from a secular or a Puritan-owned press is uncertain, but Puritans always preferred dealing with printeries commanded by like-minded religious believers.

After finding their printers, Puritan authors and publishers had to find their readers. Many complex questions about literacy and readership relate to this topic, more than can be treated here. Puritanism emerged in England at a time of rising literacy and high appreciation of Bible reading.[58] England, especially London, had a rather high proportion of literate citizens, for the time; Amsterdam had a similar unusual rate of literacy.[59] Puritans in England and the Netherlands took good advantage of this situation by appealing to the literate Christian, and in the process of so doing, further advanced the growth of literacy. In practical terms, Puritans, not having the ear of monarch or bishops, had to reach new audiences. Moreover, the Puritan theology of *sola scriptura* assumed that knowing the Bible required the ability to read for oneself, or, at the least, having a reader close by. William Tyndale, Foxe's hero of the English book, had high hopes for the outreach of his Bible work, that "if God spare my life, ere many years I will cause a boy that driveth the plough shall know more scripture than thou dost". These words, which echo Erasmus, were his dare to the prelates.[60] Thomas Cartwright blessed literacy as a Protestant tenet. Whereas Catholic oppressors are fearful of allowing the Bible in the hands of "euery Husbandman, Artificer, Prentice", Protestants desire that every man, woman, and child should be able to read.[61]

Like the German Protestants, the Puritans of England found printing to be the most advantageous way to reach the widest range of readers, from the erudite down to the common man and woman. As outsiders excluded from power, Puritans went beyond the usual English Protestant audience and aimed quite far up and down the

---

[58] John Morgan, *Godly Learning: Puritan Attitudes towards Reason, Learning, and Education, 1560-1640* (Cambridge: Cambridge Univ. Press, 1988), pp. 159-61; Lawrence S. Stone, "Literacy and Education in England 1640-1900", *Past and Present*, 42 (1969), 69-139; David Cressy, *Literacy and the Social Order: Reading and Writing in Tudor and Stuart England* (Cambridge: Cambridge Univ. Press, 1980), pp. 1-5.

[59] Geoffrey Parker, "An Educational Revolution? The Growth of Literacy and Schooling in Early Modern Europe", *Tijdschrift voor Geschiedenis*, 93 (1980), p. 214.; Cressy, *Literacy*, pp. 72-73.

[60] *Cambridge History of the Bible*, III, 141-142.

[61] Cartwright, *Confvtation*, sigs. B2-B4.

social and economic scale. For the "downscale" audience, the book must be clear, interesting, and cheap. The Separatists were the masters of reaching the lower and poorer audience with their blunt and cheaply-printed tracts. More respectable authors might not want to stoop down to the bottom of the heap, scorning those little Separatist treatises. The "Sectaries" publish them purposely like that, "knowing, and foreseeing, that bookes of that size, and of small price, are both more readily bought up on all hands, especially of the common people, whose favour they hunt and hawke after; and more greedily read, and more easily understood, then large, tedious and deere discourses".[62] Puritanism found support at several levels of society, with the plowboys who carried the Bible "at the plough in the field",[63] and with the gentry and the substantial merchants. A good many English and Scottish merchants of the European trade financed book printing or engaged, on the side, in transporting and smuggling Puritan books from Holland to England.

Wherever Puritan religion took hold, the Bible and other edifying books had an appreciative readership.[64] One result of Puritanism's emphasis on personal book reading was to sanctify religious devotions, apart from public worship, for the individual in the household. Worship and preaching were essential to religion, but the preacher had to trust that the household with proper instruction could become God's little sanctuary.[65]

The printed book was one of the major instruments for preserving the Puritan fellowship in the face of opposition. Through books, new splinters and sects of Puritanism found a voice and survived for a time, as is evident from the history of English Separatists and Anabaptists. The scattered Separatists, despised by the "world", found a bond of unity by reading books by Francis Johnson sent from Amsterdam; these were the books "aboue all bookes next to the holy Bible". In them they "reioyced exceeding".[66] Books were a good seed planted

---

[62] Thomas Rogers, *Two Dialogves*, STC 21241 (London, 1608), sig. B1v.

[63] Studley, *Looking-Glasse of Schisme*, p. 23.

[64] J.T. Cliffe, *The Puritan Gentry: The Great Puritan Families of Early Stuart England* (London: Routledge & Kegan Paul, 1984), p. 158.

[65] Morgan, *Godly Learning*, chap. 8.

[66] John Darrell (or Dayrell), *A Treatise of the Church*, STC 6286 (London, 1617), sig. A2v.

by authors and printers in the hearts of men and women. "Oh reade, reade for Gods sake..."[67]

Freedom versus order

Puritans called for "freedom" to publish their books. This Puritan desire for book freedom ran counter to the widely-recognized state requirement to maintain the political and social order through control of the press. Every country of Christendom, with the possible exception of the Netherlands, followed this prudent policy. From the inception of English printing, the government attempted to control the printing industry. Puritan attitudes toward freedom, however, were very ambiguous. The complaint against regulation and the call for book freedom was not an absolute Puritan principle, but rather a plea that good (orthodox) books be allowed without opening the door to books of erroneous opinion. Faced with too many restrictions on their message, Puritans required a situation where "it may be lawfull...to reply...and to publish". Frederick S. Siebert interpreted the issue of Puritan freedom as follows, that Puritanism's objection was not against all regulation *per se* but "against the application of these restrictions to themselves".[68]

However, the assessment that Puritanism was thoroughly hypocritical regarding freedom may be too harsh since at least a few early seventeenth-century Puritans believed that nonconformity for oneself extended into a broad doctrine of freedom of expression for everyone. Leonard Busher, a Puritan who turned Anabaptist at Amsterdam, in *Religions Peace* (1614) wrote in favor of liberty of conscience and against religious persecutions of any kind. He included a call for freedom "to wryte and print as we wold". Such a policy, he argued, will never be dangerous to the king or the state.[69] Years later, in 1643/44, an "old English Anabaptist at Amsterdame" sent a similar printed admonition to the Westminister Assembly pleading for full

---

[67] *Boanerges*, p. 2.

[68] Fredrick S. Siebert, *Freedom of the Press in England 1476-1776* (Urbana: Univ. of Illinois Press, 1952), p. 89; Henry Jacob, *A Christian and Modest Offer*, STC 14329 (n.p., 1606), p. 6.

[69] Leonard Busher, *Religions Peace*, STC 4189 (Amsterdam, 1614), pp. 28-29; William R. Estep, *Religious Liberty: Heritage and Responsibility* (North Newton: Bethel College, 1988), pp. 41-44.

liberty of conscience for all sects. It seems likely that the old
Anabaptist prophet of liberty of the 1640s was Busher, who was active
in the Netherlands well into the 1650s.[70] Busher's position on religious liberty, however, was rare.

Most Puritans, in tune with the English opinion of the time, were
fearful of opening the gates to error and anarchy. The common view
among Puritans was that some opinions simply did not deserve a
hearing; after all, St. Paul at Ephesus gave an example by presiding
over a burning of wicked books worth 50,000 pieces of silver. "So
mightily grew the word of God and prevailed" (Acts 19:19). Thomas
Cartwright noted this same incident in his commentary on the English
Remists' version of the New Testament. They teach that "superstitious, heretical, and all hurtfull bookes must be made away" (Acts 19)
but he did not comment on it one way or the other.[71] Henry
Ainsworth, Separatist, and John Paget, orthodox pastor of the English
Reformed Church at Amsterdam, exchanged arguments on this topic.
Ainsworth thought that the burning of the books at Ephesus produced
a loss beyond good sense. In those books "doe you not think there
were some good things also?"[72] Paget responded that certain books
are worthy only of burning, and he used as examples recent writings
by Bellarmine and Vorstius, having been "of late justly burned by
divers Christian Princes".[73] More freedom for books, but not the
freedom of anarchy, was the Puritan principle. Most Puritans favored
a middling position that would allow a wider range to books to come
from the presses, while at the same time restricting the flow of Catholic and Arminian opinions. Finding that proper middle position—between "hindering the books" and license to publish
error—proved to be a very difficult task.

The businessman's perspective on economic freedom for printing
came from Michael Sparke, the printer of London. Long an enemy of
the printing monopolies, in 1641 he spoke out in print strongly against
monopolies, which restrict freedom of printing, harming the honest

---

[70] Robert Baillie, *The Letters and Journals of Robert Baillie*, ed. David Laing
(Edinburgh, 1841-42), II, 121 (about a printed sheet from "an old English Anabaptist
at Amsterdame", Jan. 1, 1644), Burrage, *EED*, I, 276-79 (which states that Busher was
at Delft Dec. 8, 1642). Busher's name can be found in the archives of the Waterlander
Mennonites until at least 1651 (GA Amsterdam).

[71] Cartwright, *Confvtation*, p. 309.

[72] Henry Ainsworth, quoted in Paget, *Arrow*, p. 250.

[73] Paget, *Arrow*, p. 255.

printer and the nation by keeping prices artificially high. Monopoly price "picks the Subjects pockets". However, by 1652 Sparke in the *Second Scintilla* had grown weary of the flood of sectarian tracts, which he attributed to excessive press freedom. Sparke, like others pondering the meaning of freedom, after years of revolution, read Acts 19 about the apostolic book burnings in a new way and found it very relevant to his day.[74] Now he understood how a degree of book control was sometimes necessary.

The government's traditional program for press control relied upon regulation of the printing industry through the Stationers' Company and a licensing of all books by a board of censors. Censorship was in the ecclesiastical hands of the Archbishop of Canterbury, the Bishop of London, and their assistants. The Tudor machinery of press regulation arose from a series of proclamations and decrees (1538, 1557, 1559, and finally the finishing touches in the all-encompassing decree of 1586). Various amendments occurred, all for the purpose of closing loopholes in the law and having more firm control.[75] The stated policy of Tudor magistrates was the security and welfare of the state through regulation. At the same time, the Tudor politicians and bishops understood that management of opinion required not only repression of dangerous opinion but also proclamation of good opinions in books. The people of authority were active writers on behalf of the Prayer Book and episcopalianism.

Puritan responses were many. Some authors thought they could soften their message a little and slip through the censorship. A more resolute Puritan response was to bypass the licensing regulations altogether and bring out the Puritan side of the issues through surreptitious printing presses. This action was illegal and punishable by severe penalties. Printing disobedience, nevertheless, occurred regularly. Although worldly authorities would forbid books, Puritan authors were in tune with a higher power, and their books were assuredly under the patronage of Jesus Christ Himself (the original Puritan).[76] The annals of Puritan printing revealed many famous book martyrs, including John Field and Thomas Wilcox for the *Admonition to Parlia-*

---

[74] Michael Sparke, *Scintilla, or a Light Broken into Darke Warehouses*, Wing S4818B (London, 1641), p. 5; Susan A. Stussy, "Michael Sparke, Puritan and Printer", Diss. Univ. of Tennessee, 1983, pp. 81-82.

[75] Siebert, *Freedom of the Press*, pp. 47-63.

[76] Henry Burton, *A Replie to a Relation*, "To the Kings Most Excellent Maiesty"; Gardiner, *Documents Relating to Prynne*, p. 2.

ment (1572), and the never-to-be-forgotten Martin Marprelate (1588-89). Although the Martin Marprelate group was at last smashed, this printing enterprise inspired later generations of Puritans, who hoped for a resurrection of Marprelate's printing zeal. Marprelate was a Puritan printing legend.[77]

The most furious episodes of Puritan book controvercy occurred in the regime of William Laud, Bishop of London (1628-1633) and Archbishop (1633-1645). He resolutely supervised ecclesiastical affairs and made strict printing regulation a central activity. The Star Chamber Decrees of 1637 were Laud's masterpiece. These were designed to be the ultimate seventeenth-century program of book and printing control. Had these decrees functioned as intended, every printing press and every author's manuscript would have been minutely supervised, and each book produced would have obediently served the higher powers.[78] At the same time, for economic reasons, members of the Stationers' Company welcomed certain regulations, regarding the number of presses and the like, as a way to reduce domestic and foreign competition.[79]

Although printing regulations against nonconformity were always unappreciated by Puritans, the Laudian program was the most hateful of all, because it was so efficiently focused on repression. The Archbishop's delight in control of books made the Puritans rage—but what could they do? "It is well knowne that his watchfull eye is fixed upon nothing more then Pamphlets..."[80] When the tide finally turned in 1640, Laud's impeachment articles contained particular accusations about his book policies: "His countenancing of Books and their Authours for the maintenance of his unlimited and absolute power, wherein the power of the Parliament is denied, and the Bishops power of Prelacie set up". He was further charged with "stopping of books

---

[77] In 1640, if not before, the "Mar-Prelate" imprint once again began to appear, for example, *A Dialogue Wherin Is Plainly Layd Open the Tyrannicall Dealing of Lord Bishops against Gods Children*, Published by Dr. Martin Mar-prelat, STC 6805.3 (1640); Christopher Hill in *TLS* (Sept. 18, 1981), p. 1052.

[78] Cyprian Blagden, *The Stationers' Company: A History 1403-1959* (Stanford: Stanford Univ. Press, 1977), pp. 117-25.

[79] Sheila Lambert, "The Printers and the Government, 1604-1640", in Robin Myers and Michael Harris, *Aspects of Printing from 1600* (Oxford: Oxford Polytechnic Press, 1987), pp. 1-3, 16-17.

[80] Robert Baillie, *Ladensium*, STC 1206 (n.p., 1640), pp 27-28.

from the press, both old and new, and expunging some things out of them".[81]

Laud's decrees of the 1630s functioned on two fronts; first he upgraded the vigilance of the book censors, a corps under his supervision. Next, Laud's people had full access to the printing presses, and they were commissioned to produce many books supportive of ceremonial religion. Enforcement was in the hands of the Star Chamber and the High Commission. In this regime many books by Puritan authors, especially treatises which formerly would have gained an official imprimatur or approval, were now rejected. Among the rejected writings were eagerly sought expositions on divine sovereignty, predestination, Sabbath observance, and the Pope's antichristian activities. "Our Presses formerly open onely to *Truth* and *Piety*, are closed up against them both of late." While such writings gathered dust, unprinted, other books favoring prelacy, ceremonies, Arminianism, and neutrality toward Popery had an easy time. Faced with such a horrible situation—"deplorable Newes"—Puritans raised the alarm about an insidious book plot. The supposed mastermind behind the plots, of course, was Laud.[82]

There were many Puritan versions of the prelatical conspiracy against good books. Some of these plot-and-conspiracy stories went back to the eras of Bancroft and Abbot. The least that could be said, according to concerned Puritans, was that the bishops eternally hindered the printing of worthwhile books. They "smothered" them.[83] Hugh Broughton was a bit extreme on this matter and for many years accused his archbishop of evil and murderous designs. Broughton hovered over his books as if they were his own flesh-and-blood children. Then, Bancroft attacked the books and "imprisoneth about a thousand copies". Will he forever pursue his plot "Layd to kill me"?

---

[81] On Laud's long drawn-out impeachment, and the writing of additional articles, see Charles Carlton, *Archbishop William Laud* (London: Routledge & Kegan Paul, 1987), pp. 215-24; *Articles Exhibited in Parliament against William Archbishop of Canterbury 1640*, STC 15310 (n.p., 1640), art. II; Laud, *Works*, IV, 262.

[82] William Prynne, *Newes from Ipswich*, 3rd ed., STC 20470 (1636), p. 1. For restriction on books about Sabbath observance, see James T. Dennison Jr., *The Market Day of the Soul: The Puritan Doctrine of the Sabbath in England, 1532-1700* (Lanham MD: University Press of America, 1983), p. 94.

[83] Alexander Leighton, *An Appeal to the Parliament*, STC 15429 (n.p., n.d.), p. 114; *The Fall of Babylon*, STC 1101 (n.p., 1634), pp. 85-87; L. F., *A Speedy Remedie*, STC 10649 (n.p., 1640), pp. 66-67.

Broughton lived abroad in fear and anger.[84] Certain Puritan authors
and printers about 1618 suspected that Abbot was scheming to destroy
every Puritan book. This point of view was presented in *True, Modest,
and Just Defense* (1618), printed by the Brewster-Brewer press. "We
must, at our great charge and hazard, hire the printing of ours in some
other Land." No legal sale of Puritan books, and "if they be taken by
the Bishops, are burnt, or otherwise utterly suppressed".[85]

Puritans of the 1630s were ever ready to believe stories about
Popish or Laudian plots.[86] The most thorough case against Laud for
conspiring against good books came from William Prynne. Among
many charges, Prynne exhaustively accumulated evidence about
Archbishop Laud in matters of printing. Prynne had personal evidence,
in his own mutilated body, about Laud's "bloodiest, unjustest"
methods. *Canterburies Doome* (1646) contains this story. Laud's book
policies, according to Prynne, were only one aspect of a much broader
scheme, namely (1) to introduce ceremonies and images into the
Church of England, (2) to introduce Arminian tenets as a bridge to
Popery, and (3) to wickedly control pulpit and press as the means of
establishing his own "erronious positions". The aim was "reconcili-
ation between us and *Rome*". In pursuit of these goals, Laud ruthlessly
molded the press into his servile tool. He prohibited books that
exposed his errors of crypto-Papism and Arminianism. He prohibited
the English Genevan Bible. When some books finally received permission to be printed, they often had valuable passages purged out.[87]

Prynne presented information that Laud was not satisfied to police
the realm of England, but also extended his repressive policies to
English printing in Holland. Prynne's evidence against Laud was based
on copies of a good number of letters between the Archbishop and his
informants in Amsterdam and The Hague (Boswell's letter of September 20/30, 1633, the information of M.S., April 14, 1638, and letters

---

[84] Hugh Broughton, *An Answer untho the Complaint*, STC 3844.5 (n.p., 1609), sig.
A2v; *A Petition to the Lordes Chancelours*, STC 3877.7 (n.p., n.d.); sig. B2r.

[85] *True, Modest, and Just Defence*, sig. A3v; also *Certaine Argvments*, 1635, p. 19.

[86] Caroline M. Hibbard, *Charles I and the Popish Plot* (Chapel Hill: Univ. of North
Carolina Press, 1983), pp. 3-18 ("Popish Plotting in Perspective").

[87] William Prynne, *Canterburies Doome*, Wing P3917 (London, 1646, pp. 178, 250,
441-43; Hibbard, *Charles I and the Popish Plot*, pp. 239-42. Cf. Sheila Lambert,
"Richard Montagu, Arminianism and Censorship", *Past and Present*, no. 124 (1989),
pp. 58-68, for the view that Calvinist theological books continued to be easily
available.

from Johannes le Maire of Amsterdam). This added up to "cleare Evidence", pronounced Prynne, that Laud was an enemy of "Orthodox Books" and even "endeavoured to hinder the Printing of them abroad in Forraign parts". The result of Laud's prohibiting and purging was to produce an English equivalent of the Catholic *Index Expurgatorius*. Heretofore, such a rigid control of the press existed "onely in Romish Babel".[88]

Why did Laud persist in this course against good books? The Puritan answer was clear: For fear that the Genevan Bible and the Puritanical books "should over-much instruct the people in the knowledge of the Scriptures". He desired to keep the people in darkness and his own power intact.[89] When brought to his unhappy trial, Laud's response to the charges against him was logical in its way. He had done all in his power to protect the good order of the church and state. He repeated the old arguments of Bancroft and Abbot, that censorship alone could restrain "Anabaptisicall" and "factious and schismaticall" persons.[90] As shepherd of the sheep, a bishop must be the guardian of preaching and books. "So my care was against all underminings, both at home and abroad, of the established doctrine and discipline of the Church of England." "Where's the Fault?"[91]

Many nonconformist authors and printers tested the system with bloody, gory results. While some offenders rushed into Dutch or American refuge, escaping with their bodies intact, the slower-footed ones were brought to judgment before the Star Chamber or High Commission. Punishment of the 1630s included the whip, axe, knife, pillory, jail, and branding iron. These repressions fed Puritan outrage and produced "martyrs" of the book.[92] Such were the stories of Alexander Leighton (1630), William Prynne and printer-publisher Michael Sparke (1634), Prynne, John Bastwick, and Henry Burton (1637), and John Lilburne (1638). The bloody trail led back to Laud. Puritans promised that a final reckoning would come. Never forget "the slitting of *Bastwickes* and *Burtowns* nose, the burning of *Prinnes*

---

[88] Prynne, *Canterburies Doome*, pp. 179-85, 244, 347, 349. Most of the documents used by Prynne about Laud's foreign activities on printing are found in SP 16 and SP 84 (PRO).

[89] Ibid., p. 183 (misnumbered, follows p. 180).

[90] Bancroft letter, Feb. 9, 1605/06, Winwood, *Memorials*, II, 195; Abbot, Feb. 9, 1626/27, in Browne, *Congregationalism*, p. 78.

[91] Laud, *Works*, IV, 263-64.

[92] Carlton, *Laud*, pp. 80, 124.

cheeke, the cutting of *Lightouns* eares, the scourging of *Lilburne* through the cittie...the murtheringe of others by famine, cold, vermine, stinke, and other miseries...".[93] Persecuted book martyrs like these suffered for righteousness' sake and would be counted among the "Martyrs in white" of Revelation 7.[94]

Sustained by convictions nearly unshakable, the Puritan network of authors, printers, and financial sponsors continued their surreptitious book enterprises in secret and out-of-the-way places. Soon after the Prynne-Bastwick-Burton spectacle in Star Chamber, hidden authors produced little tracts attacking Laud and posted on crosses and pillories in Cheapside—the pillory for Laud being most appropriate in these circumstances. These anonymous tracts proclaimed that the Archbishop "had his hand in persecuting the Saints, and shedding the blood of the Martyrs".[95]

The secret, anonymous method of writing and printing was not heroic in the style of Prynne and Leighton, but much safer. Was the route of anonymity cowardly? An anonymous Puritan writer replied that there was no choice. "Consider what a dangerous and scoffing age this is."[96] To speak up publicly in print, advertised with one's own name, was "publiquely to take up Christs crosse, and so to follow him", even unto death.[97] There were other roads of discipleship than reckless martyrdom. Friends of Samuel Hieron of Modbury, Devon published at least two of his books abroad without names of author or printer, "nor was it safe at that time" to do so. Had his name been affixed, "a thousand to one", he would have suffered ejection and misery.[98] Anonymity also had the example of the Bible. The author of the book of Hebrews wrote anonymously, and who could condemn the model of Scripture?[99]

The printers of unlicensed books wisely omitted their names in most cases and tried to use common type and ornaments. Prynne once

---

[93] Baillie *Ladensium*, STC 1206, preface, sig. B3r; Foster, *Notes*, chaps. 3-5; Siebert, *Freedom*, pp. 122-25.

[94] J. Henric, *The Curtaine of Church-Power and Authoritie*, STC 13071 (n.p., 1632), p. 9.

[95] William Prynne, *A Breviate of the Life of William Laud*, Wing P3904 (London, 1644), p. 21.

[96] John Richards, *Crowne of a Christian Martyr*, STC 21009.5 (n.p., 1634), The Publisher to the Reader.

[97] Henoch Clapham, *Errour on the Right Hand*, STC 5341 (London, 1608), pp. 3-4.

[98] Quick, "Icones", I, i, p. 84.

[99] English Reformed Church, Amsterdam, CR, III, 42 (GA Amsterdam).

provided a London printer with an unusual ornamental capital letter, which he had obtained elsewhere, to use in printing one of his controversial books. The aim, of course, was to make the typography of the book puzzling and unrecognizable.[100] Another common Puritan printing strategy was the fictitious title page, giving a false name or place of printing. This might be an English-printed book, claiming that it had been printed in Amsterdam or Rotterdam, or the opposite, a Dutch-printed book claiming to be from London. The false title page emboldened the author and printer to try a touch of fantasy and bravado. Authors like these spoke: Theophilus, Cosmophilus, and Didoclavius.[101] The printer abode in exotic places: Helicon, Paradise, and Elesium. One book was printed "at the signe of the blew Bitch in Dog Lane" and "Transported ouer sea in *a cods belly*".[102] The book is done, "thankes be to God. And he only wil keepe vs from the searchers rod". Find us if you can!

> Imprinted we know where and whan
> Judge you the place and you can.[103]

Nonconformist writing and printing in England always had risks, and this led to the search for alternative printers and locations. Certain books were hazardous to write, print, and possess. "Threatened dangers make men afraid to read our bookes."[104] In these circumstances the printing presses of the Netherlands provided a great service.

---

[100] *CSPD*, Charles I, 1637, pp. 174-75, 543-44.

[101] Scot, *Vox Vera*, pp. 3-4; *Dies Dominica*, STC 26115 (n.p. 1639).

[102] See for examples, books by Thomas Scott, B.D., which used many fanciful locations on the title pages; Katherine S. Van Eerde, "Robert Waldegrave: The Printer as Agent and Link between Sixteenth-Century England and Scotland", *Reniassance Quarterly*, 34 (Spring 1981), p. 41. John Taylor, *Taylors Revenge*, STC 23804 (Rotterdam, i.e. London, 1615).

[103] Title page of *Certaine Articles*, STC 10850 (n.p. n.d.), c. 1572.

[104] *True, Modest, and Just Defence*, sig. A3r.

CHAPTER 2

THE OPEN DOORS OF DUTCH PRINTING

Whenever the opportunities for Puritan printing diminished in England, the doors opened in Holland. God always provided for His own, Puritans believed, and when one door closed, He opened a different one. "And if our fountaine be dammde up in one place, God will open it in another."[1] The Dutch Netherlands with its renowned printing resources offered many opportunities for English and Scottish nonconformists. Although not convinced of the freedom of all printing, Puritans cherished for themselves the Dutch freedom to express their ideas and to print them. Nearly from the dawn of English Protestantism, the Low Countries served as a haven for nonconformist English Christians. Safe in their Dutch sanctuary, Puritans and other dissenters could set up churches, schools, and print shops "in exile". These kept up the momentum of Puritan activity. To meet their printing needs Puritans smuggled papers for publication beyond the seas and then smuggled the printed books back to England or Scotland. Puritan believers in England, Holland, and even America received many "a choyce piece" in the form of books from Amsterdam.[2]

Printing books was one of many Puritan activities in the Netherlands. A large settlement of English and Scots lived there in the sixteenth and seventeenth centuries. By career they were merchants, artisans, soldiers, or perhaps they were abroad as students, scholars, and travellers. These overseas British people had financial resources for religious causes, which included support for refugee preachers, churches, schools, and payment for the printing of worthy books. The backbone of the Dutch Puritan movement was in the English churches of the Netherlands. Amsterdam had, off and on, ten English-Scottish churches before 1640, two of them surviving until the end of the

---

[1] Quick, "Icones", I, i, 494-95.
[2] "The Stationer to the Reader", in Henry Ainsworth, *The Old Orthodox Foundation of Religion*, Wing A810 (London: E. Cotes for Michael Sparke, 1653).

century, and Leiden had two English churches. Several of these churches were good-sized congregations with 300 or more members.[3] Even though driven abroad, the English and Scottish nonconformists conducted themselves like active participants in the home struggle, and they always seemed to have good and "probable intelligence" of all the news. Amsterdam and Leiden were the two leading cities of Puritan activity, the headquarters of a large Dutch Puritan movement in exile, but the nonconformists also found refuge at Rotterdam, Delft, Utrecht, Middelburg, and elsewhere. The Puritans of the Netherlands were ceaseless in "preaching, pressing, printing", and they practiced "presbyterian" and other forms of innovative church discipline.[4]

Overview of English printing in Holland

Printed books from the Dutch presses moved almost daily across to England and Scotland. Although Puritanical religious books were the most famous, the total output of Dutch-English printing consisted of many kinds of books. The Dutch printers excelled in quality of printing, but what commended Holland most wonderfully to Puritan writers was the relative freedom of printing. Many topics too hot for the printers of London and Edinburgh found a favorable printing reception in the Netherlands. Books on Puritan theology, Parliamentary affairs, and warnings about Arminianism and Spanish plots at Court regularly came from the Low Countries. The authorities of Britain felt obliged to keep a close eye upon all English-language printing in the Netherlands, lest dangerous opinions of any kind gain a foothold.

Whatever the message of the book, the Dutch printers were willing and equipped to handle the job—with few questions asked. By the estimate of H. de la Fontaine Verwey, the seventeenth-century Dutch Republic was so active in printing that it produced perhaps half or more of all the books of the century printed in the entire world.

---

[3] On the English and Scottish churches, see K.L. Sprunger, *Dutch Puritanism: A History of English and Scottish Churches of the Netherlands in the Sixteenth and Seventeenth Centuries*, vol. 31 of *Studies in the History of Christian Thought* (Leiden: E.J. Brill, 1982).

[4] *A Record of Some Worthy Proceedings*, STC 7751.2 (n.p., 1611), preface; SP 84/146/40.

Dutch printers did "better work for smaller wages".[5] These books came out in a myriad of languages of which English was only a small part. However, for the survival of Puritanism, this Dutch Puritan outpost of printing played a critical role. For some Puritan authors, the Dutch printed works composed 100 percent of their writings.

There was another market for English-language books from the Netherlands. Dutch printers found it very profitable to print English books for the general reader; and the printers' quality and efficiency of operation made the Dutch highly competitive in sales. Bibles, grammars, concordances, and atlases all sold well when shipped over to England due to excellent quality and reasonable price. Because such books were protected in England by monopoly, the Dutch printers of this illegal trade obligingly produced false title pages so that the books could easily blend into the English bookshops. Thousands of Bibles printed in Holland carried the title page, "Imprinted at London, 1599". Such falsification was simply considered a necessary business practice, not dishonesty or unethical deception. One Amsterdam printer boasted that his shop had printed more than a million English Bibles, enough for every English or Scottish plow boy or servant girl to have one.[6] Puritan authors often insisted on anonymous or fictitious title pages in order to protect their own safety. Since so many books appeared with anonymous or false title pages, a complete listing of English and Scottish books from Dutch presses will always remain partly conjecture.

Here and there a bit of light shines upon the anonymous dealings of the Dutch-English book enterprise. A very complete description of English printing in Holland, although covering only a few months of 1637-38, came from "The Information of Matthew Symmons". Simmons (or Symmons), an English printer working at Leiden, was forced to give information to the magistrates in late 1637 or early 1638. This insider's report showed the many aspects of Dutch-English printing; it consisted, of course, of Puritan polemics but also many unauthorized editions of standard works. Of recently printed Puritan treatises, Matthew Simmons reported the following: Books written by

---

[5] H. de la Fontaine Verwey, "The Seventeenth Century", in W.G. Hellinga, *Copy and Print in the Netherlands* (Amsterdam: North Holland Publishing Co., 1962). p. 29; idem, *Uit de wereld van het boek*, III (Amsterdam: Nico Israel, 1979), pp. 9-10.

[6] I.H. van Eeghen, "De befaamde drukkerij op de Herengracht over Plantage (1685-1755)", *AJ*, 58 (1966), p. 83.

John Bastwick, William Prynne, George Gillespie, Richard Sibbes, John Preston, Thomas Hooker, and Samuel Ward (coming from the presses of Jan Fredericksz Stam, Amsterdam; John Canne of Amsterdam; Willem Christiaensz of Leiden; and James Moxon of Delft). Two merchants of Rotterdam were producing a book by John Robinson. Simmons also reported many ordinary books aimed for the English and Scottish markets: English Bibles by Moxon, Christiaensz, and Stam; Lewis Bayly's *Practice of Piety* by Johannes Janssonius of Amsterdam; editions of Lily's *Rules* and *Grammar* by Christiaensz; and Clement Cotton's *Concordance* by Henry Tuthill of Rotterdam. These books of 1637-38 were produced in editions varying between 1000 and 5000, and some even "by tenn thousand at a time".[7]

Shipments of books in this quantity into Britain, seemingly year after year, were truly a danger, because such Puritan books could undermine official Anglican religion and the non-controversial books, cheaply priced, could undermine the prosperity of the general English-Scottish book trade. Dutch printing, a salvation to the Puritans, posed an unpleasant threat to the English printing industry.

Many English printers complained about undesirable Dutch competition, especially "the imprintinge of the English Bible and other priviledged bookes there"; and the Privy Council and other high officials gave the printers a sympathetic hearing. This situation threatened to bring unemployment in England and the unregulated printing from abroad often turned out to be "lewde and seditious bookes or phamphlettes".[8] However, no easy solution could be found. In the 1630s Archbishop Laud examined the issues thoroughly, and his analysis was gloomy. He repeated some of the old complaints of James I. A large part of the books from Holland were illegal Puritan tracts and Geneva editions of the Bible, full of alarming opinions and according to James I, "untrue, seditious,...dangerous and traitorous"—written in a "desperate way". Other ordinarily worthwhile books, such as Bibles without the notes and concordances, were also dangerous because of their excellent sales value. "For the books which came thence, were better print, better bound, better paper, and for all the charges of bringing, sold better cheap." Asked Laud: "Would any man buy a worse Bible dearer, that might have a better more cheap?"

---

[7] SP 16/387/79. The information was collected in late 1637 or early 1638; it was received in England April 14, 1638.

[8] PC *Acts* (1601), New Ser. XXXII, 14-15.

Laud's campaign against Dutch printing, consequently, was necessary for economic as well as religious reasons. "There was a great and a just fear conceived, that by little and little, printing would quite be carried out of the kingdom."[9]

On the point of Dutch printing, Michael Sparke, in nearly every other matter a critic of Laud, concurred in part. The Stationers' Company was worried. In the *Scintilla* (1641) Sparke acknowledged the great success of Dutch printers in the English market, although he blamed Laudian censorship and monopolistic practices for a major part of the problem. The "*Holland* Bible" in English by the thousands of copies came over "and sold very reasonable" at about half the English price. Latin Bibles from Amsterdam also came in, "printed well...and good paper". Sparke pointed to Cotton's *Concordance*—kept artificially expensive in England by the monopoly—and skillfully printed beyond the seas; "brought over, and sold at half their prise". The painful result? "Pitty the manufactory should be carryed thither by deare selling here."[10] It has been estimated that a quarter of all Bibles sold in England for a large part of the seventeenth century were printed in Holland.[11] Whether for economic, political, or religious reasons, the Dutch printing presses won a significant share of the English book market.

Puritan messages by book

What constitutes a "Puritan book"? The variety of "Puritan books" and treatises appealing to Puritan readers was large. For the purposes of this study, the emphasis will be on books printed in the Netherlands and written by authors of the Puritan persuasion. The little book, *English Puritanisme* by William Ames and William Bradshaw (1605 and 1610), printed several times thereafter, contains a succinct statement of many of the main Puritan concerns. Bradshaw was author of the main body of the work and Ames in the Netherlands did the preface of the re-edited version in 1610. According to Ames, the main beliefs and practices of Puritans were these: (1) They desire a purified church; (2)

---

[9] Laud, *Works*, IV, 262-63; VII, 544.

[10] Michael Sparke, *Scintilla*, Wing S4818B (London, 1641), pp. 3-5; Susan A. Stussy, "Michael Sparke, Puritan and Printer", Diss. Univ. of Tennessee, 1983. p. 81.

[11] Stanley Morison, *John Fell: The University Press and the "Fell" Types* (Oxford: Clarendon Press, 1967), p. 42.

They strive for personal and public righteousness, which calls for a reform of manners and morals, Sabbath observance, prayers, good conversation, and the shunning of stage plays, swearing, drunkenness, masking, dicing, and all unholy reveling; (3) Their absolute authority is the Bible.[12] Bradshaw's part of the book emphasized worship and the nature of the church, which he defined as non-prelatical and centered in the local congregation. Although the Ames-Bradshaw treatise could not speak for all Puritan concerns, and indeed was controversial in its ecclesiological definition of the church, the two authors raised many of the critical and enduring Puritan concerns.

Taking the *corpus* of the Dutch-Puritan printed books as a whole, several themes and topics stand out.

1 Bibles. The Dutch presses produced Genevan editions long after the English presses ceased printing that variety of Bible. There were also Bible study aids such as concordances and commentaries. These "Holland Bibles" also had a price advantage over other Bibles.

2 Books of Piety. Non-controversial volumes could be printed at home; some with high sales potential were printed on both sides of the water. Several books of pious exhortation had printings in Holland to serve the English churches in the Netherlands; among these were Thomas Goodwin, *Aggravation of Sinne* (1639), "Printed for the benefit of the English Churches in the Netherlands", and Thomas Hooker, *The Sovles Preparation for Christ* (1638), "for the benefit of the churches in the Netherlands".

3 Separatist books. Nearly all books by the Separatist giants, Francis Johnson and Henry Ainsworth, and other Separatist writers before 1640 had to be produced in the Netherlands. This was also the case with the English Anabaptists John Smyth and Thomas Helwys.

4 Puritan (Separatist and Non-Separatist) attacks on abuses in the Church of England. Fervent topics were ceremonies and prelatical tyranny. Purer forms of church government (Congregational, Presbyterian, Anabaptist, and the like) were proposed.

5 Distinctive Puritan theological doctrines. Topics that went out of favor in England in the Laudian era still had access to the printing presses in Holland. These perennial Puritan topics included predestination, strict Sabbath observance, anti-Arminianism, and fiery anti-Catholicism.

---

[12] Ames preface to *English Puritanisme* (1660 ed.). The Ames preface first appeared in the 1610 Latin ed.

6 Millenarianism and Visionary Eschatology. Thomas Brightman's prophetic books, for example, were first printed in the Netherlands.

7 Christian writings about the Jews. Hugh Broughton, while stationed in the Netherlands, wrote profusely about converting the Jews. John Harrison, Leonard Busher, and John Paget were other writers on this topic.

8 Political Analysis. Many books about Parliament, the Spanish menace, and political malfeasance—very dangerous topics—found their printing birth abroad. Thomas Scott's books about the Spanish plots at court are good examples of this type of political Puritanism.

9 Scottish affairs. Nonconformist Scots needed the Dutch presses as much as the English nonconformists (including such notable Scots as David Calderwood, Samuel Rutherford, and Robert Baillie).

10 Worship forms and aids. Although disdaining the English prayer book, many Puritans used Calvinistic worship forms and guidelines. Schilders of Middelburg printed three editions of the Puritan-approved *Booke of the Forme of Common Prayers* (1586, 1587, and 1602). About 1640 a translation of the Dutch liturgy was printed in English (Leiden, STC 16560.5).[13]

Puritan printing in the Netherlands, 1600-1640, went forward in stages, depending upon the world situation of the time. First, 1600 up to 1620, the Separatists were mostly in charge and Separatist controversies predominated. Second, 1620-30, political and religious issues regarding the Thirty Years War, Catholic plots, and Arminianism were uppermost. Third, during the 1630s, the main concerns were the English and Scottish struggles against Laud. The other topics listed above were mixed in throughout.

The puritan alliance of press and church

After a small beginning in the sixteenth century, the Dutch production of English books rose remarkably in the seventeenth century. A clandestine network of authors, printers, and financial backers developed effective channels for printing and distributing books. Existing channels of trade and travel were utilized, and the Puritan book people developed new routes for moving books. The English and Scottish

---

[13] Daniel James Meeter, "The Puritan and Presbyterian Versions of the Netherlands Liturgy", *NAK*, 70 (1990), pp. 52-74.

churches in the Netherlands closely allied themselves with the book networks. Nearly every preacher was active in writing books or aiding their publication, and the money for paying the bills often came from the members of the congregations. At Amsterdam the Brownist "Ancient Church" was always at the center of book activity, with elder Giles Thorp, and pastor John Canne, and others serving as printers. At Leiden elder William Brewster was a printer. George Waters, deacon of the English church at Dort, was a printer; and at Rotterdam, James Moxon housed his press in the English church building.[14] In addition to the churches, the brotherhood of Puritan books was able to draw substantial help from several other English and Scottish institutions in the Low Countries, especially the English-Scottish merchant groups and the English regiments. Many an English and Scottish merchant, pillars of the congregations, and sympathetic Dutch merchants, transported parcels of books into Britain and gave money to support exiled authors or pay for printing. "I sent my book over by a Dutch merchant", explained John Bastwick.[15] Sixteenth-century English merchants aided authors, such as Tyndale, in going abroad where they could write in safety, and this practice continued into the seventeenth century as well. Hugh Broughton, William Ames, and Robert Parker are examples of authors who received stipends to go abroad and write.[16]

The Merchant Adventurers at their staple ports at Middelburg, Delft, and Rotterdam always supported a preacher and a chapel. Their preachers were nearly unanimously illustrious Puritans, and several times the merchants paid to have books by their preachers put into print. This Merchant Adventurer subsidy proved to be an excellent aid to Puritan book publishing. The Scottish nonconformist John Forbes (c. 1568-1634) had several books printed by the merchants; his book on justification (1616), he said, was "wrytten at the desyr of the

---

[14] Sprunger, *Dutch Puritanism*, pp. 70-76, 308, 313-14.

[15] John Bastwick, *A Briefe Relation of Certaine Speciall and Most Materiall Passages, and Speeches in the Starre-Chamber*, STC 1570 (n.p., 1638), p. 13.

[16] John Foxe, *Acts and Monuments*, 9th ed., II (London, 1684), p. 210; Hugh Broughton, *Works* (London, 1662), preface by John Lighfoot, sig. a2v; Matthias Nethenus, "Praefatio Introductoria" (on Ames) (1658), trans. by Douglas Horton, in *William Ames by Matthew Nethenus, Hugo Visscher, and Karl Reuter* (Cambridge: Harvard Divinity School Library, 1965), p. 4.

company of Merchand Aduenturers and is now printed by them".[17]
Broughton dedicated *Reqvire of Agreement* (1611) to the Merchant
Adventurers, who were "a great help to hold the Gospel, maintaining
our best learned abroad, to restore the truth".[18] At the same time, the
army regiments offered shelter and provision for exiled Puritan
preachers, and several were authors who produced books while in
army service. The English officers could not openly countenance
nonconformist books; but all the same, their chaplains continued to
write them. One can surmise that some officers, of the stature of Sir
Edward Vere and Sir Horace Vere (1565-1635) and his spouse, Lady
Mary Vere, were not only friends of the Puritan chaplains but also of
their books. When Chaplain William Ames was in serious trouble for
Puritan nonconformity, Sir Horace interceded for him with Sir
Dudley Carleton for the sake of Ames "and wee that are his hearers".
Many authors dedicated books to Sir Horace and Lady Mary. While
he served with his sword, the author served "by his pen".[19]

All of these activities in the British churches, regiments, and among
the merchants combined into a very effective Dutch Puritan book
network. It was a "Catilinarian" conspiracy functioning throughout
England, Scotland, and the Netherlands.[20] The new Cataline Conspiracy of the Puritans, it seems, was a book conspiracy.

Initially, the English and Scottish authors relied on a few Dutch
printers who knew English and could adequately print it. Certain
Dutch printers remained active in Puritan and Bible printing throughout the seventeenth century. Relying solely on the Dutch printers,
however, presented several problems. In most cases, they were profit-
minded printing entrepreneurs who printed for English Puritans just as
they printed for any other customers. Puritans yearned for more zeal
in the printer's heart. The Dutch handling of the English language also
left much to be desired. Although the head printer might be knowl-

---

[17] Christiaan G.F. de Jong, *John Forbes (ca. 1565-1634)* (Proefschrift Rijksuniversiteit te Groningen, 1987), p. 152. De Jong, "John Forbes (c. 1568-1634), Scottish
Minister and Exile in The Netherlands", *NAK*, 69 (1989), pp. 17-53.

[18] Broughton, *A Reqvire of Agreement*, STC 3882 (n.p., 1611), Epistle Dedicatorie;
Broughton, *Works*, III, 614-15.

[19] SP 84/71/252. Among the Vere dedications were books by Henry Hexham,
soldier serving under Vere in the Netherlands. See his translations of Polyander, *A
Disputation*, STC 20095 (Dort: George Waters, 1611) and *The Refvtation*, STC 20096
(London, 1610), "Dedication."

[20] Patrick Scot, *Vox Vera*, STC 21863 (London, 1625), p. 35.

edgeable in the language, some of the assistants were not. Many English authors complained that errors by Dutch printers harmed the message of their books.

Stories abounded of incompetent printing of English books. Reports like these: The printer of one book was "much lacking in letter and altogether in our language". In another book the original copy had been badly written; then it was carelessly printed "in hast, the Compositors also straungers". Another time the "setter...knew not English", with horrible results. A certain book required a long list of errata because "there was noe Englishman to attend the Correction". Under such circumstances, "it is not possible to avoid many errata".[21] Samuel Hieron's *Aaron's Bells A-Sounding*, printed at Amsterdam in 1623, had a most unhappy birth. The Dutch printer worked from a carelessly transcribed manuscript "by such an unskilled hand". Then the Dutchman, "wholly ignorant of our English Tongue, could hardly read it; wherefore in ye print there be many miscarriages, and in one or two places...ye very sence is thereby marrde".[22]

In spite of these problems, English and Scottish authors received much good service from skilled Dutch printers. Nevertheless, many authors thought it more satisfactory to have native English printers. Eventually, a corps of English and Scottish printers of nonconformist conviction established themselves in the major Dutch cities; and their history, along with the associated Dutch printers of Puritan literature, will be told in the following chapters.

Dutch printing laws

All Puritan printing enterprises had to reckon with Dutch law and government. European countries of the seventeenth century had press laws to control the flow of printed books and systems of censorship to put teeth into the laws. The Netherlands also had such printing laws; but in contrast to England and the surrounding countries, the Dutch

---

[21] Henoch Clapham, *Theologicall Axioms*, STC 5346 (n.p., 1597), sig. Fiiii; *The Reasons which Compelled the States of Bohemia*, STC 3212 (Dort: George Waters, n.d.), "To the Reader"; Hugh Broughton, *Daniel with a Brief Explication*, STC 2787 (Hanau, 1607), p. 128; William Bradshaw, *The Unreasonablnes of the Separation*, STC 3533 (n.p., 1640), Printer's preface; William Spang, *Rerum nuper in regno Scotiae gestarum historia* (Dantisci, 1641), errata.

[22] Quick, "Icones", I, i, p. 86.

had no thorough policy of censorship to regulate the overall process of printing and bookselling. Dutch officials selectively enforced the printing laws on the books. H.A. Enno van Gelder, in the spirit of liberal historiography, has summarized the Dutch situation: "The printing press in the era of the Republic was restricted and supervised in many ways by laws; in practice the printing press was almost completely free."[23]

Freedom of printing was not an absolute right of the citizen, since the magistrates had the authority to enforce restrictive laws. S. Groenveld has questioned the common historical assessment that the Dutch Republic, in fact, had a "free press". Was the Netherlands "the Mecca of authors"?[24] It must be pointed out that certain religious and political topics strained the limits of Dutch toleration, leading to the banning of books. Over 150 Dutch books were *verboden* and banned by reasons of state in the seventeenth century, a not insignificant number.[25] Foreign religious doctrines, however, seldom moved the magistrates to wrath. Because there was no uniform national policy of censorship, local authorities operated by their own standards. This kind of system worked to the advantage of English and Scottish nonconformists, who adjusted their printing activities to the local situation. Whenever the pressure for enforcement built up temporarily at one city, Amsterdam, for example, the Puritan book people could easily move their printing and selling for a time to some other Dutch city.

The foundational press law governing printing and bookselling was the Holland *plakkaat* or edict of December 20, 1581, followed-up by the edicts of 1584, 1587, 1589, and 1594. The States General brought overall book regulation to the Republic with the edict of 1608, incorporating the policies of the previous Holland edicts, and renewed and updated by the edicts of 1615, 1618, 1621, 1624, 1639, 1646, 1651, 1669, and others. J.T. Bodel Nyenhuis in a survey of seven-

---

[23] H.A. Enno van Gelder, *Getemperde vrijheid* (Groningen: Wolters-Noordhoff, 1972), p. 151; also Van Eeghen, *AB*, V, 23-26.

[24] S. Groenveld, "The Mecca of Authors? State Assemblies and Censorship in the Seventeenth-Century Dutch Republic", in A.C. Duke and C.A. Tamse, eds., *Too Mighty To Be Free: Censorship and the Press in Britain and the Netherlands*, vol. 9 of *Britain and The Netherlands* (Zutphen: De Walburg Pers, 1987), pp. 63-86.

[25] Van Gelder, *Getemperde vrijheid*, pp. 154-55, 161-62; see W.P.C. Knuttel, *Verboden boeken in de Republiek der Vereenigde Nederlanden* ('s-Gravenhage: Nijhoff, 1914). Groenveld, "Mecca", p. 74, identified 210 prohibited books for the period of 1580-1699.

teenth-century Dutch press control laws listed at least fourteen edicts from the States General and over twenty-one from the States of Holland. Other provinces were also making book laws. The substance of these regulatory laws was to prohibit publication of rebellious and scandalous books and to require each printer to set down his name, place, year, the author, and the translator. Punishment of printers in 1581 was by a fine of 100 carolus guilders (later raised in 1615 to 300 guilders) with double fines for repeated violations. After 1615, the laws provided also for the possibility of corporal punishment.[26]

As new problems arose, the 1581 law had been updated and refined. English Puritan books, because of their effect on relations with England, played a role in several of the revisions. The States General *plakkaten* of July 7, 1615 and January 16, 1621 were the basic laws applicable to cases relating to Puritan printing. These two laws, revisions of the 1581 law, forbade the printing, the giving forth in print or writing, the selling, scattering, or carrying about of "any scandalous and seditious books" or libels, rhymes, pamphlets, and songs. The printer was required to print his name, the names of author and translator, and place and date. Because Puritan writers so often dwelt on "flaws" in the English church and state, the 1615 law resolved that books should not attack "kings and potentates, our friends and allies" (understood by all as intending to protect the good name of the King of England).[27] With the Twelve Years' Truce ending, the *plakkaat* of 1621 was still more explicit about the English concern, due to the recent uproar over the Brewster-Brewer press of Leiden. This law prohibited the printing of libellous books "in the Latin, French, English, Scottish, and other tongues as well in ecclesiastical as political affairs, touching the persons and government of kings and princes, friends and allies of the Netherlands...to the disquiet of their peaceable government".[28] These two edicts covered most circumstances of Puritan book printing and distribution.

Nevertheless, the books kept coming. The States General in 1639, fearing a reproachment between Spain and England, to the detriment

---

[26] J.T. Bodel Nyenhuis, *De wetgeving op drukpers en boekhandel in de Nederlanden tot in het begin der XIXde eeuw* (Amsterdam: P.N. van Kampen & Zoon, 1892), pp. 99-145; Nikolaas Wiltens, *Kerkelyk plakaatboek behelzende de plakaaten, ordonnantien, ende resolutien, over de kerkelyke zaken* (The Hague, 1772), pp. 391-95. Groenveld, "Mecca", pp. 77-79.

[27] Wiltens, pp. 403-08.

[28] Ibid., p. 403.

of the Republic, produced another *plakkaat*, the law of October 3, 1639. This time the revision came down on disrespectful, anti-Anglican books produced by Christiaensz and Canne at Leiden and Amsterdam. In regard to prohibited printing, the States General forbade books touching friends of the Republic, "in particular, the King of Great Britain and his principal ministers, both spiritual and political".[29] The States of Holland, which covered Amsterdam and Leiden, also enacted laws, and further regulations emanated from magistrates of the individual cities.

Book printing always had clear foreign policy implications regarding relations between the Republic and Britain. The British authorities kept a close watch on books emanating from abroad, whether by their own citizens, or by foreigners meddling in British affairs. The *Weegh-Schael* by Jacobus Taurinus (1617) greatly offended King James I and his ambassador, and the States General offered a gesture of good will to Britain by banning the book.[30] Another Dutch book about the same time, Gerson Bucerus' *Dissertatio de gubernatione ecclesiae* (1618) also provoked a diplomatic storm because of its hard-hitting comments about certain flaws in The Church of England. Because the English displeasure was intense, the magistrates of Middelberg confiscated the remaining copies of the book.[31] Wherever necessary, steps to placate foreign dignitaries were taken.

In spite of a parade of laws, and governmental intervention, which seemed to provide ample teeth for controlling nonconformist English and Scottish books, the results were meager. Putting the laws on paper was one thing; getting them to be strictly enforced was another. The Dutch authorities were very lukewarm when it came to censoring the press, in any case, and they did not often see Puritan doctrines as much of a threat. Determined pressure from a foreign government, like England, produced some temporary action. Apparently, it served the purposes of the Dutch politicians to be able to point to sternly-written laws on the books, and then they would allow them to gather dust. "How little effect these strong measures had", concluded Van Gelder.[32]

---

[29] Ibid., p. 407. Groenveld, "Mecca", p. 70.

[30] Knuttel, *Verboden boeken*, p. 129.

[31] C.A. Tukker, "Gerson Bucerus—Jacobus I—de Statenvertaling", *NAK*, 50 (1969-70), pp. 56-66.

[32] Van Gelder, *Getemperde vrijheid*, p. 156.

While the political magistrates kept an eye on political printing, the Dutch Reformed preachers sought higher standards of proper printing order. An orderly society needed to regulate the flow of opinion. Many preachers feared books containing corrupt doctrines by Arminians, Socinians, Muslims, Jews, heretics and disorderly troublemakers. Hence, there was a need for "order in the printing of books". On all sides the preachers saw great "licentiousness in the printing of all sorts of scandalous and offensive books".[33] From the churches came a demand for a very strict enforcement of the printing laws already on the law books; and as a further step, many churchmen favored some sort of a system of "preventive censorship" which would choke off the printing of unworthy books.[34] To accomplish this, the preachers urged the political authorities to enact a system of religious censors, to be called *visitatores librorum* or *censores librorum*, whereby preachers would act as ecclesiastical book inspectors empowered to license books before publication.[35] The adoption of a nation-wide system of "book visitors" would have brought the Netherlands more into line with general European censorship practice. Although Reformed classes and synods repeatedly pleaded for an extensive scheme of book visitors, and appointed such inspectors to censure theological books among their own members, the political magistrates did not choose to put the church in charge of books.[36]

There was an occasional crack-down on Puritan printing but no consistent policy of control. Most Dutch officials had no quarrel with nonconformist English and Scots, and thus no desire on their own to harass the Puritans. In spite of the laws, printers and authors in the Netherlands had considerable freedom to print whatever they wanted to—more "than they would find elsewhere in contemporary Europe"[37]—and Puritans and Covenanters benefitted greatly from this situation.

---

[33] Acta Synod North Holland, 1607, art. 21; 1620, art. 11; 1623, art. 23 (no. 99, Amsterdam classis archive, G.A. Amsterdam).

[34] R.B. Evenhuis *Ook dat was Amsterdam* (Amsterdam: Ten Have, 1965-78), II, 142-43; Van Gelder, *Getemperde vrijheid*, pp. 168-89.

[35] See, for example, Acta Synod North Holland, 1628, art. 33 (no. 100); 1638, art. 31; 1640, art. 42; 1641, art. 26; 1643, art. 25; 1646, art. 20 (no. 101, Amsterdam classis archive).

[36] Evenhuis, *Ook dat was Amsterdam*, II, 143.

[37] Groenveld, "Mecca", p. 81.

The English campaign to regulate Dutch printing

The Puritan access to the Dutch presses greatly alarmed the authorities
at home. They reasoned that press control and censorship in Britain
would not be effective so long as uncontrolled printing presses operated a few miles across the water. Dutch printing freedom produced
atrocious results: "Riotous misdemeanours...infamous *Libels*...licentious
Libertines, malcontented *Fugitives*, or Professed Enemies."[38] In the face
of lax enforcement and unmotivated Dutch magistrates, the British
government had its own actions against the foreign nonconformist
printing.

The English and Scottish governments sent many official requests to
the Netherlands for enforcement of the press laws. Central to these
activities were ambassadors Sir Ralph Winwood (1603-1613), Sir
Dudley Carleton (1616-1628), and Sir William Boswell (1632-1649).
Each ambassador had instructions to find better ways to hinder the
flood of books, whereupon the ambassador would go to the city
currently producing objectionable books, or to the States of Holland
and the States General. The object was to find the printer, suppress the
books, and "learne out...those Englishemen that did sett him on
worke".[39] Archbishop Bancroft in 1606 ordered Ambassador
Winwood into action against books; the archbishop was particularly
angry with the writings of Hugh Broughton being printed at Amsterdam.[40] Winwood in 1614 presented another strong message to the
magistrates of Amsterdam against "seditious books", and some were
seized and kept "in Custody".[41] Although the "subversive book"
issue was always on the British agenda, the ambassadors could not gain
full cooperation from the Dutch magistrates. The British urged that
the times required vigilant enforcement of the printing laws, accom-
panied by really frightening punishments, like whippings and impris-
onment, for authors and printers.[42]

When Archbishop Laud in the 1630s took over censorship matters,
the pace of anti-Puritan action quickened. The instructions to Sir
William Boswell in 1632 gave the order against "new opinion" and

---

[38] Scot, *Vox Vera*, p. 3.
[39] P.C. *Acts* (1600-1601), New Ser. XXXI, 216.
[40] Winwood, *Memorials,* II, 195; Hugh Broughton, *A Petition to the Lordes Chancelours*, STC 3877.7 (n.p., n.d.), sig. B2.
[41] SP 84/69/177; Bodel Nyenhuis, *Wetgeving*, p. 33.
[42] SP 84/148/99.

"scandalous pamphlets" in Holland. "You shal watch over their presses, and printing houses." You shall suppress the books and you shall expose "the authors, abbeter, and transporters".[43] Boswell took this challenge very seriously. On arrival at his post, Boswell immediately confronted some of the nasty books: *The Curtaine of Chvrch-Power* by Henric (1632), *The Fresh Suit* by Ames (1633). *The Crowne of a Christian Martyr* by Richards (1634), and Canne's *Necessitie of Separation.* (1634). These books were "bitter idle".[44] Such was the plague of Puritan books. "Blew books" and "blew coats" (*blauboexckens*) was what Boswell's party called them.[45]

Always "new stuff printing at Amsterdam".[46] What was to be done? "What should I do?" asked Laud.[47] The English authorities had to take the initiative. The ambassadors assembled a corps of collaborators, agents, and informers to counter the Puritan book dealers. Because so many offensive books appeared anonymously, the first step was to discover the identities of these hidden hands. To trace the printers, the English authorities relied considerably upon analysis of literary style and print type by knowledgeable scholars and "experienced printers". Moving from a book assuredly linked with a particular printer, they compared anonymous books until they matched them by style and type. And "by that character" or letter "he is condemned of the rest". This kind of comparative type analysis was used by Sir Dudley Carleton to expose Brewster and Brewer at Leiden in 1619, leading to the break-up of their print shop.[48]

Some informers were volunteers; others were paid to spy. Francis Hill, an English printer living at Amsterdam, in 1624 received pay to infiltrate the English printing shops and bring reports.[49] Other English and Scots offered information without payment, because they saw the book situation as completely out of hand; and some, no doubt, had personal and long-standing grudges against particular Puritan authors. Stephen Goffe, a chaplain to English troops, and Edward Misselden, deputy of the Merchant Adventurers at Delft, in the 1630s regularly

---

[43] SP 84/144/164v.

[44] SP 16/250/28; SP 84/146/101-02.

[45] B.P., I, 171, 139; SP 16/250/28; Van Gelder, *Getemperde vrijheid*, p. 157.

[46] Laud to Boswell, Nov. 26, 1638 (Add. MS C. 69, Bodleian Library, Oxford).

[47] Laud, *Works*, IV, 263.

[48] Edward Arber, *The Story of the Pilgrim Fathers, 1606-1623* (London, 1897), p. 209.

[49] SP 84/117/157.

passed on information about books and other aspects of Puritan activities in the Netherlands.

In time Boswell recruited informers in Amsterdam, Leiden, Utrecht, Rotterdam, and The Hague (among them John Paget, Malachi Harris, George Beaumont, and Griffin Higgs). They kept their eyes and ears open for news about books and watched for the appearance of undesirable books, "searching" and inquiring "according to your command". Boswell's informers visited "the chiefest stationers shops".[50] Malachi Harris of Utrecht had the particular assignment to watch Professor Gisbertus Voetius, who was suspected of aiding the Puritan cause through his writings.[51] At Amsterdam, *dominee* Johannes le Maire, a Dutch preacher friendly with Laud, was an invaluable source of information about books in that city.[52]

Every Puritan preacher in the Netherlands was under perpetual suspicion for writing or publishing books. Ambassador Boswell went after them harshly, hoping to intimidate and silence them. When John Davenport came over in 1634, Boswell soon quizzed him about his preaching and suspected publishing: "Whether you have not been cause, or consciouse of any English Books, or Treaties printed, or published in these parts...or now in press?" Davenport denied all involvement.[53] Hugh Peter, English pastor of Rotterdam, was also accused: "Why you have written, printed, published, commended, distributed scandalous books against the lawes...?"[54] In addition, the eye of authority scrutinized such Puritans authors residing in Holland as William Ames, Alexander Leighton, Thomas Hooker, and John Canne.

With channels of inside information, the ambassadors were able to obtain very early copies of the books, or at least some sheets from the press. These could be used to deduce more information, "that I might better discover the Author, Printer, the Publisher of it", or to send sample copies of the books at top speed to England for examination.[55]

Gathering intelligence about the books—author, printer, and publisher—was the first step toward stopping the books. When irrefut-

---

[50] B.P., I, 80, 86, 171-72, 202, 221, 230, 339-40.

[51] Ibid., I, 335.

[52] SP 84/154/44; 138/44; also see chapter 4.

[53] B.P., I, 402, 189.

[54] Ibid., I, 405.

[55] SP 16/246/56.

able evidence was in hand, the English ambassador or one of his friends would go to the magistrates of the city and demand enforcement of the printing laws. If the evidence was beyond question, and the pressure from England strong enough, the magistrates might decide to make an example of one or two printers (Brewster and Brewer at Leiden in 1619, Christiaensz at Leiden in 1638, Canne at Amsterdam in 1638). And if the Puritan books were truly abusive, the ambassador would use the outrage and shock of the occasion to push for a tightening of the laws, as in 1621 and 1639, with specific wording to cover English printing. If the books were already printed, the English authorities occasionally tried direct confrontation of the printers and booksellers. As late as 1643, the situation desperate in Britain, ambassador Boswell was demanding new action from the States General against books, because printers "from day to day are printing famous and harmful libels in this land" to the detriment of the Kingdom of England.[56]

Although never a full success, the English campaign against Puritan printing in the Low Countries reduced the flow of books and greatly frightened Puritan authors. When Laud came to trial for treason during the revolution, he had to answer the charge "that I used my power to suppress books in Holland". To the end, Laud defended these Dutch book policies as absolutely necessary for orderly government, "for till this was done, every discontented spirit could print what he pleased at Amsterdam".[57]

---

[56] Res. States General, no. 3202, fol. 601r-v.
[57] Laud, *Works*, IV, 264.

CHAPTER 3

PURITAN RENAISSANCE (OR PURITAN "BABEL"?)
AT SEVENTEENTH-CENTURY AMSTERDAM

When Puritans began their migrations to Amsterdam in the late
sixteenth century, they found intellectual stimulation as well as religious solace and economic opportunity. In the sixteenth and seventeenth centuries, Amsterdam was a mighty metropolis of world trade
and finance; its commerce "doth daily increase", and foreigners
flocked in "there to resyde and trafficq".[1] One of Hugh Broughton's
first published books at Amsterdam advertised on the title page the
world greatness of the city: "Printed at Amstelredam a city of
Marchandise knowen vnto India and all limites of the Earth."[2] In
addition to religious and economic opportunity, Puritan intellectuals
found new freedom to probe the horizons of knowledge. The combination of profitable commerce and free opinions was a strange and
dangerous world for Puritans, so much so that Ambassador Winwood
warned that Amsterdam "doth growe another Babilon, and in tyme
may be feared will prove the Babel of Holland".[3]

The Puritan settlers had to confront "Babylon" and "Babel".
Freedom meant diversity and sectarianism. The lifestyle looked like
Babylon. The voices sounded like Babel. After William Bedwell came
for a visit in 1612, he thought "Cairo" might be a better description—Egypt sounded terribly factious and wicked.[4] But where, in
truth, was Babylon? For many of the Puritan exiles, the story was
reversed. Amsterdam meant the land of freedom, and England, which
had persecuted them, was the real Babylon. Many of the Puritanical
books printed at Amsterdam changed the labels and proclaimed that
England under the prelates was today's Babylon (or Egypt).

---

[1] SP 84/61/83v (1601).
[2] Hugh Broughton, *The Familie of David*, STC 3867.5 (Amsterdam: Zacharias
Heyns, 1605), title page.
[3] SP 84/68/3v (1610).
[4] Alastair Hamilton, *William Bedwell: The Arabist 1563-1632* (Leiden: Sir Thomas
Browne Institute, 1985), p. 45.

Puritan settlers in Amsterdam established churches and worshipped God. To enrich scholarship and grow in intellectual achievement was far from the original goal for coming. "Learning I have none to boast of", asserted Separatist Henry Ainsworth; "it is ynough for me if I may know Christ & him crucified."[5] All the same, most Amsterdam Puritans believed in the necessity of a learned ministry, and in defense of their cause the English preachers almost daily expounded theology and produced books. Many of the Puritan writings were contributions to the religious and, sometimes, to the humanistic learning of the day.

The Separatist preachers of the "Ancient Church" (Henry Ainsworth of Gonville and Caius College, and Francis Johnson, M.A. Christ's College), assisted by brother George Johnson, M.A. Christ's College, and elder Matthew Slade, B.A. St. Alban Hall, were the early guardians of English, Brownist faith and learning. In the first decade of the seventeenth century they were reinforced by John Smyth, M.A. Christ's College, and John Robinson, M.A. Corpus Christi. The intellectual and spiritual center of Separatist Puritanism had shifted to Amsterdam. Non-Separatist Puritans had their religious headquarters at the English Reformed church, pastored by John Paget (M.A. Trinity). Paget's associates included a flow of Puritan travellers: Hugh Broughton, William Ames, Robert Parker, Thomas Hooker, John Davenport, Hugh Peter, and others.

This cluster of Puritanical intellectuals in exile had a lively dialogue on polemical and learned topics. Unorthodox notions flourished alongside scholarly orthodoxy. Freedom of ideas produced "Amsterdam Babylon" and "Amsterdam Babel". The more positive term of "Puritan Renaissance" can be equally well applied to this episode of Puritan history.

The reawakening included Brownist Puritans, as much as non-Separatist Puritans, which in itself was quite an achievement. From their early days, Separatists carried a large suspicion of humanistic and profane learning, for fear that it would quench the Spirit. Robert Browne, the original Brownist, had strongly warned of the dangers of vain logic and "curious Diuisions", and among Puritans all such objections to erudite study were a sure Brownist sign: "This objection seemeth to smell of Brownisme."[6] As a rule, Separatists (Brownists)

---

[5] Ainsworth, in *Certayne Questions*, STC 3848 (n.p., 1605), p. 38.

[6] *The Writings of Robert Harrison and Robert Browne*, ed. Albert Peel and Leland H. Carlson (London: George Allen and Unwin Ltd, 1953), pp. 177-80; Hamilton, *Bedwell*, p. 55.

avoided outside religious contacts because other churches, whether
English Episcopal or Dutch Reformed, were likely to be polluted with
antichristian elements. Many Separatists defined holy "Separation" to
mean that they could not hear sermons in outside churches; and,
caring little for the heritage of civilization, they avoided the use of
profane books for study or use of buildings for worship which at any
time in the past, no matter how remote, had been occupied by Jews
or Roman Catholics for worship. Better that these "idolatrous" buildings would be converted to barns and stables.[7] Separatism meant
sanctified exclusiveness. Separatist members who transgressed these
rules ran the risk of excommunication. At Amsterdam and Leiden
however, the story began to change. Puritans of all persuasions, albeit
at first reluctantly, joined the intellectual life of the Republic. The
Netherlands saw the intellectualizing and mellowing of Brownism. In
addition to traditional theological learning, these Puritans of the
Netherlands forcefully dealt with questions of philology and relationships to strange cultures. They met Jews, Arabs, and Turks. Some
delved deeply into the philosophies of Platonism and Ramism.

To many visitors, Amsterdam made an unlikely intellectual "Athens".
It had no university, and Amsterdam people threw their main energies
into trade. The merchant was not much interested in school books.
"Their best Books being those of Accounts; and Learning is commonly
as much silent among Tradesmen, as the Laws are among Men of
Arms."[8] Although higher learning centered at Leiden, Franeker and
Utrecht, the university cities, Amsterdam, nevertheless, provided much
intellectual activity outside of the formal academy setting. H. de la Fontaine Verwey has observed that "the university incorporated only a part
of the intellectual forces active in the Republic". Some great scholars
always lived "outside its circle". So it was at Amsterdam.[9] The money-
hungry "tradesmen" enhanced the life of their city by supporting a Latin
School, a city library, and the Athenaeum Illustre, which eventually
evolved into the University of Amsterdam. Doctor Samuel Coster ran
the "Duytsche Academie" and the Remonstrants in 1634 opened a seminary. The printing houses of Amsterdam contributed much to the intellectual weight, as well as to the economic prosperity, of the city.

---

[7] Henoch Clapham, *A Chronological Discourse*, STC 5336 (London, 1609), sig. B4.

[8] John Northleigh, *Topographical Descriptions* (London, 1702), p. 70.

[9] H. de la Fontaine Verwey, in W.Gs Hellinga, *Copy and Print in the Netherlands*
(Amsterdam: North Holland Publishing Co., 1962), p. 30.

The opening of the Athenaeum Illustre in 1632 highlighted Amsterdam's desire to achieve some eminence in scholarship to match its prodigious economic achievement. The first two professors were Gerardus Joannes Vossius and Caspar Barlaeus, both distinguished humanists. Vossius' inaugural oration was on "The Utility of History", and Barlaeus spoke on the happy connections between trade and philosophy. Barlaeus paid tribute to the Amsterdam magistrates for leading the city, a stronghold of Mercury and Pluto, into becoming a residence of Athena and Apollo. In Amsterdam, he declared, "an unusually good interaction existed between trade and the study of literature and philosophy...so that the merchant will be all the happier in the measure in which he can better cultivate learning".[10]

Puritans, printers, and the intellectual life of Amsterdam

When the Puritan theologian-scholars came over to Amsterdam, they were thrown into the most cosmopolitan community of northern Europe. Dutch, Germans, Danes, Norwegians, English, French, Greeks, Arabs, Armenians, Persians, Turks, and Jews produced a conglomeration remarkably stimulating to the new settlers. Seven or eight languages could be heard daily on the financial exchange, and no part of the city escaped the impact of exotic people and languages.[11] English immigrants were swept into the milieu.

The beginning of a new Puritan erudition at Amsterdam arose from the study of languages. The goal was *ad fontes*. Matthew Slade (1569-1628), Henry Ainsworth (1569/70-1622) and Hugh Broughton (1549-1612) took the lead among Puritans in Hebraic and other philological study. The most famous was Slade, renowned English intellectual, with a solid public reputation in the city. Although a convinced Separatist Brownist at the time of his immigration in 1597, and elder of the congregation, he soon renounced his Brownism and withdrew from the Ancient Church; the church reciprocated and excommunicated him. His withdrawal from the English sect earned him much respectability in the eyes of the Dutch population. He joined the Latin

---

[10] C.S.M. Rademaker, *The Life and Work of Gerardus Joannes Vossius* (Assen: Van Gorcum, 1981), pp. 242-43.

[11] James Howell, *Epistolae Ho-Elianae*, 3rd ed., Wing H3073 (London, 1655), I, 95 (1622).

grammar school as sub-rector (conrector); in 1603 he became rector of
the Latin school; later he married a Dutch wife, a step-daughter of
Petrus Plancius. At the same time he served as Amsterdam city librarian, which was appropriate since he himself was famous as a "walking
library" of knowledge. Other Puritan intellectuals-in-exile sought out
his company, and consequently, Slade stood at the center of an infor-
mal English "circle".[12] This Slade circle (composed of Slade,
Broughton, Paget, and some Dutch associates) informally gathered at
the Latin School, the city library, in the English churches, at Jan
Theunisz' inn or at the printing shops. Ainsworth's Separatist group
(himself and Francis and George Johnson) was sometimes included in
these discussions; often they were excluded.

After his excommunication, Slade joined the Dutch Reformed
church; he never rejoined any of the English churches of Amsterdam.
Nevertheless, he retained many English ties, and his lifelong outlook
on religion was strictly Calvinistic and Puritanical. His published
writings were contra-Remonstrant books directed against Vorstius (a
stand much appreciated by King James of England). He would be
honored, Slade said, to serve as one of his Majesty's "basest Var-
lets".[13] Hoping to rise in the world, Slade curried favor with high
English officials, especially with Sir Horace Vere and ambassadors Sir
Ralph Winwood and Sir Dudley Carleton. With his English friends
Slade was extremely generous of time and scholarship, and, of course,
he expected favors in return.[14] In 1612/13 Sir Henry Saville, the
father-in-law of Carleton, sent over to Slade eighteen copies of his
eight-volume Greek edition of Chrysostom, asking him to peddle the
books. Slade tried hard, and eventually sold a few as a favor to Saville
(and Ambassador Carleton). Slade, however, reported that the market
for such expensive Greek books at Amsterdam was not great; "they
who have Greeke are moniles, and they that have money are Greek-

---

[12] On Slade, see the biographical chapter in Willem Nijenhuis, *Matthew Slade
1569-1628: Letters to the English Ambassador* (Leiden: Sir Thomas Browne Institute,
1986), pp. 3-30; C.P. Burger Jr., "Een Metselaar-Latinist", *Het Boek*, 20 (1931), pp.
305-10; H.F. Wijnman, "De geleerdenkring van Mathaeus Sladus", in A.E. D'Ailly
(ed.), *Zeven eeuwen Amsterdam* (Amsterdam: N.V. Uitg. Mij. "Joost van den Vondel",
n.d.), II, 439-43.

[13] Nijenhuis, *Slade*, p. 85.

[14] For Slade's 39 surviving letters to Winwood and Carleton (SP 84), from the
years 1614-24, see Nijenhuis, *Slade*; C. van der Woude, *Sibrandus Lubbertus: Leven en
werken* (Kampen: J.H. Kok, 1963), pp. 251-56.

les."[15] Through his energetic efforts, he arranged for his son Cornelis to gain the position of conrector at the school (in lieu of an inheritance); after the father's death, Cornelis in 1628 advanced to rector.[16]

Hugh Broughton, Slade's friend, lived for several years at Amsterdam in the early seventeenth century. A very learned Hebraist, he had a degree from Magdalene College, Cambridge, and was former fellow of St. John's and Christ's. Although splendidly gifted in scholarly matters, he was such an outspoken Puritan that he found it necessary to live abroad (Germany, Switzerland, and the Netherlands). After sojourning in Amsterdam, Broughton for several years, approximately 1605-1611, served as preacher of the English Merchant Adventurers at Middelburg; but much of this time, in fact, he managed to spend in Amsterdam in company with Slade and Paget. He kept contact with "the learnedest men then extant", and at Leiden he had particularly valued the scholarly company of Franciscus Raphelengius and Joseph Scaliger, "both as good Linguists, as any in this world". He aspired to take his place, at least in reputation, along side these luminaries.[17] Slade had worked to secure a pastorate for Broughton at the new English Reformed Church (1605) which Slade helped to establish but never personally joined as a member. Although Broughton was a leading candidate for minister, he instead preferred the position at Middelburg. By the end of 1605, he had removed, being "of late at Amsterdam".[18] His Middelburg position, apparently, allowed him a good deal of freedom to travel about.

With Broughton out of the way, the English Reformed pastorate went to John Paget, who served 1607-37. Paget was not an intellectual giant like Broughton or Slade, but he certainly exhibited curiosity and knowledge about many areas of learning. Paget's biography by his nephew Robert Paget, English pastor at Dort, tells about how he gained a deep mastery of Biblical languages, and "he could to good purpose and with much ease make use of the Chaldean, Syriack, Rabbinicall, Thalmudicall, Arabic and Persian versions and commen-

---

[15] HMC, Buccleuch and Queensberry, I, 123; SP 84/80/55 (Nov. 10/20, 1617).

[16] Will of Matthew Slade, 1624, NA 573 (Lamberti), fols. 99-100; BL, I, 345.

[17] On Broughton, see BL I, 103-04; DNB; and The Works of the Great Albionean Divine, ed. John Lightfoot, Wing B4997 (London, 1662), intro. and I, 254.

[18] Alice C. Carter, The English Reformed Church in Amsterdam in the Seventeenth Century (Amsterdam: Scheltema & Holkema NV, 1964), pp. 21-22; K.L. Sprunger, Dutch Puritanism (Leiden: E.J. Brill, 1982), p. 92. Broughton and Ainsworth, Certayne Questions, 1605, reports on the title page that Broughton is "of late at Amsterdam."

taries".[19] Young Robert Paget, it should be said, inherited his uncle's library and in time also became renowned for his knowledge and library of Jewish books.[20] Due to the linguistic skills of Ainsworth, Slade, Broughton, and Paget, the Christian scholarship of the Hebrew language and culture in early seventeenth-century Amsterdam took on an English, and even a Puritan, flavor.

A very important aspect in Puritanism's scholarly achievement was the close relationship with the booksellers and printers of Amsterdam. The seventeenth-century Netherlanders were the leading book handlers, publishers, and printers of Europe; Amsterdam was "the metropolis of the book trade".[21] Von Zesen's description of Amsterdam in 1664 reported that there were forty presses at work, all sending forth books in the varied languages of Europe.[22] Many Puritan authors, stifled at home, hurried to these publishers and printers.

Several Amsterdam booksellers and printers were keenly interested in English-language printing. Dutch printers of the seventeenth century penetrated the English market with Bibles, atlases, maps, and scholarly books. The first English newspapers or news sheets were printed at Amsterdam, beginning in 1618. The best of the printers were themselves amateur men of letters, the *geleerde drukkers*, learned printers in the esteemed tradition of Aldus or Plantin. Some delved into the languages of classical antiquity; more often they excelled in the modern practical skills of astronomy or cartography.[23] For this heroic age of printing, Elizabeth Eisenstein's description of the scholarly printer may well apply to the Amsterdam printer. Such a printer or publisher was an urban entrepreneur seeking profits, but with a wider vision:

> It seems more accurate to describe many publishers as being *both* businessmen *and* literary dispensers of glory. They served men of letters not only by providing traditional forms of patronage but also by acting as press agents and as cultural impresarios of a new kind.

---

[19] Robert Paget, "The Publisher to the Reader", in John Paget, *Meditations of Death*, STC 19099 (Dort, 1639), sig. *4v.

[20] J. van den Berg, *Joden en Christenen in Nederland gedurende de zeventiende eeuw* (Kampen: J.H. Kok, 1969), p. 38.

[21] H. de la Fontaine Verwey, *Uit de wereld van het boek* (Amsterdam: Nico Israel, 1979), III, 9-10.

[22] Violet Barbour, *Capitalism in Amsterdam in the 17th Century* (Ann Arbor: Univ. of Michigan Press, 1966), p. 65.

[23] De la Fontaine Verwey, *Uit de wereld van het boek*, III, 10.

In fact, "the profit motive was combined with other motives that were self-serving *and* altrustic, and even evangelistic, at times". The printing-publishing shops were not necessarily typical workshops "because they served as gathering places for scholars, artists, and literati; as sanctuaries for foreign translators, emigrés and refugees; as institutions of advanced learning, and as focal points for every kind of cultural and intellectual interchange".[24]

The leading Dutch publishers and printers with close ties to the Amsterdam Puritans were these: Jodocus Hondius (1563-1612), his sons Jodocus Hondius II and Henricus Hondius, his son-in-law Johannes Janssonius (married to Elizabeth Hondius), Zacharias Heyns, Jan Theunisz, Henricus Laurentius, Joris Veseler, and J.F. Stam (the latter two to be considered further in chapter 4). Willem Jansz Blaeu and his son Joan Blaeu did outstanding printing of atlases and navigational books for the English market. The Blaeus were famous for quality printing. At the peak, their printing establishment consisted of nine or ten presses, each elegantly dedicated to one of the nine muses.[25] Several Amsterdam printers and publishers had first-hand English experience by having lived in England, among them the Hondius family, Heinrik Moej, and Heyndrick Godewyn, plus Gillis Rooman at Haarlem and Richard Schilders at Middelburg).[26]

The geographical center of Amsterdam printing was "op 't Water" (the Damrak). Here were the shops of W.J. Blaeu, Johannes Janssonius, Henricus Laurentius, J.A. Colom, Dirck Pietersz Pers, J.E. Cloppenburgh,and paper merchant Peter Haeck. Jan Theunisz was only a few steps away on the sidestreet Oudebrugsteeg. The book and printing shops bustled with activity. Although not nearly so large or elaborate as the Plantin or Aldus establishments, the Amsterdam shops carried on some of the same functions of "institutions of advanced learning" for Dutch and foreign scholars, authors, artists, and translators. At the printery of Blaeu there was "a room for men of letters and proof-readers".[27] In a similar way, the Hondius business was widely famous as a scholarly printing shop. Jodocus Hondius had his shop, "In

[24] Elizabeth L. Eisenstein, *The Printing Press As an Agent of Change* (Cambridge: Cambridge Univ. Press, 1982), I, 22-23.

[25] C. Koeman, *Joan Blaeu and His Grand Atlas* (Amsterdam: Theatrum Orbis Terrarum Ltd, 1970), pp. 13, 17.

[26] Briels, *ZB*, pp. 14, 25.

[27] David W. Davies, *The World of the Elseviers 1580-1712* (The Hague: Nijhoff, 1954), p. 135; Eisenstein, *Printing Press*, I, 22-23.

de Wackere Hondt", on the Dam. A talented man in publishing, engraving, cartography, and globemaking, Hondius at first did not print his own books; later the firm established its own presses.[28] His family and personal connections put the Hondius printing in the stream of the business and intellectual life of the city. Petrus Montanus, sub-rector of the Latin School, was his brother-in-law; rector Matthew Slade was a close friend; Hugh Broughton was a customer and author. The Hondius shop attracted visitors from far and wide; people wanting to converse with him, said Montanus, came four or five at a time.[29] Hondius' door was always open to English visitors and customers; he knew English people and ideas from his ten-year residence in London (1583-93). Hondius was the publisher of several English works and, perhaps, of some of Broughton's Hebrew books. The relationship of Hondius and Broughton went back to previous days in London, when Hondius had done engravings for two of Broughton's books.

The extent of Hondius' publishing of English Puritan books is uncertain, because many of the Puritan books carried no imprint. Moreover, because he relied on a variety of printers, his work is difficult to identify on strictly typographical grounds. One treatise by William Bradshaw, *A Shorte Treatise of the Crosse in Baptism*, is imprinted "Amsterdam: Printed by I.H. 1604". Jodocus Hondius (J.H.) seems like the obvious publisher but not the printer. The myriad of false title pages and other deceptions, however, makes any attribution questionable (more on this in chapter 4). Bradshaw's topic, the evils of ceremonialism, was certainly congenial with the Calvinistic opinions of Hondius.[30]

From Slade, Broughton, and Hondius, the English connection led quickly to another important "learned printer", Jan Theunisz (or in Latinized form, Johannes Antonides, 1569-1638). An Anabaptist, member of the Waterlander Mennonites, he had a remarkable career as a scholar-printer, which began in Leiden working for the master

---

[28] On Hondius and his printing presses, or lack thereof, see H.F. Wijnman, "Jodocus Hondius en de drukker van de Amsterdamsche Ptolemaeus-Uitgave van 1605", *Het Boek*, 28 (1944-46), pp. 8, 24, 30.

[29] Briels, *ZB*, pp. 322-25; Kleerkooper and Van Stockum, I, 263-65; Wijnman, "Jodocus Hondius", pp. 21-23.

[30] On the printing of Bradshaw's books and the question of Hondius' possible involvement, see infra, chap. 4 and articles by Mark H. Curtis, *The Library* (1964) and H. F. Wijnman, *Het Boek* (1944-46).

printer, François van Raphelingen (Raphelengius). Here he learned the art of Hebrew and Greek printing and even took up type-founding (becoming the first north Netherlandic "lettergieter").[31] After having his own shop at Leiden for several years, Theunisz established himself as a printer at Amsterdam, primarily from 1604 to 1608. Thereafter, although continuing to live in Amsterdam, he seldom printed.[32] His printing skills in eastern languages enabled the Puritan authors like Broughton to bring their Hebrew scholarship into print. Broughton published twelve or more books at Amsterdam which were wholly in Hebrew or had some Hebrew words.

Various scholars credit Theunisz with printing these first Hebrew books of Amsterdam, with Jodocus Hondius and Zacharias Heyns acting as publishers. This topic, however, has been the subject of an extensive scholarly debate between H.F. Wijnman (in favor of Theunisz as the printer) and L. Hirschel (in favor of Hondius and Heyns as the printers and publishers). In summarizing the debate, L. Fuks and R.G. Fuks-Mansfeld (1984) leaned toward the Hondius hypothesis but left the issue somewhat open and "problematic".[33] The argument on behalf of the Theunisz hypothesis as the first printer of Hebrew at Amsterdam seems to be the stranger one. In addition to the known skill of Theunisz in printing Hebrew at Leiden, another example of a Theunisz book with extensive Hebrew text printed at Amsterdam has now been identified. This is by Broughton, *The Familie of David*, imprinted "Amstelredam...by Ian Theunisz. 1606" (STC 3867.7).[34] An earlier edition of 1605 carried the imprint

---

[31] Briels, *ZB*, p. 141.

[32] According to Gruys and De Wolf, he printed at Leiden 1600-1604 and at Amsterdam 1605-1627. On Theunisz, see *NNBW*, IX, 1117-22; Wijnman, "Jan Theunisz alias Joannes Antonides" (1569-1637), *AJ*, 25 (1928), pp. 29-123; C.P. Burger Jr., "Jan Theunisz", *Het Boek*, 17 (1928), pp. 115-26.

[33] L. Fuks and R.G. Fuks-Mansfeld, *Hebrew Typography in the Northern Netherlands 1585-1815: Historical Evaluation and Descriptive Bibliography*, 2 vols. (Leiden: E.J. Brill, 1984-87), I, 95-96; L. Hirschel, "Jodocus Hondius en Hugh Broughton: Bijdrage tot de kennis der eerste Hebreeuwsche uitgaven in Amsterdam", *Het Boek*, 17 (1928), pp. 199-208; L. Hirschel, "Uit de voorgeschiedenis der Hebreeuwsche typographie te Amsterdam", *AJ*, 31 (1934), pp. 65-79; Wijnman, "Jan Theunisz alias Joannes Antonides", *AJ*, 25 (1928), pp. 29-133; Wijnman, "Moet Jodocus Hondius of Jan Theunisz beschouwd worden als de eerste drukker van Hebreeuwsche boeken te Amsterdam?", *Het Boek*, 17 (1928), pp. 301-13; Wijnman, "Jodocus Hondius", *Het Boek*, 28 (1944-46), pp. 1-49.

[34] This edition is at Lambeth Palace Library.

"Amstelredam...by Zacharias Heyns. 1605" (STC 3867.5) Whatever the
role of Heyns may have been, he moved to Zwolle in 1605, leaving
the field open for Theunisz. Moreover, another book by Broughton
has the touch of Theunisz, the answer to Rabbi Abraham Reuben,
which Theunisz translated from Hebrew into Dutch, and probably
printed as well. This was the *Antwoort. Op een Hebreuschen brief van een
Jode...Uytten Hebreeusche in Nederduytsher tale overgheset door Ian Theu-
nissen* (published by Humphrey Bromley, c. 1606). A later Broughton
book, *Eenighe schoone ende sekere bewijsredenen* (1611) was translated into
Dutch from English by "een liefhebber der waerheyt" (perhaps a
reference to Theunisz).[35]

Theunisz and his English friends pioneered in another scholarly
endeavor at Amsterdam, the linguistic study of Arabic. He had learned
some rudiments of Arabic while working with Raphelengius at Leiden, but he immensely improved his skill by practicing the language
with Arab visitors to Amsterdam. Theunisz rented out rooms and kept
an inn in his house; one of his boarders was 'Abd-al-'Aziz ibn
Mohammed, the secretary of the Moroccan ambassador to the Dutch
Republic (1609-10). At the same time Theunisz was also learning
Ethiopian. Slade and Paget joined Theunisz in Arabic studies and in
collecting Arabic books and manuscripts. 'Abd-al-'Aziz ibn
Mohammed made an Arabic translation of the four Gospels and
inscribed it: "In usum amici Johannis Paget."[36] With his newly
sharpened skill, Theunisz in 1612 applied to be professor of Arabic at
Leiden University, and, in fact, worked for one year as "lector in the
Arabic language". However, he lost the Arabic professorship after one
year of teaching, due to harsh opposition from several Leiden professors, who wanted a more "respectable" academic professor not an
Anabaptist tradesman-printer who had never finished his university
degrees. Thomas Erpenius gained the position as professor of Arabic in
1613.[37]

The Theunisz house on the Oudebrugsteeg always functioned as a
center of intellectual conversation. After 1608 he did little printing and

---

[35] The Bromley-Theunisz book is a translation of Broughton's *Parsjégen Nisjtawan*,
1606; Wijnman, "Jan Theunisz", *AJ* (1928), pp. 66, 115.
[36] H. F. Wijnman, "De Hebraïcus Jan Theunisz. Barbarossius alias Johannes
Antonides", *Studia Rosenthaliana*, 2 (1968), pp. 1-5.
[37] Ibid., pp. 18-21, 151-60; W.M.C. Juynboll, *Zeventiende-eeuwsche beoefenaars van
het Arabisch in Nederland* (Utrecht: Kemink en Zoon N.V., 1931), pp. 53-57;
Hamilton, *Bedwell*, p. 39.

concentrated on making a success of his "public house". "The Ox in the Wedding" (*D'Os in de Bruyloft*) became known far and wide for its crowd of visitors and for its ingenious mechanical "waterworks" organ, six stories high, which featured music and moving statues. Englishman William Brereton visited him in 1634 and described him as "a lusty old man, whose beard reacheth his girdle". Another Theunisz business was a gin distillery. At times he taught Hebrew at Coster's Academy under the surname Barbarossius.[38] As his lively career progressed, his religious piety declined, and the Waterlander Mennonite congregation disciplined him several times and banned him in 1626, but later restored him. Pious people disparagingly referred to him as an *afvallich Mennonist*, an apostate, backslidden Mennonite.[39] Theunisz's printing of Hebrew books for Broughton and his study of Arabic with Slade and Paget made him a valued figure in this circle of English-Dutch intellectuals.

Some other Dutch printers with English Puritan connections should be noted here. Johannes Janssonius, the son-in-law of Hondius, did much scholarly printing for Doctor William Ames (1576-1633), an exiled Puritan who had secured a professor's chair at Franeker University. Janssonius printed a steady stream of Latin books for Ames (Guilielmus Amesius) including the important 1658 *Opera Omnia*.[40] Ames was a friend of John Paget, although they differed on church government, and a frequent visitor to Amsterdam. Ames was the only expatriate Puritan to gain a position at a Dutch university. Broughton in 1605 had tried at Franeker but failed to get in.[41] Janssonius also printed Latin works for William Twisse, Matthew Slade, and John Bastwick, and Mercator atlases. Willem Jansz Blaeu and his son Joan Blaeu, although most of the time Remonstrants, printed one of Ames'

---

[38] Sir William Brereton, *Travels in Holland, the United Provinces, England, Scotland and Ireland*, ed. Edward Hawkins, Chetham Society, I (1844), p. 56; Brereton called him "Yantunus, who hath been professor in Leyden of the Arabic language". Wijnman, "De Hebraïcus Jan Theunisz", p. 175.

[39] On the Mennonite Career of Theunisz, see W.J. Kühler, *Geschiedenis der Nederlandsche Doopsgezinden*, 3 vols. (Haarlem: H. D. Tjeenk Willink & Zoon, 1932-56), II, 62-63, 158-60, 175; Piet Visser, *Broeders in de geest*, 2 vols., (Deventer: Uitgeverij Sub Rosa, 1988), I, 68-70, 108, 188; R.B. Evenhuis, *Ook dat was Amsterdam* (Amsterdam: W. Ten Have, 1965-78), II, 281. He was banned in 1626 and restored in 1634.

[40] Kleerkooper and Van Stockum, I, 295-301.

[41] Van der Woude, *Lubbertus*, pp. 390-91.

anti-Arminian books, *Anti-Sinodalia Scripta* (1633).[42] Another learned printer, Henricus Laurentius (Hendrik Laurensz), printed quite a number of books by English and Scottish authors in English, Dutch, and Latin. His authors included Thomas Brightman, John Fowler, William Ames, Dudley Fenner, Thomas Cartwright, and Samuel Rutherford.[43]

The scholarly confederation of Puritan and Dutch intellectuals and the "learned printers" often excluded Ainsworth and other Separatists. When Separatist and non-Separatist discussions occurred, they were most often hostile. Ainsworth had to rely upon the printing services of Giles Thorp, a trusted friend from the Separatist church. Although very knowledgeable in Hebrew, Ainsworth did not write or publish in Arabic or Hebrew, except for an occasional Hebrew word. Thorp's books have, at most, only a few scattered Hebrew words. Apparently, Thorp could not handle the language or did not have much of the type. A study of the typography of some of Broughton's English-language books suggests that he too—although a vehement anti-Separatist—went to Thorp for printing.[44]

The printer's or publisher's shop, presided over by a Hondius, Heyns, Theunisz, Janssonius, or Blaeu, promoted day-to-day scholarly interchange. As authors came and went, they would meet each other, as if by chance. "When I met you at the printers", Ainsworth reported to Broughton, "and had by occasion some litle speech hereof".[45] They could not meet in the same church, but the print shop and the city library were neutral ground. Broughton first encountered Rabbi David Farar at a print shop, probably that of Theunisz.[46] On John Evelyn's trip to the city in 1641, he eagerly sought out the inn of Theunisz—by then under new management—so that he could see the much talked-about waterworks machine, and then he canvassed the

---

[42] J. Keuning, *Willem Janszoon Blaeu* (Amsterdam: Theatrum Orbis Terrarum Ltd, 1973), pp. 28, 36.

[43] On the high interest in English Puritan books by Dutch readers, see W.J. op 't Hof, *Engelse pietistische geschriften in het Nederlands, 1598-1622* (Rotterdam: Lindenberg, 1987).

[44] STC, s.v. Broughton.

[45] Ainsworth and Broughton, *Certayne Questions*, p. 5.

[46] L. Hirschel, "Een godsdienstdisput te Amsterdam in het begin der 17e eeuw", *De Vrijdagavond*, 6 (5689 / June 21, 1929), p. 179; Wijnman, "Jodocus Hondius" (1944-46), p. 34.

booksellers, visiting the Hondius and Blaeu shops, "well-known to the Learned", to buy books.[47]

Other times the English scholars gathered at Slade's Latin school, as when Broughton debated with Jews in 1608, or they met at the city library, of which Slade was director, located in the Nieuwe Kerk. This remarkable library, another sign of Amsterdam's reach for scholarly achievement (in imitation of Alexandria's famous Museum), contained a rich collection of many fields of knowledge. According to H.F. Wijnman, this was the "center of the scholarly life of Amsterdam" in the late sixteenth and early seventeenth centuries. The books were written in Dutch, German, Hebrew, Syriac, Arabic, Ethiopian, Latin, Greek, and "in almost all languages of the world". The library was open to all readers.[48] The Puritan intellectuals often used its resources, and many a "chance" meeting led to stimulating and argumentative conversation. When Ainsworth and Broughton were debating about Hebrew topics, Ainsworth "bringth, to the Church Library" his Hebrew dictionaries, so that he "might seem to have some learning".[49] Paget and Ainsworth crossed paths at "the library of the great church" where, Paget reported, "I have divers times found you".[50] Such library learning was "study without Prayer...like to be but a prophane study".[51] Still, in Puritan, and even Separatist eyes, it could be enlightening.

Through their connections with the Amsterdam printers, Puritans gained the voice denied them at home. Their books spoke to the world. By means of the Frankfurt fair and the book catalogues, some of the books were distributed internationally. Broughton proclaimed: "Francfurt Mart shall beare me witnesse." The Frankfurt catalogues advertised many of Broughton's Hebrew books, which were printed at Amsterdam and handled by the Officiana Commeliniana, with

---

[47] Evelyn, *Diary* (Oxford Univ. Press ed., 1955), I, 34-35. Wijnman, "Jan Theunisz" (1928), pp. 37-38.

[48] Wijnman, "Geleerdenkring van Sladus", p. 441; Paul R. Sellin, *So Doth, So Is Religion: John Donne and Diplomatic Contexts in the Reformed Netherlands, 1619-1620* (Columbia: Univ. of Missouri Press, 1988), pp. 52, 210; Herman de la Verwey, "The City Library of Amsterdam in the Nieuwe Kerk 1578-1632", *Quaerendo*, 14 (1984), pp. 163-206.

[49] Broughton, "Admonition to Mr. Francis Blackwell", *Works*, III, 725.

[50] Paget, *An Arrow against the Separation*, STC 19098 (Amsterdam, 1618), pp. 159-160.

[51] Clapham, *Chronological Discourse*, sig. C1, summarizing Separatist concerns.

offices at Heidelberg, Amsterdam and Leiden. In Broughton's heated controversy of books with Archbishop Bancroft, "*Francfurt Mart*, may quietly trie betweene vs".[52] Giles Thorp had books listed in the fair catalogues several times. The Separatists promised a Latin version of Ainsworth's *Communion of Saints* in the fair catalogue (listed in 1608 as "Tractatus de communione, quam habent fides cum Deo and Angelis", apud Cornelium Nicolai"); but this was premature and Ainsworth never got out a Latin edition into print. A French version, *La Commvnion des Saincts*, par Giles Thorp, appeared eventually (1618). Ainsworth's enemies scoffed at his slow pace: "Cry vnto the Christians in every nation, and kindred and tongue"—if you dare![53]

Puritan Hebraists and the Jews

Of all the newly encountered people at Amsterdam, none made a greater impact upon Puritanism than the Jews. Since England had no active Jewish community, Jews having been expelled in 1290, Amsterdam was the meeting place for Puritans and Jews. The Sephardic Jews from Portugal and Spain and the Ashkenazic Jews from Germany and Poland had found their way to Amsterdam. By 1612 Jews numbered about 500. No public synagogues at first were allowed. The Jewish area of town, although not a rigid ghetto, was in the new, unfashionable quarter, the Vloonburg, taken into the city when it expanded the walls in 1593. Later, this was called the Waterlooplein area.[54]

Many English Brownists lived in the same Vloonburg quarter of town. The first Brownist meeting place was a house church in the home of Jean de l'Ecluse (or Lescluse) on the Lange Houtstraat. Next, in 1607 the Ancient Church built its own worship building, nearby on

---

[52] Broughton, *A Defence of the Booke*, STC 3858 (n.p., 1609), sigs. B4v, D4v; C.P. Burger Jr., "Amsterdamsche boeken op de Frankforter mis 1590-1609", *Het Boek*, 32 (1935-36), p. 183.

[53] Paget, *Arrow*, p. 86; Kleerkooper and Van Stockum, p. 1468; *Catalogus Universalis* (Frankfurt, autumn 1608, Blr, and autumn 1618, D4r). C. Nicolai (i.e. Cornelis Claesz) was one of the most important booksellers of Amsterdam; see B. van Selm, *Een menighte treffelijcke boeken: Nederlandse boekhandelscatalogi in het begin van de zeventiende eeuw* (Utrecht: Hes, 1987), chap 4.

[54] M.H. Gans, *Memorbook: History of Dutch Jewry from the Renaissance to 1940* (Baarn: Bosch & Keuning N.V., 1977), p. 29; Jonathan I. Israel, *European Jewry in the Age of Mercantilism 1559-1750* (Oxford: Clarendon Press, 1985), pp. 61-64.

the Lange Houtstraat. All around them were Jews, "being neighbours vnto the Brownists and dwelling hard by them". The Jews worshipped inconspicuously on the Houtgracht in a house synagogue (1610).[55] After the Johnson-Ainsworth Separatist church split in 1610, the Ainsworthians temporarily met in a building once used as one of the Jewish house synagogues—"in the Idol-temple of the Jews". The Brownist l'Ecluse, who moved to various locations in the Vloonburg, kept an inn for travellers; "tis not far from the *Synagog* of Jews."[56] The English settlers had daily rubbed shoulders with Jews, and the English found them exotic and fascinating. John Evelyn could hardly wait to see them when he came to the city. "The first thing, I went to see was a Synagogue of the *Jewes* (it being *Saturday*) whose Ceremonys, Ornaments, Lamps, Laws, and Scholes, afforded matter for my Contemplations."[57]

Stringent restrictions upon Jews loosened over the years, to allow public synagogues, schools, and a Hebrew printing press. Menasseh Ben Israel began printing Hebrew books in 1627, picking up where Theunisz and Hondius had left off. Humanists welcomed the inflow of new knowledge from the Jews. "Plainly, God desires them to live somewhere. Why not here, rather than elsewhere?" Certain strict Dutch Reformed churchmen tried to resist the inroads of Jewish influence, but to no avail. In due time, a "Hebraic patina" faintly touched seventeenth-century Amsterdam.[58]

The Puritan study of the Hebrew language and Jewish religion proceeded in earnest at Amsterdam. The Christian Hebraists, in the steps of Reuchlin, proclaimed four great values of Hebraic study: (1) Mastering the Hebrew language for the sake of humane, classical knowledge—a Hebrew Renaissance to match the earlier Greek and Latin Renaissances; (2) Aiding a deeper Christian study of the Bible and theology; (3) Converting the Jews to Christianity; and (4)

---

[55] Gans, *Memorbook*, p. 30; A.M. Vaz Dias, "Een verzoek om de Joden in Amsterdam een bepaalde woonplaats aan te wijzen", *AJ*, 35 (1938), pp.186-89; John Fowler, *A Shield of Defence*, STC 11212 (Amsterdam, 1612), p. 23. On relationships of Jews and Puritans, see also R.G. Fuks-Mansfeld, *De Sefardim in Amsterdam tot 1795* (Hilversum: Historische Vereniging Holland, 1989), pp. 87-91.

[56] Paget, *Arrow*, p. 26; Howell, *Epistolae Ho-Elianae*, I, 11 (1619).

[57] Evelyn, *Diary*, I, 31 (1641).

[58] Gans, *Memorbook*, pp. 25-28, 78 (quoting Busken Huet).

Through converting of the Jews, helping to bring in the Millennium.[59] The Puritan Hebraists, motivated chiefly by the goals of
converting the Jews, and enhancing knowledge of the Bible, saw
Hebrew study as a means to the greater Christian good. Amsterdam
was the "school" for gaining first-hand knowledge of the Jews and
their store of learning.

The most prominent Puritan Hebraists of Amsterdam were Hugh
Broughton, Matthew Slade, Henry Ainsworth, and John Paget. None
of these, except Broughton, had been particularly known before
immigration for unusual expertise in the Hebrew language or the
Talmud. All of them, no doubt, had studied Hebrew at their universities in England; at Amsterdam, however, they gained the motivation
and the resources to go deeply into this study. Language lessons,
discussions, and debates occurred. Also in seventeenth-century Amsterdam, the tools of Jewish scholarship increased greatly through the
printing of Hebrew books and new editions of the Talmud from
Jewish scholars. The writings of Maimonides, the twelfth-century rabbi
from Egypt, under the title *Mishneh Torah*, first became easily available
in print at Amsterdam. The *Mishneh Torah* in Latin and Hebrew
became "the sourcebook par excellence for an intense and still grow-
ing Christian interest in 'normative' Judaism".[60]

Ainsworth, Broughton, and fellow Puritan scholars were directly at
the center of the Christian Hebraic movement. They were some of
the first at Amsterdam to distinguish themselves in Hebrew linguistic
study and in the substance of the *Mishneh Torah*.[61] Broughton liked
to boast about his incomparable Hebrew skills—"Doctor of the
world"—which rather irritated his acquaintances. Was "our learned
Broughton"[62] always infallible? Henoch Clapham, pastor at Amsterdam, praised him "as sufficient for the holy tongue as any publikely
knowen off in Europe; he also could read it without stumblinge".

---

[59] Aaron L. Katchen, *Christian Hebraists and Dutch Rabbis: Seventeenth Century
Apologetics and the Study of Maimonides' Mishneh Torah* (Cambridge: Harvard University
Center for Jewish Studies, 1984), pp. 13-14, 29-30. See also Peter T. van Rooden,
*Theology, Biblical Scholarship and Rabinial Studies in the Seventeenth Century: Constantijn
L'Empereur (1591-1648) Professor of Hebrew and Theology at Leiden* (Leiden: E.J. Brill,
1989), chap. 3, "On the Use of Hebrew."

[60] Katchen, *Christian Hebraists* p. vii.

[61] Ibid., pp. 35-36.

[62] Ainsworth in *Certayne Questions*, p. 38; Thomas Brightman, *A Most Comfortable
Exposition of Daniel*, STC 3753 (n.p., 1635), p. 49.

Clapham also considered himself knowledgeable in Hebrew, although not in the same league as Broughton.[63]

Ainsworth had a tremendous reputation for Hebrew scholarship, especially among his Separatist brethren, being superior, they said, to anyone at Leiden University, and had "not his better for the hebrew tongve in the vniversitie. Nor scarce in Europa".[64] Many other Puritans at Amsterdam, learned scholars and some ingenious laymen, claimed skill in Hebrew. John Smyth of the English Anabaptist congregation taught that the preacher should work directly from the Hebrew-Greek text for preaching, rather than trusting to printed translations; indeed all members "must endeavour to their vtmost" to learn Hebrew and Greek.[65] Sabine Staresmore, an English merchant and sometime preacher, proclaimed his interest in Hebrew, having "not much skill in the Hebrue tongue, yet...I have looked upon the Hebrue Bible".[66] The Separatist and non-Separatist Puritan congregations were well supplied with persons, knowledgeable in Hebrew, or at least a smattering of it.

Hugo Grotius predicted, regarding the Jews, that "the scholars among them may be of service to us by teaching us the Hebrew language".[67] This, indeed, occurred. Tasting the richness of Hebrew learning led to the desire for more. Puritan preachers, curious for more knowledge, sought out conversations and debates with rabbis. Broughton and Rabbi David Farar debated about the value of the Old Testament and New Testament; Ainsworth challenged "some of his rabbies" about the prophecies of the Messiah. At Amsterdam the Jews were not reticent and spoke out openly against Christianity—to the distress of Puritans.[68] Meanwhile, the English Hebraists carried on

---

[63] Henoch Clapham, *Bibliotheca Theologica*, STC 5331 (Amsterdam, 1597), "The Proem".

[64] William Bradford, "A Dialogue or the sume of a Conference...1648", *Publications of the Colonial Society of Massachusetts*, 22 (1920), p. 136. On Ainsworth, see Michael E. Moody, "'A Man of a Thousand': The Reputation and Character of Henry Ainsworth, 1569/70-1622", *Huntington Library Quarterly*, 45 (1982), pp. 200-14.

[65] John Smyth, *Works*, ed. W.T. Whitley, 2 vols. (Cambridge: At the Univ. Press, 1915), I, 299.

[66] Sabine Staresmore, *The Vnlawfvlnes of Reading in Prayer*, STC 23235 (n.p., 1619), p. 16.

[67] Gans, *Memorbook*, pp. 25, 28.

[68] Daniel Neal, *History of the Puritans*, 5 vols. (London, 1822; reprint ed., Gregg, International, 1970), II, 42; Israel, *European Jewry*, p. 84; Fuks-Mansfeld, *De Sefardim*, pp. 88-91.

many debates among themselves about philological and historical questions. Ainsworth and Broughton argued, by sending letters back and forth through messengers, about the high priest Aaron's ephod—was it made of wool or silk? This required a close study of Hebrew words. How was the translator of Hebrew to "expresse the Consonants, Vowels...Accents"?[69] Broughton had a long-running controversy with scholars in England regarding the phrase, "he descended into hell", from the Creed. He took the emphatic position that Christ's was not a physical descent into the fiery hell; rather, based upon a philological examination of the Hebrew *sheol* and the Greek *hades*, that Christ went to the place of the dead (heaven or hell and in Christ's case, of course, heaven).[70]

Ainsworth and Broughton used Hebrew scholarship in their sermons and other pastoral work. Broughton urgently insisted that every earnest Christian must learn some Hebrew, the better to read Scripture with "a seriousness, and searching more then ordinary". According to reports, some of his disciples indeed were excited into studying Hebrew in their homes, with good results, "nay, a Woman might be named, that hath done it".[71]

The scholarly fruit of Hebrew study, for Broughton and Ainsworth, apart from pastoral work, led to a large output of books. Henry Ainsworth, whose office was "teacher" of his congregation, not a university professorship, did translations and commentaries of the Five Books of Moses, incorporating in them the "Greek and Chaldee Versions, and moniments of the Hebrewes".[72] In addition, Ainsworth produced his own translations of the Song of Solomon and the Psalms, "Englished both in Prose and Metre". All of these were printed by Giles Thorp or his successors at the Thorp printery. Also an avid Bible translator, Broughton produced his own translations and commentaries of Daniel, Ecclesiastes, Lamentations, Job, and the Apocalypse. With this wealth of experience, it was a bitter blow for him to be bypassed and excluded from the work of the official Bible translation of 1611,

---

[69] Paget, *Arrow*, p. 466; Broughton, *Works*, III, 723.

[70] Broughton, *Works*, II, 355; III, 727-46, 747-52; Dewey D. Wallace Jr., "Puritan and Anglican: The Interpretation of Christ's Descent into Hell in Elizabethan Theology", *Archiv für Reformationsgeschichte*, 69 (1978), p. 280.

[71] Broughton, *Works*, preface by Lightfoot.

[72] Henry Ainsworth, *Annotations upon Leviticus*, STC 214 (n.p., 1618), title page.

especially since he had been one of the earliest to urge such a translation project.[73]

For the Puritan Hebraists the most glorious and eternal outcome of their work was to be conversion of the Jews to Christianity. Ainsworth may be the exception here, since he said little about conversion. Broughton, with his vast Hebrew erudition, led the way in confronting the Jews with the Christian message. The Broughton method was to overwhelm by arguments and summon the adversary to Jesus the Messiah. Broughton was *homo furiosus et maledicus*[74]—and he always spoke with "wondrous boldness, and freeness". His pen was like a "thunderbolt", his mouth could destroy.[75] Once while visiting a synagogue in Germany, a Jew asked Broughton, "Did not our Minister sing like an Angel?" Broughton: "No...he barks like a Dog." Broughton was indeed brave but foolhardy.[76]

Broughton's principal debates with Jews were these: (1) With Rabbi Elias at Frankfurt synagogue in 1589; (2) A second time with Elias, about 1599 at Basle, "a Rabbin most desirous of christianity"; (3) With Rabbi Wolf at Hanau; (4) With Rabbi David Farar at Amsterdam in 1608. Broughton also achieved a great spiritual encounter, via letter in 1596, with Rabbi Abraham Reuben of Constantinople. In every meeting with Jews, he preached that Jesus is the Messiah and that the Old Testament invariably points toward the fulfillment of the New Testament.[77]

The fruits of these debates were always meager in terms of victories for Christ. Rabbi Elias seemed almost persuaded, thought Broughton, almost "desirous of Christianity"; but he would not take the decisive step. The others were hard of heart, hoping to "overthrow the Gospel". When Rabbi Elias in 1589 departed from their meetings still

---

[73] See Broughton's letter to Sir William Cecil, June 21, 1593, where he urged Cecil to sponsor a new Bible Translation, Lansdown MSS. 75, no. 4, fols. 8r-9v (British Library).

[74] The descriptive phrase is from Joseph Scaliger; *BL*, I, 103.

[75] Broughton, *A Petition to the King*, STC 3877 (n.p., n.d.), sig. A2; *Works*, Lightfoot preface.

[76] Broughton, *Works*, Lightfoot preface.

[77] Ibid.; Broughton, *A Revelation of the Apocalyps*, STC 3884 (n.p., 1610), pp. 337-38; Broughton, *A Reqvire of Agreement to the Groundes of Divinitie Studie*, STC 3882 (n.p., 1611), Dedication and p. 1.

doubting Jesus, he flattered Broughton by asking for more information, "with desire to bee taught by printing".[78]

Books would carry the message. Broughton immediately grasped a
larger strategy, to teach the Jews by printing. To this end, he invited
the printers of Europe to join with him in a campaign to convert the
Children of Israel. The next step in his Jewish strategy occurred in
1596 when he received the Hebrew letter from Rabbi Abraham
Reuben of Constantinople, who can not be accurately identified
today. The pious rabbi implored him "to haue our Gospell opened in
Ebrew". It seemed obvious to Broughton that if the New Testament
could be put into the Jews' language, they would certainly believe in
Jesus. Broughton would work wonders; even some Jews confessed, he
will "turne all our nation".[79]

Why speak to only one rabbi at a time in one isolated debate or by
a single written letter? Why hinder the swift spreading of the Gospel?
The printing press could produce "a thousand copies" of books for the
Jews instead of "one poor letter".[80] Broughton set the printing
presses, first of Basle, then of Amsterdam into full motion: 1,000
copies here, 36,000 copies there; then another 3,000 copies, in seven
different languages "thus far a doore is opened". By his alliance with
the printing press, Broughton announced a grand missionary strategy,
"To fill the world with bookes of our faith...to fill the world quick-
lie".[81]

By 1605, Broughton's efforts had shifted to the Netherlands. To
achieve this work of the Lord, he proposed setting up at Amsterdam
a little academy of scribes, scholars, and "learned Printers", with
himself at the head. They would correlate the Christian and Talmudic
literature, translate the New Testament into Hebrew, produce suitable
dictionaries, and print them up in huge quantities. Much money
would be required. In a petition to "Any of the Lords of the Privy
Council" (1604-05), he requested a "princely allowance" to buy up
Hebrew and Talmudic reference books, to pay himself a generous
salary, and "to hyre common Ebrew setters at *Venice* or *Basill*".

---

[78] *Reqvire of Agreement*, p. 1; *Ovr Lordes Famile*, STC 3875 (Amsterdam, 1608), title
page.
[79] Broughton, *Defence of the Booke*, dedication and sig. D3v; *Reqvire of Agreement*, p.
1. The Rabbi Abraham Reuben letter led to extensive writing on Broughton's part.
[80] Broughton, *Works*, III, 840.
[81] *Reqvire of Agreement*, p. 2; *Ovr Lordes Famile*, "To the Kinges Maiestie".

Broughton promised, "The Bible and the Thalmud shalbe opened by Gods helpe".[82]

The call for printers skilled in Hebrew touched on a difficult problem. Up to 1605, Broughton had found few printers of Hebrew in Holland, except for the university printers at Leiden. Most printers of England and Holland could not work in Hebrew "for want of skil & letters".[83] This was the reason for his earlier printing activities at Basle, Geneva, and Frankfurt. The call for princely patronage never produced any funds for his proposed Broughtonian Hebrew academy and staff of Hebrew printers. Instead, ordinary Amsterdam printers and publishers (most likely the shops of Hondius, Heyns, and Theunisz) had to carry the load. Although short of printers, Broughton found several English supporters willing to help with finances. "From Amsterdam I sent forth more books", said Broughton.[84] As for those dull spirits, like archbishops and bishops, who thwarted his plans for a royal subsidy, Broughton had only contempt. "Anathema" on them.

During the years of 1605-1611, while Broughton was pastor in Middelburg, but often in Amsterdam, he put forth at Amsterdam over a dozen books with some Hebrew typography (done in four sets of type). L. Fuks and R.G. Fuks-Mansfeld have highlighted seven of them with extensive Hebrew texts: *A Comment upon Coheleth or Ecclesiastes* (n.p., 1605, STC 3849); *Familia Davidis* (Amstelodami: Zacharias Heinsius, 1605); *The Familie of David* (Amstelredam: Zacharias Heyns, 1605, STC 3867.5); a treatise about the sequence of the Jubilee years (entirely in Hebrew; Amsterdam, 1606); A Hebrew letter of Abraham b. Reuben from Constantinople and the answer of Broughton (entirely in Hebrew; Amsterdam, 1606); a Hebrew treatise on biblical history, with Latin translation, *Responsum ad epistolam Judaei* (Amsterdam, 1606); and two Hebrew letters unto great men of Britain about converting Jews (Amsterdam, 1606).[85] Two other similar books should also be emphasized here, the second version of *The Familie of David* (Amstelredam, Ian Theunisz, 1606, STC 3867.7) and *Certayne Questions concerning Silk or Wool* (Amsterdam, 1605, STC 3848). Broughton was always a prolific writer, but these Middelburg-Amster-

---

[82] *Revelation of the Apocalypse*, p. 338; *An Advertisement of Corrvption in Ovr Handling of Religion*, STC 3844 (n.p., 1604), p. 110; HMC, Salisbury XVII, 575-76.

[83] Broughton, *An Exposition vpon the Lords Prayer*, STC 3867 (n.p., n.d.), p. 1.

[84] L. Hirschel, "Hondius en Broughton" (1928), p. 208.

[85] Fuks and Fuks, *Hebrew Typography*, I, 94-99; cf. Hirschel, *AJ* (1934) and Wijnman, *AJ* (1928).

dam years were the pinnacle of his productivity (the *STC* lists over 30
titles printed in the Netherlands for that period). Of all of these, the
books on Jewish conversion were his greatest priority. These books "I
dispersed in many thousand copies by Sea & Land over Europe &
Asia".[86]

Although Broughton made exceptional use of the printing press for
scholarship and evangelism, his relationship with printers, like all of his
personal relationships, was strained. The *furiosus* and *maledicus*
Broughton demanded perfection in workmanship, while being rather
stingy in settling his bills. He insisted to the printers, "that to misse in
one letter is a corruption of the whole worlde" (a rabbanic proverb),
and when the printer missed the mark, he was indeed "furious".[87]
When his London printer garbled the Hebrew lines in his commentary
on *Daniel* (1596), Broughton exploded. "I...haue bene iniuried by a
Printer, who hath corrupted my commentaries." No malicious adversary could have sabotaged him as much as this careless printer. Nothing satisfied Broughton except to order a thousand new copies of the
Hebrew portion of the book from Raphelengius of Leiden.[88] On
several occasions he had to call down damnation from heaven upon
printers who crossed him or printed books written against him. After
one unpleasant book attacking him, Broughton rejoiced at heaven's
vengeance in punishing the bookseller and the printer. "God killed the
printer"; then, "God called...the stationer."[89] The printers of two
other hostile books paid the price and "descendeth to Hell".[90]

Printers always wanted money, "pieuish printers, and greadie of
vnhonest gaynes". They chased after him demanding to be paid. Printers
once cut off his work at Geneva, and they followed him to Amsterdam
in 1608, in the midst of his Hebrew study, and told the Dutch printers
about "how they used me in Geneva". Broughton's Amsterdam printer

---

[86] Broughton, *A Comment vpon Coheleth or Ecclesiastes*, STC 3849 (n.p., 1605),
dedication.

[87] Broughton, *An Epistle to the Learned Nobilitie of England*, STC 3862 (Middelburg,
1597), sig. H1r.

[88] Ibid., sig. H1r. Cf. the two versions of Broughton's *Daniel his Chaldie Visions and
His Ebrew*, STC 2785 (1596) and 2786 (1597), both at the Huntington Library. In the
former version, sig. K1vv, the columns of Hebrew text are reversed, with the marginal
note added, "Here the reader must helpe the printe: where the text of the right
colume should chaunge place with the left". In the latter edition (2786), these pages
are replaced with the correct rendering.

[89] *Ovr Lordes Famile*, (*Works*, II, 370).

[90] Broughton, *Advertisement*, p. 42.

took their advice, turned peevish, and "telleth me, he will not print my book unlesse I pay him".[91] Here at stake was the most urgent work of a century—and all the printers could think of was payment.

In spite of heroic efforts, Broughton's results from his Jewish projects were most disappointing. He blamed printers, the lack of funding, and the Jews themselves. If they reject Christ, they are "dog Jewes". "They have Satan breathing in them". He may have "won" some of his debates with Jews, and overwhelmed them with a flood of books, but his harvest of souls for Christ was piteously small. Broughton could only point to three definite conversions, two Italian Jews and one Jew in England.[92]

Broughton's "mission" to the Jews blended with a larger movement of Jewish outreach, supported by other English and Dutch persons of Amsterdam. The English "vision" for the Jews corresponded with a Dutch "visie".[93] Many Puritan books printed at Amsterdam spoke to Jewish topics in discussions of evangelism and millenarianism. For Puritan millenarians, the Jews had a special place in the speculations about the "last days". The conversion of Jews to the Messiahship of Jesus was accounted as a definite step in the return of the Lord. The sooner they were converted, the sooner Jesus would return for the end of the age, hopefully by 1650.[94] Thomas Brightman (1562-1607), the learned prophetic scholar, exerted an influence at Amsterdam, without ever visiting the city. Several of his prophetic books were printed at Amsterdam; the cost, apparently, was borne by Puritanical admirers in the city. Brightman's commentaries on the Revelation and Daniel appealed because of their tantalizing, visionary view of the future in which the Christianizing of the Jews was central, and also because of their prophetic denunciation of the Church of England.[95]

---

[91] Broughton, *Epistle*, sig. H2r; *An Answer to the Iniurious Complaint of R. C.*, STC 3844.7, in *Works*, III, 785. Broughton did not mention the name of the Amsterdam printer who was demanding payment (Hondius? Theunisz?).

[92] Broughton, *Epistle*, p. 43; *Reqvire of Agreement*, p. 1.

[93] W.J. op 't Hof, *De visie op de Joden in de Nadere Reformatie tijdens het eerste kwart van de zeventiende eeuw* (Amsterdam; Ton Bolland, 1984), pp. 56-71, 99-100; J. van den Berg, *Joden en Christenen in Nederland*, pp. 25-43. An English version of some of Van den Berg's writing can be found in Peter Toon, *Puritans, the Millennium and the Future of Israel* (Cambridge: James Clark, 1970), pp. 137-53.

[94] David S. Katz, *Philo-Semitism and the Readmission of the Jews to England 1603-1655* (Oxford: Clarendon Press, 1982), chap. 3.

[95] Paul Christianson, *Reformers and Babylon: English Apocalyptic Visions from the Reformation to the Eve of the Civil War* (Toronto: Univ. of Toronto Press, 1978), pp. 100-06.

Other Amsterdam Puritans had a burden for the Jews. Such was Humphrey Bromley, the English candle seller and amateur Hebraist of Amsterdam; he was swayed by Broughton and paid to have one of Broughton's books put into Dutch translation and printed (1606). In this way Bromley furthered the work of converting the Jews. To neglect this work would make us "worse than the Turks". John Harrison's *Messiah Alreadie Come* (printed at Amsterdam in 1613 and again in 1619) made an appeal to the Jews to accept Jesus. Harrison claimed to have "a little tast" of Hebrew from living in Barbary.[96] Amsterdam Puritans saw to the printing of books like these. Another book in this spirit was Sir Henry Finch's *The Calling of the Jewes*. A Dutch version, *Een schoone prophecye*, appeared in Holland in 1623.[97]

Some unintended consequences followed from meeting and studying about the Jews. The borrowing of Jewish practices or doctrines and mingling them into Christianity was called "Judaizing". Such Judaizing occurred in Amsterdam, just as it had in England. The Puritan Hebraists (Broughton, Ainsworth, and Paget) did not intend for this to happen. The chief Judaizer of England was John Traske (1585-1636), and his followers were the "Traskites".[98] In the Amsterdam English churches the most frequent Judaizing tendency was Saturday Sabbatarianism; this and other Jewish practices emerged in the churches every few years. A hint of Judaizing had sprung up in the Separatist church in 1602. Details are scanty, except that Thomas Wolsey, a prisoner in Norwich, wrote a letter to the Separatist church at Amsterdam "in which he endeavours to prove it unlawful to eat *blood, things strangled,* and *things offered to idols* now in the times of the Gospel". The officers of the church (Francis Johnson, Henry Ainsworth, Daniel Studley, and Stanshal Mercer) responded with a letter to Wolsey denying that the Old Testament laws on food were any longer obligatory. These dietary laws, they said, "we hold to be temporary, and was then a figure for the time present, but is now disannulled...". Must we at Amsterdam "enquire at the shambles

---

[96] Bromley edition of Broughton's response to Rabbi Abraham Reuben's letter, *Antwoort. Op een Hebreuschen brief van een Jode* (Amsterdam: Humphrey Bromley, n.d.), epilogue by Bromley; John Harrison, *The Messiah Already Come*, STC 12858 (Amsterdam, 1619). p. 68.

[97] Kn. 3394.

[98] Katz, *Philo-Semitism*, pp. 18-32. On Traske, see also B.R. White, "John Traske (1585-1636) and London Puritanism", *Transactions of the Congregationial Historical Society*, 20 (1968), pp. 223-33; and Henry E.I. Phillips, "An Early Stuart Judaising Sect", *Transactions of the Jewish Historical Society of England*, 15 (sessions 1939-45), pp. 63-72.

touching every little beast & bird that we buy, whether it were duely slaine or no, and the blood let out, according to the law, *Levit.* 17.13"? Must we "come to the Jews superstition, that buy not their flesh at the shambles of the Gentiles, but slay them themselves?"[99] Of course not!

The Traskite opinion on Saturday-sabbatarianism and Jewish practice gained new strength at Amsterdam with the immigration of several of Traske's people in the 1620s. Traske himself recanted his Judaizing doctrines in 1619, but "Traskism" carried on. The best-known Amsterdam Traskites of English background, were Hamlet Jackson and Christopher Sands. They fraternized with Jews and "turned directly Jew". Jackson was more extreme; he renounced the Messiahship of Jesus and was circumcised by Dutch Jews; Sands stopped short of circumcision and was content to be a Gentile Saint, observing some but not all legalities. They honored the seventh day instead of Sunday. Jackson declared that he would "rather question Pauls writings, then the fourth Commandment". Sir William Brereton in 1634 met an Englishman and his wife "lately turned Jew". The large majority of Amsterdam English people viewed all of these happenings with abhorrence, "the most horrid, fearful, scoffing blasphemer of Christ and Christian Religion, that was to be found or heard of in those places". Had they done it "merely to enrich themselves"?[100] Another manifestation of Traskism was the publication at Amsterdam of Theophilus Brabourne's *Defence of That Most Ancient, and Sacred Ordinance of Gods, the Sabbath Day* (1632). Although Brabourne did not personally visit Holland, some Judaizers of Amsterdam saw to the publishing of the book.[101]

Paget's English Reformed Church had its own cases of Sabbath Christians; one was Thomas Adams, who had to be disciplined for "obstinate" opinions about the "Satursdays Sabbath".[102] To counteract

---

[99] Henry Ainsworth et al., *A Seasonable Treatise for This Age*, Wing S2245 (London, 1657), title page, pp. 3, 17. The contents of the book were dated Dec. 7, 1602, but the book itself was not published until 1657.

[100] Ephraim Pagitt, *Heresiography*, 6th ed., Wing P182 (London, 1662), pp. 180, 190-92, 196; Brereton, *Travels*, pp. 60-61; Katz, *Philo-Semitism*, pp. 28-30; Katz, *Sabbath and Sectarianism in Seventeenth-Century England* (Leiden: E.J. Brill, 1988), pp. 12-13.

[101] Katz, *Philo-Semitism*, pp. 34-35. Two of Brabourne's books, apparently, were published in the Netherlands, *A Discourse upon the Sabbath Day*, STC 3474 (n.p., 1628), and *A Defence of the Sabbath Day*, STC 3473 (n.p., 1632).

[102] ERC Amsterdam, CR, III, 129 (1642).

these horrid opinions, numerous orthodox books supporting strict
Sunday observance and warning against Judaizing doctrines appeared
at Amsterdam and Leiden in the 1630s. These were for the benefit of
English congregations in the Netherlands and for the churches of
England. Among these anti-Judaizing treatises were George Walker's
The Doctrine of the Sabbath (Amsterdam, 1638 and 1639) and Thomas
Young's *Dies Dominica* (Leiden, 1639), the latter written under the
pseudonym of Theophilus Philokuriaces.

Puritans could very easily argue that the study of Jewish religion
was dangerous. What could Christians learn from the Jews, "the
professed enemies of Christe"?[103] The Puritan debate over the value
of Hebrew language and Jewish religion for Christians was carried on
for several years by Henry Ainsworth and John Paget, pastors of the
"Ancient" (Separatist) Church and the English Reformed Church.
Although critical of much in Judaism, Ainsworth found much to
admire. He had given great effort to master the Hebrew language,
and, as a consequent blessing, he now discerned many Jewish insights
applicable to the study of the Old and New Testaments, "God having
given him a gift in opening the mysteries contained in the Law of the
Shadows".[104] He used the "original Hebrue" language for his *Book
of Psalmes Englished* (1612), and the *Annotations vpon the Five Bookes of
Moses* (1622; printed earlier in sections in 1616, 1617, 1618, and
1619). He admitted to borrowing from rabbinical commentaries "of
the ancienter sort, and some later of best esteem for learning".[105]

Ainsworth's most relied-upon texts for translation and commentary
were, apart from the Scriptures themselves, the Greek Septuagint, and
from Hebrew scholarship the "Chaldee paraphrases" and the works of
Maimonides. Such resources provided two benefits: (1) historical
information about the external practices of the Jews, and (2) linguistic
information about the exact meaning of words, phrases, and language,
showing how they foreshadow the New Testament, and "so the
testimony of the adversary against himself, helpeth our faith".[106] In
the preface to his *Annotations upon Genesis* (1616), he explained that
Moses, a Hebrew, wrote in the Hebrew language; thus by mastering

---

[103] Fowler, *Shield of Defence*, p. 23.

[104] Ainsworth, *Seasonable Treatise*, preface by T. W. (Thomas Wall).

[105] *The Book of Psalmes: Englished Both in Prose and Metre*, STC 2407 (Amsterdam,
1612), preface and pp. 1-3; Ainsworth, *Annotation upon Genesis*, STC 210 (n.p., 1616),
preface.

[106] Ainsworth, *Annotations upon Genesis*, preface.

the language, "the mysteries of godlynes therin implied, may the better be discerned". Seeming discrepancies in the variant Hebrew texts must be struggled with and reconciled, and Christians would benefit greatly from penetrating into these Hebrew "mysteries". Ainsworth approved of a saying of the Hebrew doctors, that "*the Law hath seventie faces*", that is, seventy ways to be opened and applied "*and all of them trueth*".[107] For a strict Separatist, Ainsworth's eager views on Hebrew scholarship are quite remarkable.

His opponent, John Paget, also fancied himself a fine scholar of the Hebrew language, but he could not take such a generous position as Ainsworth. He sharply challenged Ainsworth's stand on Christian-Jewish scholarship; *The Arrow against the Separation* (1618) not only attacked Ainsworth's Separatism but also his standing as an interpreter of Jewish topics. To enlarge on the matter, Paget wrote a large appendix for the *Arrow*, "An Admonition Touching Talmvdiqve and Rabbinical Allegations" (pp. 339-476). This elaborates on seven "scandals" of the Talmudists and Cabalists.

Among Ainsworth's many dangerous tendencies, two were most deadly. First was his use of variant Hebrew Old Testament texts, thus implying errors in the sacred Scripture. "Before this time, I never heard of any Christian, that durst avouch so peremptorily", as if God were "like *Janus Bifrons*, the idoll with two faces", looking two ways at once. Second, Ainsworth respected the Talmudists too much. "You runne vnto the *Thalmud*". For Christians to depend on and praise the Talmud detracted from the honor of God's Scriptures, which were sufficient and perfect in themselves. "What have we to do with the opinions of these fabulous and blasphemous Thalmudists?" Paget urged: "Cannot the controversie betwixt vs be decided by the word of God, and by the voyce of the holy scriptures?"[108]

Like Broughton, Paget was very harsh toward the Jewish people of the past and present. They were "blinde and obstinate Jewes". He warned that they are "wicked persons, despisers of Christ". The Talmud could be to Christians a "black darknes...vtter darknes...a hellish dungeon".[109] Paget, intent on keeping his English Reformed Church free from Jewish taint, considered Ainsworth far too lax in

---

[107] Ibid.

[108] Paget, *Arrow*, pp. 372, 106-07, 419. Paget cited a large number of Jewish sources in marginal notes as he rebutted Ainsworth.

[109] Ibid., pp. 26, 287, 449.

defending Christianity against Judaizing. Ainsworth wrote a response to Paget in "An Advertisement to the Reader, Touching Some Objections Made Against the Sinceritie of the Hebrew Text, and Allegations of the Rabbines" in the *Annotations upon Deuteronomie* (1619).

Amateur scholars, crackpots, and secret knowledge

While pastor John Paget and pastor Henry Ainsworth tested and debated the erudite doctrines of Jewish learning, they uneasily observed another arena of activity, occupied by English amateurs and self-educated prophets pursuing their own roads to knowledge. Humphrey Bromley and Thomas Leamer were two of these self-proclaimed "scholars" of the lower road of Puritanism. They and their disciples tasted Amsterdam's Babylonish freedom and found it good. This grassroots Puritan movement, outside the bounds of orthodox opinion, went beyond the control of the respectable English churches and caused Paget and Ainsworth much grief and worry.

The first of the notorious Englishmen was Humphrey Bromley (fl. 1605-49), an English wax chandler living "on the Newen dyke". His business was selling wax and candles. A long-time resident of Amsterdam, he had married a Dutch wife and joined the Dutch Reformed Church. In 1607 he became a founding member of the English Reformed Church in the Begijnhof. His sister also became a member of the English church. Regardless of the church in which he claimed membership, Dutch or English, Bromley was always a fringe member and most troublesome because of his strong-willed, unpredictable opinions.[110] Another unorthodox Puritan was Thomas Leamer (fl. 1592-1627). He was a merchant and mariner from England living "op't Ruslant in de Colonel".[111] Leamer and Bromley would have lived and died in obscurity except for their ability to write and publish books which gave them a local reputation. Although they did not

---

[110] ERC Amsterdam, CR, I, 3, 16 (Bromley was one of the 68 original members); *NNBW*, IX, 100-01. Bromley was the center of many discipline cases in the Dutch Reformed Kerkeraad in 1605-06 before transferring to the English Church. On Bromley's disciplinary record in the Dutch church, see Herman Roodenburg, *Onder censuur: De kerkelijke tucht in de gereformeerde gemeente van Amsterdam, 1578-1700* (Hilversum: Verloren, 1990), pp. 193, 366.

[111] On Leamer, see *NNBW*, II, 790-91; Leamer, *Een klaer vertoninge*, Kn. 2030, title page; Evenhuis, *Ook dat was Amsterdam*, II, 237-41.

work together as a team, each pursuing his own course, they emerged out of the same Puritan fringe underworld at Amsterdam.

The Bromley-Leamer type of Puritanism was thoroughly eccentric. During the working day, the dilettante scholars would be merchants or tradesmen, but in spare hours they were preachers and authors. Not trained in formal logic and lacking university degrees, they nevertheless hungered for knowledge—immediate, useful knowledge. They wanted access to the secrets and mysteries of heaven and earth. They wanted illumination and desired fast results. The ardent, grassroots prophets sought truth in all available places: the Bible, theology, the Hebrew language, astrology, alchemy, the Talmudic lore of the Amsterdam rabbis, the Cabala, and the incomparable Doctor Paracelsus. This Puritanism of the people, like other lay movements of Europe, promised a holy immediacy with God and Nature, without having to rely on the supervision of learned theologians like Paget and Ainsworth.[112] The established preachers of the churches, of course, were alarmed at this insurgency and tried to head it off; all the same it flourished. The scoldings of the preachers did not silence the Bromleys and Leamers. After all, Doctor Paracelsus had predicted and advised that the edicts of the intellectual elite can be safely disregarded.[113]

The preachers of the English churches were the arbiters of respectable opinion. Above all, the Puritan preachers warned, be wary of the Cabala and its "curious speculations".[114] The Cabala gave access to secret, mysterious learning, and revealed ultimate meanings of numbers and letters. Henry Ainsworth himself, in spite of his deep-rooted suspicions of mysticism, gleaned a few helpful doctrines from the examples of the Cabala, especially on the hidden meaning of words. In his translation of the Psalms, he discovered meaning at two levels. He translated Psalm 14:7:

> Who will give out of Sion, the salvation of Israel?
> When Jehoveh returneth the captivitie of his people:
> Jacob shall be glad. Israel shall rejoyce.

---

[112] On the widespread European popular interest in Paracelsus, the Cabala, and other mysterious learning, see Miriam U. Chrisman, *Lay Culture, Learned Culture: Books and Social Change in Strasbourg 1480-1599* (New Haven: Yale Univ. Press, 1982), pp. 224-25; Frances Yates, *The Rosicrucian Enlightenment* (London: Routledge & Kegan Paul, 1972), passim; Walter Pagel, *Paracelsus: An Introduction to Philosophical Medicine in the Era of The Renaissance*, 2nd ed. (Basel: S. Karger, 1982), pp. 35-44.

[113] Pagel, *Paracelsus*, p. 44; Chrisman, *Lay Culture, Learned Culture*, p. 227.

[114] Paget, *Arrow*, p. 51.

At one level, this spoke of God's transcendent power. However, at another level of mystical understanding, the words themselves revealed a hidden message. Ainsworth was struck by the double use of the word ISRAEL. This amazing word, Ainsworth announced, contains the first letters of the names of Abraham and his wife Sarah, of Israel and his wife Rebecca, and of Jacob and both of his wives Leah and Rachel.[115] Thus, the blessing of Bible study was increased. Although this is a very mild example of word play for pious purposes, it does suggest that Ainsworth in some instances did "imitate" the "cabalists".

Paget severely castigated Ainsworth for this Cabalistic commentary; Paget demonstrated how one could achieve nearly the same results with the word SEPARATION (almost all of Ainsworth's Biblical names plus Johnson with an I, Smyth, Robinson, and Ainsworth himself.) But what would that prove? Paget urgently warned all Christians to flee from this dangerous heap and separate the "wheate" from the "chaffe" of knowledge.[116] Ainsworth sampled the Cabala only a little; Paget advised to shun it entirely. The grassroots scholars were more adventuresome. They were creating their own "enlightenment".

Bromley was adventuresome and self-taught in many fields. The candle business was not a sufficient challenge for him; he aspired to be a scholar and man of knowledge. His first learned venture was into Jewish matters. At that time Hugh Broughton was actively promoting evangelism among the Jews, and Bromley caught Broughton's vision for Jewish conversion. Bromley's contribution to Broughton's Jewish project was to publish and sell in 1606 a Dutch version of Broughton's letter to Rabbi Abraham Reuben: *Antwoort. Op een Hebreuschen brief van een Jode.* Translated for him by Jan Theunisz, it carried the Bromley imprint: "Amstelredam: Men vintse te coop by Humphrey Bromley Engelsman, was-vercooper ende caersmaecker op de Nieuwe-dijck int Wapen van Spangien" (i.e., available for sale at Humphrey Bromley, Englishman, wax-seller and candle-maker on the Nieuwendijk at the Arms of Spain).[117] Although Bromley personally

---

[115] Ainsworth, *Annotations upon the Book of Psalmes*, 2nd ed., STC 2411 (n.p., 1617), sig. E3r.

[116] Paget, *Arrow*, pp. 51-52. On Christian uses of the Cabala, see *Encyclopedia Judaica*, X:643-46.

[117] Bromley's *Antwoort* is not dated. The Univ. of Amsterdam copy has the date 1606 pencilled in. This date seems to be the correct one. The epilogue by Bromley refers to "1573 years" since the death of Christ (i.e. 1606). Also, the acta of the Amsterdam kerkeraad for May 26, 1606 refer to a recent book by Bromley; III, 145.

knew little Hebrew and had to depend on Theunisz, he felt a great desire to invest his money in God's work and thus to do his little part in the winning of the Jews "to the true and sunshiny path of Christianity".[118]

As an astute shopkeeper and entrepreneur with candles and books to sell, Bromley used his publication to advertise both of his products. On the title page, he announced the selling of the Dutch book in hand, and he also offered editions of Broughton's book in Hebrew, Greek, and Latin. On the back of the title page, to avoid wasting blank space, he advertised his candles and wax products: Bromley's table candles, wedding candles, book candles, and so on. Obviously, the book had cost him plenty of money, but he still hoped to turn a profit overall while advancing his religious ideals. This book was just the beginning of his career in disseminating knowledge.

After gaining a small reputation for Hebrew study—being "a poore Englyshman of some knowledge"—Bromley branched into fresh fields of information. He played theologian and attempted to be a conciliator in the Arminian-Calvinist disputes of 1617-18; this proved to be dangerous. He received threats: "knock him on the head", and the like.[119] In addition, he explored bigamy, quick salving, and all kinds of occultic mysteries. Bromley was not a good church member and he refused pastoral admonition. Paget and the church elders saw Bromley as presumptuous and reaching far above his proper station in life. Who was he to pretend to be a scholar? The English church sought to bring him back into line and restrain "his rediculous and unlawfull practices". In 1620 the elders suspended him from the Lords Table for grievous sins. Among the crimes were that Bromley advocated speaking with angels and good spirits out in a wood—based on the authority of Doctor Paracelsus. There were gory reports that Bromley had a "box wherin was mans flesh cut from a mans heart on the gallowes, wherin wormes did creepe".[120]

In 1623 the English elders had to step in again, this time for his alchemistic bragging and claims for "a golden art and the philosophers stone to make gold". He advertised having a "Philosophers Tower"

[118] *Antwoort*, epilogue by Bromley.

[119] SP 84/76/126; G. Brandt, *Historie der Reformatie, en andere kerkelyke geschiedenissen* (Amsterdam, 1671), II, 484, which identified Bromley as the Englishman involved; Evenhuis, *Ook dat was Amsterdam*, I, 238-39.

[120] CR, I, 99, 108-09; II, 1-4, 11-12; Carter, *English Reformed Church*, pp. 61-64.

which was open to the public. The church officials scolded Bromley for "his vainglory and ambition in making ostentation of skill in philosophy and hanging up tables in many boastfull phrases". His printed "tables" or posters were emblazoned with "sayings of the Holy Ghost".[121] Such antics were terribly embarrassing to the English Church, which felt responsible for upholding the good name of the English nation, but nothing could silence Bromley, not even excommunication (which he endured until 1649). Sometimes he travelled to Leiden to mingle with the scholars at the university and to peddle some of his wares; on one trip he had "certain monstrous and embalmed babies", which he sold to the university for 25 florins.[122] He was a shameless profaner of the Sabbath. In 1630 Bromley appealed to the public with a second book, *Den Engelschen-Stats-Roep*.[123] Bromley is a good example of the curious, self-educated Puritan who strayed off the established paths. The last word on Bromley is 1649, when the church lifted his excommunication.

Equally infamous was Thomas Leamer. This English merchant had lived abroad in the Netherlands and Germany since about 1592.[124] Formerly joined with the Separatists and then the Anabaptists, he soon drifted into total, outright heresy. The Dutch Reformed consistory investigated and condemned him many times, having reports that "he seeks to establish his own church here". Pastor John Paget pronounced that Leamer was "the Monster of Lemarisme". Leamerism, feared by English Puritan and Dutch Reformed, consisted of a hideous mixture of Mohammedanism, Judaism, Papism, Lutheranism, Anabaptism, Libertinism, Brownism, and Arianism—a veritable walking library of false religions.[125] Although Leamer never established his own recognized church, as some had feared, he attracted a circle of disciples, and Paget in 1610 expressed concern about some of his English Reformed members who had slipped away to Leamer's heretical conventicle (a short-lived house congregation). He attracted some Germans, French-

---

[121] CR, II, 36-37.

[122] P.C. Molhuysen, *Bronnen tot de geschiedenis der Leidsche Universiteit* (The Hague: Nijhoff, 1913-24), II, 95 (res. curatoren, 1620).

[123] Kn. 4110. Published by Aert Meuris, The Hague, 1630.

[124] "Memorie van Thomas Leamer", Remonstrant MS 519 (Gem. Bib. Rotterdam), p. 31.

[125] Christopher Lawne, *The Prophane Schisme of the Brownists*, STC 15324 (n.p., 1612), pp. 55-56; Paget, *Arrow*, p. 383-84, Acta Kerkeraad Amsterdam, III, 167, left side.

men, and English people; some of his group were "Arians". He "infects many".[126] The English embassy in the Netherlands had a report about Leamer in 1610; "an Englishman, who hath dwelt many yeares at Amstelredam." Of good moral honesty, but "true it is, that his religion is somewhat strange, for he adhereth to none of ye professions which are within that Town...but hath opinions aparte".[127]

In the theological realm, his inventive mind delved into many ideas quite out of the ordinary. He proclaimed an Arianistic view of Christ, which gave great offense to the orthodox. Leamer also preached a combination of millenarianism and mysticism, expecting a speedy end to the age; "not only Antichrist shall be overthrown, but that Christ shall come down from heaven within 20 years, and reign as King over all the earth, where he shall remain visible and known to all the world." Thus the world would end by 1631.[128] Following the examples of the expert Puritan theologians of Amsterdam for Hebrew study, Leamer set out to emulate and surpass them. He studied on his own about the Hebraic language and Jewish doctrines available in Amsterdam; and he memorized some rudiments of the Hebrew language (the alphabet at least). Hebrew became for him the magic language with the hidden key to all knowledge. And knowledge must be put to use.

His proudest discovery was applying Hebrew letters to navigation. By his cabalistic calculations from the letters and characters of the Hebrew alphabet, he "professeth to shew vs the course of the sun, the waye to the Indies, with other secrets of Astronomie".[129] ELOHIM (God) was a magic word. Leamer's plan was to inscribe the letters of the word ELOHIM as markers on nautical instruments and then use these Hebrew letters to calculate east and west navigation to produce just as sure a method as using the North Star for north-south navigation. If this had worked, he would have had a great invention. The Netherlands greatly desired a methodology for measuring east-west navigation. The States General was offering a prize of 25,000 florins to the inventor of such a procedure or instrument. Leamer applied for the prize but did not qualify for it.[130]

---

[126] Acta Kerkeraad Amsterdam, III, 236v, 237 (June 24, 1610) 177v; IV, 399.

[127] SP 84/67/185.

[128] HMC, Downshire, III, 48.

[129] Paget, Arrow, p. 384.

[130] NNBW, II, 791. Willem Jansz Blaeu was one of the commissioners appointed to judge Leamer's case for the prize; Keuning, Blaeu, p. 25.

With Leamer, Bromley, and their sort loose in Amsterdam, the forces
of confusion were on the move. When they put their opinions into
print, the confusion was multiplied. If only they could be denied use
of the printing presses! The Dutch Reformed churchmen spent considerable time in consistory tracking down and counteracting Bromley
and Leamer books. The consistory investigated Bromley's book of
1606, the *Antwoort*, and they did not expect anything good to come
from him.[131] Today, only one of Leamer's books is known, *Een klaer
vertoninge hoe men door het uyr-werck van Elohim ofte den groten EYGHE-
NAER...so sijn meridiaens lengde te weten comen can* (Kampen, 1612).[132]
Petrus Plancius in 1612 reported to the consistory brethren that this
blasphemous book was being sold openly at the book printers. It was
found good to ask the burgomasters to take action (which petition, of
course, led nowhere).[133] On several earlier occasions (1604, 1607,
1609), the consistory had discussed other printed books of Leamer or
his close associates which were disseminating Chiliastic and Arian
heresies.[134] These earlier Leamer books have not been identified.
Every time the Dutch tried to silence him, Leamer would print a
pamphlet or provoke a public disputation to further air his views.

Leamer's *Klaer vertoninge* reveals his great enthusiasm for Hebrew
learning. The very language of the Hebrews provided him with a key
to long-hidden knowledge. His book promised to measure the merid-
ian through *Elohim* "by sun, moon, and stars in all places of the world,
on water or on land". This book was written and published with
corrections by Thomas Leamer, Englishman, lover of truth. How had
he learned this mysterious knowledge? "Through his own industry,
long observation by night and day, together with great cost, effort, and
labor, with the Lord's help and grace, he found the true and genuine
knowledge..." By using the word *Elohim* and other Hebrew words, all
natural creation being related to the Creator, he calculated the longi-
tudes and latitudes for traveling east and west.[135] He used no
Hebrew characters in the text itself, but he explained how the translations and calculations were to be made.

---

[131] Acta Kerkeraad Amsterdam, III, 145v.
[132] Kn. 2030 (published by Albert Lieffertsz).
[133] Acta Kerkeraad Amsterdam, IV, 25-26.
[134] Ibid., III, 113v-114, 177r-v, 216.
[135] Leamer, *Klaer vertoninge*, fol. M.

Leamer was always aggressive and confrontational. His enemies frequently challenged him to·explain his credentials for teaching about the Hebrew language. Although self-taught in Hebrew, he still considered himself more skilled in Hebrew-Dutch translation than most of the best scholars and preachers of Amsterdam. He even proposed to the Dutch government that he should be supported "at public cost" to have a school to teach each year six or seven Dutch scholars in the proper understanding of the Hebrew language and its relationship to the stars. He wanted to create a little "Leamer Academy". Established scholars and politicians with money would have nothing to do with his schemes and some mocked him as an ignoramus. Regardless of the abuse, Leamer reminded the Amsterdam people that his knowledge was useful information at the service of the country for navigation, not erudite fantasy.[136]

Leamer and Bromley found the road of bookish scholarship filled with obstacles. Leamer's astronomy, when tested, could not be verified, or even comprehended. Was it science or religious ranting? Abraham Costerus of Hooge en Lage Zwaluwe wrote a devastating response against him in *De grouwelijke ongehoorde blasphemien ende raserijen van Thomas Leamer, Engelsman* (Rotterdam, 1613). A strident condemner of the Jews, Costerus resented Leamer's heavy reliance on Hebrew learning.[137] Established scholars of Hebrew were embarrassed by Leamer's unorthodox notions and they felt obliged, for the sake of scholarship and Christian religion, to discredit him. They announced that they easily found "more than 100 errors" in his work.[138]

Leamer stood his ground, David against the Goliaths, and when attacked, always challenged his opponents to a public debate. He provoked several notable scholars of Amsterdam into meeting him in public disputation. He once offered to meet the preachers of the Amsterdam consistory in "public disputation" of all issues. The invitation was disregarded, however.[139] Matthew Slade of the Latin School publicly debated with Leamer in 1609 regarding his Arianistic proposition that Christ was created on "the first day". The record and tran-

---

[136] Ibid., p. 53r; Abraham Costerus, *De grouwelijke ongehoorde blasphemien...van Thomas Leamer*, Kn. 2085 (Rotterdam, 1613), fol. A.

[137] *BL*, II, 143.

[138] Wijnman, "De Hebraïcus Jan Theunisz", pp. 174-75.

[139] Acta Kerkeraad Amsterdam, II, 113v (July 15, 1604).

script of this debate runs to 117 pages.[140] Another time, in 1614, Jan
Theunisz had a turn at meeting Leamer face to face, with Slade
presiding. Theunisz tried to demolish Leamer by ridiculing his ignorance of Hebrew; according to Theunisz, the Englishman could not
even correctly handle the first word of the Hebrew scriptures ("In the
beginning").[141] On another occasion, Leamer proposed a competition: It would be Leamer versus Petrus Plancius, Matthew Slade, and
Rudolph Snellius, notable scholars all, "to demonstrate that I can
explain and translate more Hebrew than those three can".[142] Apparently, Leamer's public statements were plausible enough, in the judgment of many, to make him worth listening to. The experts, however,
regarded him as an astronomy crackpot, a man "fantastical therein, as
in other apprehensions".[143] Leamer was a heretic. He was uppity and
arrogant. But, what did he care about their opinions of him? Even
being excommunicated did not trouble him. He died in about
1627.[144] Leamer and Bromley are known to us because of their self-
financed publications. Various others of the same circles now are
unknown, because they never finished their books or failed to get
them into print.

The "Puritan Renaissance" of learning at Amsterdam on its various
levels produced a diverse picture, from the impressive linguistic and
philosophical scholarship of the preachers, rooted in the union of
"Reason and Religion",[145] to the curious speculations of Bromley
and Leamer. The search for knowledge however, was very selective.
Puritans appreciated learning about languages, philosophy, the historical and theological contexts of the Jews, and new cultures. Ainsworth,
the Separatist, showed how this information could fit into the old
framework of truth; "service" to God, he said, is "all manner work,
labour, industry of body or mynd", which helps to forward religion.
This meant, Paget pointed out, all kinds of endeavor; and study in the

---

[140] Leamer's version is in Remonstrant MS no. 519 (Gem. Bib. Rotterdam);
Wijnman, "De Hebraïcus Jan Theunisz", p. 175.

[141] GA Amsterdam, NA 377 (Jacobs), fol. 414; Wijnman, "Geleerdenkring van
Sladus", pp. 450–51.

[142] Leamer, Klaer vertoninge, p. 53; Costerus, Grouwelijke blasphemien, fol. A.

[143] SP 84/67/185.

[144] Leamer was referred to as dead in a document of June 2, 1627;
NA 634 (Sibrant Cornelisz), fol. 87.

[145] Paget, Arrow, "To The Christian Reader".

library "must be acknowledged a worship of God".[146] Nevertheless, there were many gaps and missing links in Puritan culture at Amsterdam. One looks in vain for any appreciation of what Amsterdam had to offer in art, architecture, literature, poetry, and drama.

---

[146] Henry Ainsworth, *An Arrow against Idolatrie*, STC 221 (n.p., 1611), p. 12; Paget, *Arrow*, p. 160.

CHAPTER 4

PURITAN PRINTING AT AMSTERDAM

For Puritans Amsterdam was certainly a city of books. Amsterdam served the scholarly needs of Puritanism; and the polemical and controversial spirit was equally well served by the Dutch presses. Most Puritan printing enterprises were intimately linked with the English churches which provided a base of support for writing and publishing books. English congregations multiplied at Amsterdam, with an aggregate membership of several hundred. The mother church of English religion in the Low Countries was the "Ancient Church" (1596), pastored by Francis Johnson and Henry Ainsworth. In 1610, this venerable, but unstable, church split into two rival congregations, one headed by Johnson, the other by Ainsworth. In addition, many splinter Separatist groups branched off from the main church or organized as new Separatist-Brownist immigrants came over from England. The saying was, "The Sun of Brownisme shines in Netherlande".[1]

Taking the period up to 1610 alone, the following English congregations existed: The Ancient Church, and after the split the Johnson church and the Ainsworth church; the Henoch Clapham church (1590s); the George Johnson church (1603); the Thomas White church (c. 1603-05); the John Robinson "Pilgrim" church (1608-09, thereafter at Leiden); and two English Anabaptist congregations, one led by John Smyth, and other by Thomas Helwys. The non-Separatists had their church, the English Reformed Church, pastored by John Paget.[2] This multiplicity of rival preachers and congregations produced an environment brimming with writing and printing. Each preacher and church was determined to get its story into print.

English Puritan polemical book printing at Amsterdam went through three broad phases: (1) Separatist controversial printing, which predominated 1596-1620, (2) political Puritanism, mixed with anti-

---

[1] Henoch Clapham, *The Syn against the Holy Ghoste*, STC 5345 (Amsterdam, 1598), sig. Biiiv.

[2] See K.L. Sprunger, *Dutch Puritanism* (Leiden: E. J. Brill, 1982), chaps. 3 and 4.

conformist religion—the 1620s and era of the Thirty Years' War, (3) English and Scottish struggles against Laud and other Episcopal "tyranny"—the 1630s.

Giles Thorp: English separatist printer

After the Separatists established their church at Amsterdam, one of their first tasks was to publicize their cause through printing. The confession of faith of 1596, published at Amsterdam, declared that they wrote and printed "to stop the mouths of impious and unreasonable men"[3] and "for the manyfestation and clearing of the truth off God from reproche off men".[4] Other foundational books of Separatist faith followed. Pastor Johnson saw personally to the reprinting of Barrow's *Plaine Refutation of Gifford*, an act of penance for once having burned 1000 copies of that pious book before his Separatist conversion. Johnson caused the book "to be New printed and sett out at his own Charge".[5] Without doubt, these Separatist books from Amsterdam were effective in persuading readers. The Amsterdam books were powerful in expression and single-minded in making their point. They presented their message "with more simplicitie and plainenesse". Hearts were warmed and "the way was prepared vnto Separation".[6]

When the Separatist group first came over to Amsterdam, they entrusted their printing to whatever Dutch printer would take their work. Eventually some of their own members, headed by Giles Thorp, set up an English shop which handled their printing work. A.F. Johnson's article on Thorp dated his printing work from 1604 to about the end of 1622.[7] Although the beginning and ending dates are hazy, contemporary records support approximately that span of time for Thorp's activities. He died in 1622 or 1623.[8]

---

[3] *A True Confession of Faith*, STC 18433.7 (1596), preface.

[4] *The Confession of Fayth*, STC 18434 (1602), preface. See also *The Confession of Faith*, STC 18435 (1607), preface.

[5] William Bradford, "A Dialogue or the sume of a Conference...1648", *Publications of the Colonial Society of Massachusetts*, 22 (1920), pp. 121-22.

[6] The testimony of Mat. Saunders and Cuth. Hutton in Lawne, *The Prophane Schisme of the Brownists or Separatists*, STC 15324 (London, 1612), p. 56.

[7] Johnson (1951), pp. 219-20.

[8] Thorp died in 1622 (or possibly 1623), based on somewhat obscure references in Ainsworth, *Certain Notes*, STC 227 (n.p. 1630), sig. A3v and postscript; see Michael E.

Under his own imprint, Thorp printed ten books in the English, Latin, and French languages: Ainsworth, *The Commvnion of Saincts*, STC 228 (1607), Ainsworth, *An Epistle Sent vnto Two Daughters of Warwick from H.N.*, STC 18553 (1608), Ainsworth, *A Defence of Holy Scriptures*, STC 235 (1609), Richard Clyfton, *The Plea for Infants and Elder People*, STC 5450 (1610), Hugh Sanford, *De descensu domini nostri Jesu Christi ad inferos* (1611), Ainsworth, *The Booke of Psalmes*, STC 2407 (1612), Ainsworth, *An Animadversion to Mr. Richard Clyftons Advertisement*, STC 209 (1613), John Harrison, *The Messiah Alreadie Come*, STC 12857.8 (1613) and STC 12858 (1619), and Ainsworth, *La Commvnion des Saincts* (n.d., c. 1618). These ten books, however, are only a small part of the output from Thorp's press. Most of his printing was done anonymously. On the basis of typography and documentary records, one can calculate Thorp's corpus of printing 1604-22 as in the range of 60-65 books (see Appendix I). The majority of English-language books printed in Amsterdam during Thorp's period had his sure but anonymous touch. Mr. Thorp "hath had a hand in the printing".[9]

Thorp was a member of the Ancient Church and had the congregation's confidence in all matters relating to printing. There was little likelihood of more English printers coming to town, reported Matthew Slade in 1619, so long as there was already "Thorp, also a Brownist setled here".[10] Printing was only one part of the larger religious cause which Thorp served. He was a totally dedicated Separatist Puritan, and it is very likely that he learned printing as a means of serving the church, no evidence existing of an earlier "secular" printing career. A pillar and core member of the Ancient Church, he gave service as deacon (1612) and elder of Ainsworth's church (1615, to his death). One sample of Thorp's work as elder was his visit, along with Ainsworth, to the consistory of the English Reformed Church in 1615 to consult about a discipline case. Paget credited the two Separatist officials with bringing "light" to the situation.[11] Thorp's spiritual gifts, like Ainsworth's, were greatly appreciated: "Did you but know

---

Moody, "'A Man of a Thousand': The Reputation and Character of Henry Ainsworth, 1569/70-1622", *Huntington Library Quarterly*, 45 (1982), p. 212.

[9] John Fowler, *A Shield of Defence*, STC 11212 (Amsterdam, 1612), p. 8.

[10] SP 84/92/41. Slade referred to "William Thorp" but surely meant Giles Thorp. See Willem Nijenhuis, *Matthew Slade 1569-1628: Letters to the English Ambassador* (Leiden: Sir Thomas Browne Institute, 1986), p. 97.

[11] John Paget, *An Arrow against the Separation of the Brownists*, STC 19098 (Amsterdam, 1618), p. 32; CR I, 84.

the wholsom counsell of Mr. Thorp our Elder." Pastor Ainsworth and elder Thorp were "those worthy Governours" of the church.[12]

In addition to praying and printing the Separatist word, Thorp also did some writing about church affairs in Amsterdam. He was author of a "writing" or "booke" called "The Hunting of the Foxe" (part 1), produced about 1610. This circulated from hand to hand among the English people of Amsterdam, and it contained many juicy details about church scandals among the Johnsonians. No copy has survived, and it is possible that it was only a handwritten tract, not in print.[13] Whether in manuscript or in print, it went far and wide. The Dutch Mennonite pastor, P.J. Twisck of Hoorn, had access to Thorp's book ("het schrijven van Meester Gillis Thorp") in 1620 when writing volume 2 of his *Chroniick*.[14]

Thorp's press was always at the service of Ainsworth, just as it had earlier, before the church split, been the servant of Francis Johnson. Thorp's name appears in various legal documents associated with the Ancient Church. In 1613 Thorp was one of the officers negotiating to buy the church building from the Johnson faction.[15] In 1615, along with other prominent Brownists, he was a beneficiary in the will of John Beauchamp, a fellow church member and well-to-do Separatist merchant of the city. Thorp was to receive Beauchamp's best cloak; Ainsworth, 500 guilders.[16] During Thorp's lifetime, the English press devoted itself almost exclusively to printing works by pastors of the Ancient Church, thirteen books by Ainsworth alone, or other Separatist spokesmen. A few non-Separatist authors were taken on at the press—some of Hugh Broughton's Jewish scholarship, for example—but such exceptions were definitely a small part of Thorp's work. He printed some books that differed a little from his personal Separatist creed, but he could not tolerate opinions totally contrary to his own convictions. Printing for him was an act of religious service. After Thorp's death, his successors at the printery accepted a much broader range of Puritanical authors and topics for printing.

---

[12] Ainsworth, *Certain Notes*, postcript by Sabine Staresmore; John Robinson, *An Appeale on Trvths Behalf*, STC 21107 (September 18, 1624), sig. Clv.

[13] Paget, *Arrow*, p. 334; Lawne, *Prophane Schisme*, pp. 11-12; Burrage *EED*, I, 169.

[14] P.J. Twisck, *Chroniick van den onderganc der tyrannen*, 2 vols. (Hoorn, 1619-20), II, 1575. Since the writing was used so widely, it may indeed have been a printed book. Its loss to us is one of the tragedies of Puritan historiography.

[15] RA 2164, fol. 95v (GA Amsterdam).

[16] NA 613A (Ruttens), Feb. 23, 1615 (GA Amsterdam).

The Ancient Church had several members helpful to Thorp in matters of books and printing. First of all, Pastor Ainsworth had worked at a bookstore as a porter when first coming to Amsterdam.[17] Elder Francis Blackwell for several years was a financial supporter of Thorp, until the church split, and perhaps even helped with the actual printing shop work. Mr. "F.B." (i.e. Francis Blackwell) "put forth" and published the Ainsworth-Broughton book, *Certayne Qvestions* (1605), one of the anonymous Thorp books. Broughton complained that Blackwell had sided too much with Ainsworth; "you print for him".[18]

A large Blackwell-Thorp business venture comes to light in a notarial document of 1609, where Francis Blackwell, "English merchant living here", sold to Barent Otsen (Otsz), book printer and citizen of the city, "an entire printery" for 550 carolus guilders. This *geheele druckerye* consisted of two presses and 1232 pounds of cast letters, with all the respective and pertaining fonts, all in a room with a key. The document further states that "Gillis Thorp", English printer, was one of the holders of the public obligation or note, signed by Otsen; and thus Thorp received part of Otsen's payment.[19] This press launched the printing career of Otsen, who was an Amsterdam printer 1609 to 1631.[20] Blackwell and Thorp had been co-owners of the print shop, but many questions exist about the nature of the presses being sold. Obviously, it was not Thorp's primary equipment, because his work went on thereafter without much noticeable change in type, ornaments, or format. One of Thorp's sets of initials, according to Johnson, was first used in 1609.[21]

Had another English printer been functioning in Amsterdam up to 1609, also supported by the Ancient Church? A possible explanation would link the extra Blackwell-Thorp printing press at Amsterdam with William Jones, "Puritan printer and propagandist", who printed Puritan books surreptitiously at some unknown place between 1604 and 1608. One of the books printed by Jones had the imprint:

---

[17] Brook, *Puritans*, II, 299.

[18] Hugh Broughton, *Works*, ed. John Lightfoot (London, 1662), III, 722 ("An Admonition to Mr. Francis Blackwell").

[19] NA 265 (Van Banchem), fol. 18 (Jan. 16, 1609). On Otsen, see J.C. van der Kogel, *Barent Otsz. 1585-1647 boeckdrucker 1609-1631 t'Amsteldredam, inde nieuwe druckery* (doctoraalscriptie, University of Amsterdam, 1987).

[20] Gruys and De Wolf, p. 131.

[21] Johnson (1951), p. 225.

"Amsterdam: Printed by I.H. 1604."[22] Several other of the Jones books refer to printing across from England "on this side the seas".[23]

Jean de l'Ecluse (Lescluse or Lecluse) was still another member of the Ancient Church skilled in printing. Although not a partner with Thorp or a regular worker in his shop, he had various connections with Puritan printing at Amsterdam. Ecluse, a French emigré from Rouen, could comfortably handle English and French printing. A former member of the French Protestant, or Walloon, church of Amsterdam, and before that, a member of the French church at London, Ecluse experienced a Brownist conversion and about 1595 went over to the Separatist Ancient Church, temporarily at Naarden at the time. Thereafter he was unswervingly committed to Brownist religion—the "inordinate Brownist"—and rose to become an elder and occasional preacher of the church. At times, he made his living by printing, but he tried other trades as well. The local records refer to him as "book printer from Rouen" (1604, 1609); as a "cardmaker" of cards and playbooks for gamblers (1612); later as a "schoolmaster" (1616).[24] In 1600 he was under investigation at Amsterdam for printing three suspicious theological books.[25] For most of his printing career he worked for others (including Jodocus Hondius and Hendrik Laurensz in 1611).

Because Ecluse did not print under his own imprint, his printing career is indeed shadowy. His skill with languages made him valuable, and he could take credit for several translations. He translated Ainsworth's *Communion of Saincts* into French.[26] One need not look

---

[22] Jones is the subject of an article by Mark H. Curtis, "William Jones: Puritan Printer and Propagandist", *The Library*, 5th ser., 19 (1964). Curtis surmised, among other possibilities, "Perhaps Jones operated his press in the Low Countries until 1608" (p. 58). The Bradshaw book was *A Short Treatise of the Crosse*, STC 3526 (Amsterdam: Printed by I.H. 1604). Was I.H. a reference to Jodocus Hondius?

[23] See especially William Bradshaw, *A Proposition. Concerning Kneeling*, STC 3524 (n.p. 1605), "The Printer to the Reader"; *A Short Dialogve*, STC 6814 (n.p. 1605), "The Printer to the Reader"; Nicholas Fuller, *The Argvment of Master Nicholas Fvller*, STC 11460 (n.p. 1607), "The Printer to the Reader"; *Informations*, STC 14084 (n.p. 1608), "The Printer to the Reader".

[24] See *NNBW*, VIII, 1034 and Hoop Scheffer, "De Brownisten", pp. 227-29, 386, 388, 392; Fowler, *Shield of Defence*, pp. 5, 7-8. Also see Hoftijzer, *Engelse boekverkopers*, p. 24.

[25] *NNBW*, VIII, 1034.

[26] The French ed. was advertised by Cornelis Claesz in his 1608 catalogue and also in the autumn 1608 Frankfurt fair catalogue, but, apparently, the book did not

far for the intended audience for this French translation. This was one more try at winning over his old brethren of the Walloon church. Ecluse was one of the printers of Thomas Brightman's *Apocalypsis Apocalypseos* and also one of the translators and printers for the English version, *A Revelation of the Apocalyps*. He said: I had "a hand both in the translating and printing of M. B. book". Brightman's *Apocalypsis* had a complex publication history. The English version was "printed by Iudocus Hondius and Hendrick Laurenss" at Amsterdam in 1611; apparently, Ecluse worked for one or the other of them.[27] Other publishers were also involved with the Brightman books. The first Latin edition (1609) was handled, but not necessarily printed, by Cornelius Nicolai (Cornelis Claesz) of Amsterdam.[28]

The Brightman book confronted Ecluse with a dilemma. Ecluse, like Thorp, was an ideological printer. Thorp accepted for printing only work which he could conscientiously print with conviction. Profit was not the highest motive. Whereas Thorp could pick and choose his work, Ecluse had little control over his printing fare. He worked on what his "masters" gave him to do. When Brightman's Latin version, *Apocalypsis Apocalypseos* (printed 1609), came over to Hondius and Laurensz to be edited and printed in Latin and English, Ecluse found it distasteful in the extreme. The apocalyptic message itself was not objectionable, in fact even wholesome doctrine—The Seven Churches, the Seven Trumpets, and the Seven Vials with their identification of the Church of England with the lukewarm Church of

---

actually appear until 1618 or later (see supra chap. 3 and infra chap. 6, no. 45); *Het Boek*, ll (1922), p. 331.

[27] Jean de Lecluse, *An Advertisement to Everie Godly Reader of Mr. Thomas Brightman His Book*, STC 15351.7 (n.p. 1612), p. 3; reprinted in T.S. Crippen, ed., "A Rare Separatist Pamphlet", *Transactions of the Congregational Historical Society*, 6 (1914), pp. 251-64; Fowler, *Shield of Defence*, p. 7. A more complex explanation would have Ecluse working for printers a step removed from Hondius and Laurensz, in case they were only publishing or bookselling at this time.

[28] Fowler stated that Brightman's Latin version of 1609 (Shaaber B673) had Ecluse involved "in the printing" (*Shield*, p. 7). The Latin version of 1609 had two imprints: "Prostat Francofurti apud Viduam Leuine Hulsii", *Catalogvs Vniversalis*, Frankfurt, spring 1609, sig. Blv; and "Ambstelrodami apud Cornelium Nicolai", ibid., sig. B2r. The edition of 1612 (Shaaber B674) was available in the Commelin shop—"Prostat in Officina Commeliniana"—, spring 1612, Frankfurt cat. printed in Leipzig, sig. B2v. See also Appendix I, K, on H. Laurensz.

Laodicea (Rev. 3)—but Brightman's handling of Separatism as a "wicked and blasphemous" error was quite intolerable to Ecluse.[29]

When the employers of Ecluse assigned him to work on translating and printing into English, the anti-Separatist passages proved more than he could endure. Without permission, he single-handedly revised and printed several of Brightman's passages to water down their critique of Separatism. This story went around Amsterdam:

> For being appoynted by his maisters...to print this booke and that without any leave...causeth his glosses to be printed in the margent of this booke. He there sets downe in opposition vnto Mr. Brightman, his contradictions of him, his interrogations, his exclamations against him: *O England etc. O Brightman etc. Let God and his angelles and all the world judge...* He defaces and disgraceth the work committed vnto him, offendeth his maisters, wronges the reader, and iniureth the authour of the booke.[30]

When his tampering was discovered, he was speedily ordered to correct his printing fallacies and redo the ruined portions of the book at his own expense. It was "a publique scandall". He did "fret and chafe" but he had no choice. "Divers sheetes must needes be printed againe and he must endure the paine and labour for the setting of the same."[31]

The Hondius-Laurensz edition of Brightman's book, *A Revelation of the Apocalyps*, finally appeared in 1611. The unchastened Ecluse retaliated by writing a small book of his own against Brightman's anti-Separatism, *An Advertisement to Everie Godly Reader of Mr. Thomas Brightman His Book, Namely, A Revelation of the Apocalyps* (printed by Thorp, 1612). For a printer to passively print other people's errors, he believed, was to partake in "other mens synns". No one could accuse Ecluse of being a printing or religious neutralist.[32]

From the time of Giles Thorp onward, printing at Amsterdam had a slightly Brownist flavor. After Thorp, other Brownists carried on the work of English printing, namely, Sabine Staresmore, Richard Plater, and John Canne. Several Dutch printers had Brownist blood. Printer

---

[29] Thomas Brightman, *A Revelation of the Apocalyps*, STC 3754 (Amsterdam, 1611), pp. 102, 131.

[30] Fowler, *Shield of Defence*, p. 7.

[31] Ibid.; Paget, *Arrow*, p. 88.

[32] Lecluse, *Advertisement*, p. 3; Fowler, *Shield of Defence*, p. 7.

Steven Swart (active 1663-83)[33] married Abigael May, daughter of
Henry May, the younger. The Mays were a famous Brownist family.[34] After Swart's death, Abigael, the widow Swart, carried on
printing under her own name.[35] Her uncle, printer Joseph Bruyning
(Browning), "from London", was a brother of Henry May's wife
(Susanna Bruyning May, the mother of Abigael Swart). Bruyning
joined the printers guild in 1639 and died in 1672.[36] Widow Bruyning (Mercy Arnold Pelham) continued the Bruyning printery for a
good many years after Joseph's death. A son from Joseph Bruyning's
first marriage, Joseph Jr., was also an Amsterdam book dealer and later
he moved to Boston in New England, becoming one of the most
important booksellers of the city. The Bruynings had many Brownist
associations.[37] (See Appendix I, N.) Bookseller Johannes Broers,
(active 1690-97), who took over the Bruyning bookshop, married
Lydia Duyrcoop, daughter of Tabitha Thorp (granddaughter of Joseph
Thorp, Brownist member).[38] Swart, Widow Swart, and Widow
Bruyning were habitual partisans of English nonconformist causes and
produced many books and newssheets for the Whiggish Puritans. In
the 1680s, although not formal Brownist members, they were frequent
attenders at the Separatist (or Independent) church.[39] At The Hague,
bookseller Jan de La Cluse (de l' Ecluse), active in the 1660's, carried
on the name of the Brownist Ecluse family of Amsterdam.[40] For a

---

[33] On Swart see Hoftijzer, *Engelse boekverkopers*, pp. 19-31 and passim. Hoftijzer's
book gives a thorough history of the Swart and Bruyning families and their Brownist
activities. Van Eeghen, *AB*, IV, 135-38; Alice C. Carter, *The English Reformed Church
in Amsterdam in the Seventeenth Century* (Amsterdam: Scheltema & Holkema, 1964), p.
221.

[34] Abigael's father, Henry May (Hendrick May), the younger, was son of another
Amsterdam May, Henry May, the elder. There were at least two generations of
"Henry May". All the Mays were Separatists. See Hoftijzer, *Engelse boekverkopers*, "De
bruinistenfamilie May te Amsterdam", pp. 23-25.

[35] Ibid., pp. 31-32.

[36] Ibid, pp. 25-26. Bruyning's first wife was Experience Johnson. Kleerkooper and
Van Stockum, pp. 111-112; Van Eeghen, *AB*, III, 59-60, 135, 138.

[37] Hoftijzer, pp. 26-28.

[38] Van Eeghen, *AB*, III, 47-48; Hoftijzer, p. 177.

[39] Add. MS. 37,981, fol. 2v; SP 84/216/154; Hoftijzer, chap. 6.

[40] Jan de La Cluse (Johannes de l'Escluse) was born at London about 1634; his
parents were Johannes le Cluse and Dorothea Ballard. There is a strong likelihood that
he was a descendant of Jean de l'Ecluse, printer of Amsterdam and Brownist leader.
Ecluse of the Hague could hardly have been the son of Ecluse of Amsterdam who
married four times but, so far as is known, not to a Dorothea Ballard; E.F. Kossmann,

long time, many hands continued the printing that Giles Thorp had begun.

Successors of Thorp: the continuation of English printing by Plater, Staresmore, and others, 1622-35

Although there is a clear continuity of English-language printing from the same presses, based on similarity of types, initials, and ornaments, throughout the period of the 1620s and 1630s, the names and work periods of the various printers are uncertain. Most of the books were printed without imprint, and the printers changed frequently. The most important of them were Richard Plater, Sabine Staresmore, and finally John Canne. The *Short Title Catalogue* refers to many books from this significant period as done by the "Successors of G. Thorp".

In addition to Thorp, Plater, Staresmore, and Canne, a conglomeration of less well-known English printers lived and worked in Amsterdam. This corps of experienced printers probably provided some of the laborers working anonymously in the English book shops. English printers, booksellers, and bookbinders included:[41]

> 1600 – Heyndrik (Henry) Godewyn, book printer from Ipswich, England, 25 years old, betrothed October 2, 1600 (member of the English Reformed Church).[42]
> 1600 – Heinrik Moej, "from Dunnen in England, bookseller, 30 years old, living 8 years on the Dam", betrothed April 8, 1600 (perhaps the same as "Hendrick Moody").[43]

De boekhandel te 's-Gravenhage tot het eind van de 18de eeuw ('s-Gravenhage: Nijhoff, 1937), pp. 237-39. Hoftijzer proposed that Ecluse of The Hague was descended from Ecluse of Amsterdam, perhaps a grandson; see *Engelse boekverkopers*, pp. 24, 174. See also Marika Keblusek, *Boekverkoper in ballingschap: Samuel Browne, boekverkoper/drukker te Londen, 's-Gravenhage en Heidelberg 1633-1665* (doctoraalscriptie, Univ. of Leiden, 1989), I, 80. The younger Ecluse was associated in business with Samuel Browne, who supported Anglican, royalist publications.

[41] Unless otherwise noted, the information from this listing of printers comes from the archives of the ERC, Amsterdam (CR and membership lists). Some others who may have had a book trade connection were Joshua Philip, book-keeper (1628), and John Bortman, printer of caps (1634).

[42] Briels, *ZB*, p. 289; CR I, 73.

[43] Briels, *ZB*, 25, 71. On Hendrick Moody, see Tiele, no. 489 (1602).

1607 – William Boseman, "printer...now makes tobacco pipes" (joined the English Reformed Church June 17, 1607).

1610 – Thomas James, bookbinder (joined the English Reformed Church July 7, 1610).

1611 – Christopher Hill, bookbinder (joined the English Reformed Church May 4, 1611).

1614 – Pursevaul Morgan, printer (joined the English Reformed Church 1614).

1618 – James Reve, printer (joined the English Reformed Church June 13, 1618).

1618 – Randall Evans, "prynter of maps, dwelling by Mr. Johnson boekseller upon the water" (joined the English Reformed Church July 1, 1618).

1621 – John Reynolds, printer, married at Amsterdam April 24, 1621, "dwelling near the Exchange" (formerly a printer at Leiden).[44]

1622 – William Wilkinson, "printer, dwelling by St. Theunisport" (joined the English Reformed Church, Dec. 14, 1622; later moved to Leiden).

1624 – Francis Hill, printer living in Amsterdam in 1624.[45]

1631 – Richard Raven, printer of one book at Amsterdam, 1631 (STC 23050).

1634 – Cuthbert Atkenson, printer (joined the English Reformed Church February 15, 1634).

1641 – John Crosse, bookbinder (member of English Reformed Church, 1641).[46]

1641 – David de Liege, Engelsman, *lettersetter* (Englishman, compositor).[47]

The first of the "successor" printers to become publicly active was Richard Plater, who was in charge of the printery approximately 1623-29. (See Appendix I, B.) His Amsterdam printing experience went back well into the Thorp era. In 1613, Plater married Janneke Hodry; in the records he was listed as a *letterzetter* (compositor), aged 24, from Bockingham (i.e. Buckinghamshire?). At this early period of his life he was a Separatist; however, in 1621 he and his wife Joane

---

[44] D. Plooij and J. Rendel Harris, *Leyden Documents Relating to the Pilgrim Fathers* (Leyden: E.J. Brill, 1920), fols. xlvi, lxxii; D. Plooij, *The Pilgrim Fathers from a Dutch Point of View* (New York: New York Univ. Press, 1932), pp. 60-61.

[45] See no. 51 below.

[46] Membership list, no. 90. John Crosse is no. 256 and also listed on the loose sheet at end; Van Eeghen, *AB*,V, 117, no. 273.

[47] David de Liege gave an attestation at Amsterdam, Dec. 3, 1641, NA 1058 (Van de Ven), fol. 173r.

(Janneke) renounced Separatism and joined Paget's English Reformed Church. The Platers lived "on the Buorse streete". He advertised his shop as being "by the Long Bridge" (the Beursstraat, by the Langebrug). One book of 1627 has the imprint Richard Plater, "by de cleyne Raembrugh inde Twee vergulde Vysels".[48]

Plater printed five books with his name between 1625 and 1629: Samuel Bachilor, *Miles Christianvs, or the Campe Royal*, STC 1106 (1625); John Forbes, *A Frvitfvll Sermon*, STC 11130 (1626); *Een generael en waerachtigh verhael* (1627), trans. from French, Kn. 3732; Henry Ainsworth, *The Commvnion of Saincts*, STC 231.5 (1628); Samuel Bachiler, *The Campe Royal*, STC 1106.5 (1629). Most of the anonymous printing by the "Successors of G. Thorp" done at Amsterdam in the 1620s was probably under his direction. Apart from his imprint, Plater's work can also sometimes be identified by his use of a combination of initials formerly used by Thorp and Brewster, and the Brewster bear ornament.[49]

Plater obviously had assistant printers. One of his associates was printer William Wilkinson, who with his wife Mary joined the English Reformed Church December 14, 1622. Richard Plater was one of his witnesses at the joining; thus it seems very likely that the two worked together. By 1627 Wilkinson had moved to Leiden.[50] Another possible associate was Francis Hill. In 1624 he was living at Amsterdam "op Princgracht [Prinsengracht] reght tegen over den Baerstraet". At that point in life, Hill was an unemployed printer, "since I left printing". Nevertheless, he knew all the inside information about English printing in the city, and he took pay from Sir Dudley Carleton to be an informer about printing affairs. He had sample pages from the presses, and he personally was acquainted with authors David Calderwood, Alexander Leighton, and William Ames (all three of whom had books printed by the Thorp-Plater press) and with the Reverend John

---

[48] CR, II, 4-5; De Hoop Scheffer, "De Brownisten", p. 391. A daughter named Thankfull was born 1626. See Kn. 3732.

[49] Plater had the distinctive Brewster bear with the break (1b). On the difficulty of identifying printers' ornaments, such as the bear, see J.A. Gruys, "Ornamental Bears and Other Animals: An Excursus on some Head and Tail Pieces", in Harris and Jones, (ed. Breugelmans), pp. 161-69, also pp. 64-65.

[50] CR, II, 27. Wilkinson was on the 1623 membership list, but on the 1629 membership list (ERC no. 85), his name was crossed off and marked "gone". He was recorded at Leiden in 1627; see chap. 5.

Paget—"I beeing at Mr. Pagetts". After returning to London, Hill had
a long career as a bookseller in Little Britain.[51]

Two other English printers in Amsterdam may have been connected with Plater and earlier with Thorp. John Reynolds, a former
printer with William Brewster at Leiden, moved to Amsterdam in
1619 and married Persis Bailey in 1621; they lived "near the
Exchange" (the same neighborhood as Plater, who also lived near the
Bourse or Exchange). Another contemporary of Plater was Richard
Raven.[52] He printed a book by Josiah Speed, *Loves Revenge* (At Amsterdam: Printed by Richard Raven, 1631), which used some initials
similar to Plater's.[53]

A.F. Johnson pointed out in his article on Thorp that the press
from 1622 onward began using some type, initials, and ornaments (for
example,the bear with the break) from the Brewster press of Leiden,
producing a mixture of Leiden and Amsterdam printing. Who transferred the type from Leiden to Amsterdam? John Wilkinson and
Sabine Staresmore are two printers who changed their residence from
Leiden to Amsterdam about the same time that this transfer of type
occurred.[54] Thomas Brewer, the partner of Brewster, moved to Amsterdam in the mid 1620s, and before that, he had substantial business
dealings there.[55]

A fascinating but shadowy character in the Amsterdam printing field
was Sabine Staresmore (fl. 1616-47). A professed Brownist while in
Holland, he was one of the most travelled and peripatetic of the faith.
Originally from Leicestershire, he crossed back and forth many times
between England and Holland. At various times in his life he was a
member of Henry Jacob's semi-Separatist church in London,
Robinson's Separatist church at Leiden, and the Separatist church at
Amsterdam. His dabbling in Jacobitism, as well as regular Brownism,
raised questions about his genuine dedication to the cause; his detrators
declared that he was not a real separated Christian. Nevertheless, he
proclaimed himself Separatist.[56] One of his trips from London to

---

[51] SP 84/117/157, 84/118/24 and 70; McKerrow, p. 137; Plomer (1641-67), p. 98.

[52] Harris and Jones, *Leyden Documents*, fol. xlvi; Harris and Jones (ed. Breugelmans),
pp. 20-21.

[53] STC 23050.

[54] Johnson (1951), p. 230; Stephen Foster, *Notes from the Caroline Underground*
(Hamden: Archon Books, 1978), p. 88.

[55] NA 199 (Bruijningh), fols. 25lv, 276r.

[56] Greaves and Zaller, *BD*, III, 201-02; Moody, "'A Man of a Thousand'", p. 205.

Amsterdam occurred April 21, 1629, "having lived there for divers yeares last past".[57] His main occupation was that of merchant, not printing; a notary document of 1625 referred to Sabijn Staresmore, "English merchant now in Amsterdam".[58] In the 1630s he became heavily involved in printing.

The necessity of defending the Separatist cause pushed self-made authors like Staresmore into literary action, "with his tong and pene to send letters...also in print".[59] He was the author of the book, *The Vnlawfvlnes of Reading in Prayer* (printed by Thorp, 1619), in which he warmly defended the Separatist position on Spirit-filled praying. Next he entered into printing. When and where he learned printing is uncertain, but by the 1630s he was known about Amsterdam as "the Printer of the Brownists". His printing activities, certainly, had begun somewhat earlier. Although he printed no books under his own imprint, books emanated from "his Printery".[60] At least four can be traced back to him: *The Loving Tender* (1623), no copies surviving; Ainsworth, *Certain Notes of M. Henry Aynsworth His Last Sermon*, STC 227 (1630); William Ames, *A Fresh Svit against Human Ceremonies*, STC 555 (1633); and John Davenport, *A Just Complaint against an Unjust Doer*, STC 6311 (1634). A case can also be made that he either printed or published *A Treatise of the Lawfvlnes of Hearing of the Ministers in the Church of England* by John Robinson (1634).[61] (See Appendix I, C.)

Apart from the first of these books, dated 1623, Staresmore's printing activity centered on the period of 1630-35 (the post-Plater period). As other English printers died or ceased printing, he took over the trade, so much so that by 1634 Staresmore was "the only English printer in the towne".[62] Most of his printing was dull and unattractive, lacking sharpness and ornamentation. Without his work, however, such as it was, radical Puritans would have been left without

---

[57] PC *Acts* (1628-29), p. 409.

[58] NA 351B, fol. 37.

[59] A.T., *A Christian Reprofe against Contention*, STC 23605 (n.p. 1631), p. 3.

[60] Ibid., p. 3; Paget, *An Answer to the Unjust Complaints of William Best*, STC 19097 (Amsterdam, 1635), preface, sig. (*)2v.

[61] *The Loving Tender* and *Certain Notes* are connected to Staresmore by A. T., *Christian Reprofe*, p. 3; see also Paget, *Answer*, preface, and SP 16/246/56. Also on Staresmore's publishing activities, see Stephen Foster, "The Faith of a Separatist Layman: The Authorship, Context, and Significance of *The Cry of a Stone*", *William and Mary Quarterly*, 34 (1977), pp. 380-81; and Moody, "'A Man of a Thousand'", pp. 213-14, no. 58.

[62] Foster, *Notes from the Caroline Underground*, p. 23.

an English printing voice at Amsterdam. After 1635 Staresmore faded
from the Amsterdam scene. His activities continued in England.

John Canne and the "richt right press"

Next the Puritan printing mantle passed to John Canne (c. 1590-
1667). "There is one Canne a minister hath a printing house and he
hath printed manie English bookes."[63] He strengthened the old
church-press connection inasmuch as he headed both, as preacher of
the Separatist church and master printer of the printery. "He has a
press in his house for printing."[64] Canne lived a dangerous and adventuresome life, going back and forth between England and the
Netherlands several times, in and out of jail, and espousing extreme
opinions, including Separatism, Independentism, and Fifth Monarchism. At this stage in his life, the 1630s, he was a Separatist zealot.

Canne was the most articulate of the English printers serving at
Amsterdam. In fact, he was as much author as printer, often using his
writing skills on behalf of his "flock" at the Ancient Church. He
strongly presented the Separatist case in his writings; these included a
sermon "The Right Way to Peace" (printed in 1632) and *A Necessitie
of Separation* (1634). The Amsterdam Separatists were sorely in need of
a defender of the faith, because the fortunes of the church had sunk
very low. Numbers were declining and Canne acknowledged that they
had a reputation for "heresie, schisme, pride, obstinacy, disloyalty,
sedition". The Enemy saw their weaknesses "and published them all to
the world", to our "shame, sorrow, and infamie". However, Canne
was a stalwart soldier of the faith, always willing to put up a strong
defense through the spoken or printed words—"I have published them
now unto the world".[65]

Canne preferred the anonymous style of printing and omitted his
name from all of his numerous printings, except for one Bible of
1647. He hoped for safety in silence. His output, however, was large,
40 or more books 1637-40, and a few additional ones during the

---

[63] SP 16/387/79; Greaves and Zaller, *BD*, I, 122-23; *BL*, II, 116-17.

[64] SP 84/153/293; John F. Wilson, "Another Look at John Canne", *Church History*,
33 (1964), pp. 34-48.

[65] John Canne, *The Right Way to Peace: or Good Covnsell for It*, STC 4574.5 (Amsterdam, 1632), sigs. A2v, A3r, A5r, p. 30.

1640s. (See Appendix I, F.) Some of his books can be identified from records of his arrest and trial for illegal printing in 1638. He was charged at Amsterdam with printing the following books: his own *Necessitie of Separation from the Church of England* (1634, STC 4574, which he "caused to be printed" but did not personally print); *A Brief Relation of Certaine Speciall and Most Materiall Passages and Speeches in the Starre-Chamber* (on Bastwick, Burton, and Prynne, 1638, STC 1570.5); *Newes from Scotland* (1638, STC 22013); and "a part of" George Gillespie's *Dispvte against the English-Popish Ceremonies* (1637, STC 11896, done jointly with Christiaensz of Leiden).[66] The latter two books are questionable as Canne books; both were removed from his final judgment.[67] The Matthew Simmons report of printing in 1638 identified several additional Canne books; Prynne's *Quench-Coale* (1638, STC 20474), *A Guide unto Zion* (1638, STC 26125) and various devotional books by Thomas Hooker, John Preston, Richard Sibbes, and Samuel Ward.[68]

Many of Canne's books are recognizable by his use of distinctive ornaments. He frequently used a round title page ornament with the words "Richt Right", from which arises the nickname for his printery, the "Richt Right Press". However, in some of the early books of 1637 and 1638, the ornament reads "Right Right". Did it become damaged through use? He also frequently used a headpiece with the motto *Cor unum via una*. In addition, the Canne printery used initials formerly used by Thorp and Brewster, or very similar ones.

Canne, the printer, possessed very few skilled credentials of the trade, apart from what he could learn on the job. His critics questioned whether he was competent to do printing;[69] however, since no other English printer was available in Amsterdam, Canne dutifully pressed on. One unfortunate piece of work, his 1644 printing of the English-language King James Bible, was so badly done, containing over 6000 errors, "that they are not fit to be imported into England and ought to be burned". The contracted buyer of the Bibles

---

[66] Names of the books mentioned in the sentence against John Canne, in Boswell's report, SP 84/153/271. Canne disputed that he printed some of these.

[67] SP 84/154/151v.

[68] SP 16/387/79. Most of the books by Hooker, Preston, and Sibbes can be identified (see appendix I, F); the Samuel Ward book, however, has not been identified.

[69] Van Eeghen, *AB*, IV, 137; NA 848 (Steijns), doc. 140, June 23, 1644. Edmund Blake, merchant, mentioned in the notarial document, was Canne's most severe critic.

(Edmund Blake) sued Canne, rather than take delivery. Blake also complained to the English Parliament.[70] Canne's reputation suffered, but his enthusiasm for Gospel printing survived.

A jack of many trades, besides preaching and printing, Canne had a "*Brandery* or Aqua vitae shop" and some kind of "Alchymists laboratory". None of these ventures was financially successful, although they appealed to his curious spirit. "O miserable men, that follow so blinde a guide," warned John Paget.[71] The report of Canne's "alchemy" raises a question about the direction he was travelling in his thinking and printing. In addition to printing for Separatists and non-Separating Puritans, in the Thorp-Plater tradition, Canne put out in 1639-40 a few mystical and utopian tracts, mixed in with the usual fare. He printed several small reformist utopian treatises by English preacher John Dury (Durie), from the Comenius-Hartlib circle. Comenius "labours in humane Learning for the reformation of Schooles", Dury "in divine matters, to promote the counsels of peace Ecclesiasticall. He doth worke upon the faculty of reason, and I upon the consciences of men."[72] In this category of books was also a translation of Sebastian Franck's *Forbidden Fruit*. Franck (1499-1543) was a radical German reformer and spiritualist, and his message appealed to the search for mystical illumination and hidden knowledge, the spirit rather than the letter. Franck taught liberation from traditional forms; "we doe not force or include the Majestie of the word of God within the narrow prison of the Letters."[73] These were strange books for a strict Calvinistic Separatist preacher, which Canne was assumed to be. In view of Canne's later Fifth Monarchism—and some reports say Anabaptism—these books may be a clue of his testing of new ideas. Because of Canne's strong sense of conviction, it is unlikely that he would have printed books with messages strongly opposed to his own views.

---

[70] Van Eeghen, IV, 137; Hoftijzer, *Engelse boekverkopers*, p. 104. This Bible was probably Wing B2207, "Amsterdam, printed for C.P.". C.P. most likely stands for Charles Pelham.

[71] Paget, *A Defence of Chvrch-Government* (London, 1641), pp. 146, 160 (misprinted as 152).

[72] John Dury, *Vertues Reward*, STC 24844a.3 (n.p., 1639), p. 20.

[73] Sebastian Franck, *The Forbidden Frvit*, STC 11324 (n.p. 1640), p. 172; *Mennonite Encyclopedia*, II, 363-67. On the interest in Franck among some radical Puritans of spiritualist concerns, see Nigel Smith, *Perfection Proclaimed: Language and Literature in English Radical Religion 1640-1660* (Oxford: Clarendon Press, 1989), p. 114.

After 1640, Canne directed his main efforts in writing and printing to Bible projects, primarily his 1644 and 1647 editions. He prepared a full apparatus of marginal notes for his own edition of an annotated Bible, which had a long popularity among pious readers. This octavo annotated edition of the Bible appeared with the note, "John Canne: Amsterdam, 1647".[74] The Bible printing business, in spite of being the Lord's work, had many unpleasant complications for Canne, involving him in lawsuits with merchants who bought and sold his Bibles. The 1644 "small print" edition (the "6,000 error" Bible in 24° format) had inspired a legal action against him; finally the widow of Charles Pelham bought them up and the title page thereafter read, "Amsterdam, printed for C.P."[75] There was another legal squabble about his Bibles in 1649.[76] Canne kept up his Amsterdam work until at least 1647 (perhaps 1649) and then, "after 17 years Banishment", returned to England.[77] Following the Restoration, Canne once again retreated to Amsterdam and resumed printing; 2000 of his printed Bibles were sold at Amsterdam in 1663. He died about 1667.[78]

Although Canne was not a great printer, and hardly ever made a profit, he excelled in devotion to printing as a religious calling. Printing for him was evangelism. In a series of letters to William Sykes, a financial backer, Canne appealed to a grandiose vision surpassing profits and worldly reputation. Admittedly, he "never got penny" from his printing, except on occasional jobs, and he and his family had to scrape along in dreadful poverty. But every sacrifice was worth it because he was doing Christ's work: "That the glorious kingdome of Jesus Christ might be advanced... I live by faith."[79] This was John Canne's printing credo.

---

[74] A.S. Herbert, *Historical Catalogue of Printed Editions of the English Bible 1525-1961*, rev. ed. of Darlow and Moule (London: British and Foreign Bible Society, 1968), no. 601, p. 197; cf. Wilson, "John Canne", p. 47.

[75] NA 848 (Steijns), doc. 251; Van Eeghen, *AB*, IV, 137; Herbert, *Bible*, no. 582. Charles Pelham, husband of Mercy Arnold Pelham, died in 1643 (Hoftijzer, p. 26); Widow Pelham and her brother Elias Arnold made the deal for the Bibles. According to Herbert and Wing, there was a 1644 "C.P." edition (B2207) and also a 1645 ed. (B2211). Herbert recorded the Bibles as 24°, Wing as 16° and 12°.

[76] Kleerkooper and Van Stockum, p. 1135.

[77] Sprunger, *Dutch Puritanism*, p. 69.

[78] NA 2157 (d'Amour), fols. 21-23; *BL*, II, 116.

[79] Champlin Burrage, "Was John Canne a Baptist?", *Transactions of the Baptist Historical Society*, 3 (1913), pp. 230-31.

Dutch printers of Puritan books

Having the notorious Mr. Canne or Mr. Thorp for a printer was not to every author's taste. Canne's disheveled reputation and below-standard workmanship were likely to tarnish the quality of any book. When a printing alternative was needed, certain respectable Dutch printers of Amsterdam stood ready to take on the work. John Paget, for one, always avoided dealing with Brownist printers in order to flee from the slightest appearance of evil. He advised David Calderwood in 1637 to beware of John Canne's printing. "Mr. Canne, preacher to the Brownists, maintaines a presse and prints English bookes, but I think he is not for your use." Instead, "there is an other printer, a Dutchman that prints English very correctly with a good letter. He is enclined to Arminianisme, yet I conceave he deales very truely and faithfully for the worke that he is entrusted withall."[80] This Dutch printer was Jan Fredericksz Stam. Better a whiff of Stam's Arminianism, Paget believed, than to get mixed up with Brownists.

In recommending Stam, Paget was giving good advice. J. F. Stam, and his predecessor Joris Veseler, were dependable printers, capable of doing good English printing. Joris Veseler (or Veselaer, 1589-1624) was an active printer at Amsterdam with his own shop and imprint 1618-24; one of his first was Paget's *Arrow against the Separation* (1618). Originally from Antwerp, he had lived at Amsterdam since 1609; in 1613 he was betrothed to Aachjen Jakobs van Dordrecht and listed himself as a *letterzetter* or compositor. When he got on his own, the Veseler printery was located "by the South-Church, at the signe of the HOPE".[81] In addition to printing some controversial Puritan books, Veseler proved willing to print for a variety of other parties out of favor. Several of his books were pro-Arminian—at a time when such books were banned—and this caused him to be imprisoned and fined in 1621.[82] Veseler was one of the first Amsterdam printers to aim for the English market, pioneering with Petrus Keerius in the printing and selling of English-language corantos.[83] (See Appendix I, G.)

---

[80] Wodrow MS, Folio XLII, fol. 253 (National Library of Scotland).

[81] Paget, *Arrow*, title page; Kleerkooper and Van Stockum, pp. 864-81; Briels, *ZB*, pp. 513-16.

[82] Briels, *ZB*, p. 513. W.P.C. Knuttel, *Verboden boeken in de Republiek der Vereenigde Nederlanden* ('s-Gravenhage: Nijhoff, 1914), pp. 29-30, 81. P.J. Koopman of the Univ. of Amsterdam has a study of Veseler underway.

[83] STC 18501.1-18507.17.

After Veseler died in 1624, his widow carried on the work of the press independently until 1628. In 1628 she married J. F. Stam "of Gouda"; whereupon, the Veseler printery "by the South-Church" became the Stam printery. One of his early publications, a coranto of 1628, carried the imprint, "By Ian Frederiksz. Stam, inde Druckerije van Veselaer".[84]

Within a few years, Jan Fredericksz Stam (1602-1667) became one of the biggest printers of English books in the Netherlands. (See Appendix I, H.) The Stam imprint appeared 1628-64, with the English books coming in the earlier years. "He printeth much English as Bibles", was the report of Matthew Simmons in 1637-38.[85] Whether he had any particular English connections, apart from those he had inherited from Veseler, is not known; likely he had an English printer or two working for him. Religiously, he tended toward Arminianism; but Puritan authors, nevertheless, gave him their business. His Puritan authors included Alexander Leighton, Henry Burton, John Paget, and William Prynne. Undoubtedly, his largest volume of English printing was in Bibles. On a few occasions, these were printed with his own name, notably the 1633 edition, "for Thomas Crafoorth. By Iohn Fredericksz Stam". In most cases his Bibles came forth with false title pages, pretending to be the work of Barker of London. The total quantity of his Bibles must have been immense. Stam's step-daughter, Susanna Veseler, married another Amsterdam printer, Jan Jacobsz Schipper, and they carried on the Veseler-Stam printing tradition. After Schipper's death, Susanna, the "Widow Schipper", continued the printing business, much of it in English Bibles.[86]

Another Amsterdam network of printers of English books was the Hondius-Janssonius connection: Jodocus Hondius (1563-1612), his son Henricus Hondius (1597-1651), and his son-in-law, Johannes Janssonius (1588-1664). Henricus Hondius and Janssonius teamed up to produce an English edition of Mercator's *Atlas*, translated by Henry Hexham, for the English market.[87] Janssonius did a huge business in Bishop Bayly's *Practice of Pietie*, which he printed "by tenn thousand at a time".[88] (See Appendix I, J.) Other Dutch printers also had Puritan

---

[84] Dated Nov. 17, 1628, Kn. 3796.
[85] SP 16/387/79.
[86] Van Eeghen, *AB*, IV, 96, 103.
[87] Briels, *ZB*, pp. 322-26; Kleerkooper and Van Stockum, pp. 295-320.
[88] SP 16/387/79.

customers. Hendrik Laurensz printed for several Puritan authors at his shop "vpon the water at the signe of the writing booke".[89] (See Appendix I, K.) Joost Broersz, active at Amsterdam 1634-47, produced one important book valued by Puritans, a 1639 reprint of Bishop Poynet's *Short Treatise of Politike Power*, and several editions of English Bibles.[90] (See Appendix I, L.)

Dutch booksellers provided a service by handling and distributing some of the Thorp-printed Puritan books. The Frankfurt fair catalogues advertised Puritan books to international readers under the names of established Amsterdam publishers (Laurensz, Janssonius, Commelin, Cornelius Nicolai, and others), although in most cases they had not done the printing.[91]

Two groups of Puritan books by Dutch printers present special difficulties. The first of these groups is the early Amsterdam writings of Hugh Broughton regarding his missionary activities with the Jews. Fuks and Fuks call these books "Broughtoniana". These were printed in a mixture of the Latin, Greek, Hebrew, Dutch, and English languages. Seven of these Broughtonian books were listed in the fair catalogues for Frankfurt and Leipzig (spring and autumn 1606), "Amsteldami apud Commelinum". Although the Officina Commeliniana marketed the books, the actual printers and publishers are not precisely known, but the best case is for a combination of Jodocus Hondius, Zacharias Heyns, and Jan Theunisz (See chapter 3).[92]

The second group of Puritan books lacking much historical documentation is from 1640. The STC refers to them as "Cloppenburg Press" books. (See Appendix I, M.) At least fourteen books are in this group; however, they do not have an identifiable imprint, except for some smart aleck phrase like, "Seen, Allowed, and Printed, by us" or,

---

[89] Briels, *ZB*, pp. 225, 458; Gruys and De Wolf, p. 107; Fowler, *Shield of Defence*, title page.

[90] Kleerkooper and Van Stockum, pp. 106-07; Confessieboek, no. 303, p. 310v, Mar. 17, 1639 (GA Amsterdam). On Broersz, see H.M. Borst, *Joost Broersz: Biographie (1609-1647) en Bibliographie (1634-1647) van een Amsterdamse drukker* (doctoraalscriptie, Univ. of Amsterdam, 1988).

[91] On selling books by catalogue, see chap. 6.

[92] L. Fuks and R.G. Fuks-Mansfeld, *Hebrew Typography in the Northern Netherlands 1585-1815* (Leiden: E.J. Brill, 1987-87), I, 95-96; *Catalogvs Vniversalis*, Frankfurt, spring 1606, sig. Blv, "Amsteldami. 4", 1 book; Frankfurt, autumn 1606, sig. E4, 6 books; Leipzig, autumn 1606, sig. Blr, 6 books. See also Simoni, *Catalogue*, s.v. Broughton.

"Published, by the worthy Gentleman Dr. Martin Mar-Prelat".[93] No documentary references linking these books to the Cloppenburghs, or even to Amsterdam, has been found; thus the case must rest on typographical analysis. These books of 1640 were authored by Henry Burton, William Prynne, Samuel How, Lewis Hughes, and a variety of anonymous writers. Several of the books were written in support of the Scottish Covenanters. Twelve books contain a selection of similar ornaments (headpiece with crowned rose with initials I.R., headpiece with a vase at the center, and tailpiece with open scrollwork).[94] The crowned rose headpiece was used earlier by printers in England, and no information has come to light linking any of these ornaments to Holland, nor do the usual diplomataic sources mention the books.[95] Two of the books, lacking the other ornaments, have an editor's or printer's mark used earlier by J.E. Cloppenburgh.[96] Regardless of questions about printer, these fourteen books should be studied as a group, but whether they should be identified with Amsterdam is questionable. They are the kind of books that ordinarily emanated from Holland; however, thus far, evidence from the archives is lacking and the typographical information is weak.

---

[93] Samuel How, *The Sufficiencie of the Spirits Teaching*, STC 13855 (Seen, Allowed, and Printed, by us, 1640); *A Dialogve, Wherin Is Plainly Layd Open the Tyrannicall Dealing of Lord Bishops*, STC 6805.3 (Published, by the worthy Gentleman Dr. Martin Mar-Prelat, 1640).

[94] In the Folger Library copy of *Ovr Demands of the English Lords Manifested*, STC 21926 (Printed by Margary Mar Prelat, 1640), on the inside cover, there are notes about the Cloppenburgh Press and its various ornaments (signed E. A., 3/11/31). These provide a good summary of the case for attributing most of these to the Cloppenburgh press.

[95] Richard Field, John Norton (Eliots Court Press), and M. Bradwood used the crowned rose headpiece; see A.E.M. Kirwood, "Richard Field, Printer. 1589-1624", *The Library*, 4th ser., 12 (1931-32), pp. 1-39 and Henry R. Plomer, "Eliots Court Press", *The Library*, 4th ser., 3 (1923), pp. 194-209. My thanks to P.J. Koopman for information and discussion about Cloppenburgh. He has not found these so-called Cloppenburgh ornaments in work of the Cloppenburghs.

[96] The two books in this group have a title page ornament (printer's or editor's mark) with the motto: "En laet het boeck deser wet van uwen monde niet comen. Josu. 1"; J.E. Cloppenburgh used this mark sometimes.

What to print? The publication strategies of editors, publishers and financial backers

The Puritan book printing enterprise was a loose network of authors, many of them resident in England or Scotland, and Amsterdam-based printers, publishers, and financial patrons. When the books had been printed and paid for, some were sold locally and the remainder had to be transported to readers in Britain or moved onward to America. The printer, unless he had a personal conviction about some particular books, took orders from a customer who had a need for the books.

The decision about "what to print" rested with an author who could pay the printing bill or with a local "editor" or "publisher" who would see the book through the press and arrange for financing. Often the editor would write an endorsement or preface to the book and get the material ready for the printer. Many a preface told about finding an unpublished manuscript which was judged most worthy of publication, or, if a reprinted book, having an old copy which was the model of the new edition. Such a person was the "setter forth" of books. He "procured the printing".[97] (See Appendix III.)

The original Puritan book publishers at Amsterdam were the Separatist Church, or "Company", as a whole, guided by Johnson and Ainsworth. Until the early 1620s (both Ainsworth and Thorp died about 1622), the main topic of English printing at Amsterdam was the issue of Separatism, either its defense or condemnation. Thorp's press, at the behest of the church, directed itself to printing books supportive of Separatist religion. There were very few exceptions to this rule. Johnson and Ainsworth were the chief authors and their messages were blunt and terrifying: "The horride estate" of the English church and state; the necessity of Separation. To their disciples, they were the fulfillment of the "Two witnesses" clothed in sackcloth from Revelation, chapter 11:3-4, prophesying through their words and books; "Fire proceedeth out of their mouth, and devoureth their enemies."[98]

The Separatist books did not go unanswered. The most active anti-Separatist at Amsterdam was John Paget of the English Reformed Church. Back in England, he had been outspoken against prelatical ceremonialism and for this was ejected from Nantwich, Cheshire. Once in exile, he saw the greatest danger as Separatism. At Amsterdam

---

[97] SP 84/155/145; BP, I, 139.
[98] Testimony of ex-Separatists, in Lawne, *Prophane Schisme*, pp. 56, 44.

he preached anti-Separatism for over thirty years, and in addition took the lead in many book activities. His goal was to stop the spread of the Separatist tide and reverse it. Paget was the author of several pro-Presbyterian books against Brownists, Independents, Papists, and Anabaptists. The Papists and Anabaptists, he once implied, were worthy of death, and the others were not much better.[99] He got his own books into print; and from his pastoral position in the church, he orchestrated and edited an anti-Brownist book campaign. His campaign consisted of: Lawne, *The Prophane Schism* (1612), *Brownisme Tvrned the In-side Out-ward* (1613) also by Lawne, Fowler, *Shield of Defence* (1612), Ames, *Second Manuduction* (1615), Paget's own *Arrow against the Separation* (1618), and similar books. Henry Ainsworth and William Best named Paget as the mastermind behind the "disguised pamphlets that come out of your congregation". Paget, no doubt, was actively involved in putting these books together. He gathered the material, although "under other mens names, to publish it in print".[100] His furious books were lie "oyle""on the flames.[101]

Paget further arranged book affairs and gave printing advice to many scholars who needed Amsterdam printers, such as Robert Parker of Doesburg, William Ames of Franeker, David Calderwood of Edinburgh, and Mr. Sh. (Sherwood?) in England, The latter's second reply to Doctor Downame (*A Replye Answering a Defense*, 1613, STC 20620) was committed to Paget "for the overseeing of the presse". "Mr. Sh." gave Paget permission to edit and revise the manuscript as he saw fit.[102] Paget well understood the mighty power of the press. A well-printed book was like the "sound of Trumpet from an high pinacle of the Printers Tower, and blowen abroad into many Countries".[103]

Associated with Paget in publishing affairs was Thomas Allen, schoolmaster for the English Reformed Church from 1636 to 1654.

---

[99] SP 84/80/26.

[100] Best, *The Chvrches Plea for Her Right*, STC 1973.5 (Amsterdam, 1635), pp. 4, 10; Paget, *Arrow*, p. 331; Walter, H. Burgess, *John Robinson* (London, 1920), pp. 124-25.

[101] John Davenport, *An Apologeticall Reply*, STC 6310 (Rotterdam, 1636), preface.

[102] Robert Paget, "The Publisher to the Christian Reader", in John Paget, *Defence of Church-Government*; Halkett and Laing, *A Dictionary of Anonymous and Pseudonymous Publications in the English Language*, ed. John Horden, 3rd ed. (London: Longman, 1980), I, no. A142 and R72. Richard Sherwood, the likely author of this treatise, was deprived in Lincoln diocese in 1605. See Kenneth Fincham, *Prelate as Pastor: The Episcopate of James I* (Oxford: Clarendon Press, 1990), p. 324.

[103] Paget, *Answer*, preface.

Paget commended Allen for having "good knowledge of the printers, and is much employed for correcting of the presse, for English bookes. He is religious, and about such business very diligent and officious."[104] Schoolmaster Thomas Allen, who died at Amsterdam in 1660, should not be confused with minister Thomas Allen of Norwich (an exile in the Low Countries in 1636, but not particularly connected with printing).

Puritan printing at Amsterdam took a turn of direction about 1620. For one thing, the Separatist church began to splinter further into new factions, with the result that the single-minded Brownist focus of the printers began to dissipate. Non-Separatist Puritans, like Plater, had charge of the printing for a period of years, and they allowed a much broader range of authors and topics to come forth. Moreover, the world itself was changing. Holland's truce with Spain broke down, and in the Holy Roman Empire the Thirty Years' War began. In England, King Charles I fell into irreparable controversy with Parliament. There was talk of collaboration between England and Spain. On every hand, the forces of Catholicism and political absolutism were running rampant. For Puritans these were frightening times, and the authors, editors, and publishers needed to address these political issues along with the old religious ones; Separatism was too narrow a topic when the world itself seemed to be falling apart.

In the 1620s many Puritanical books from the Amsterdam presses generously mixed religion and politics. How to win the Spanish-instigated wars? How to stand firm against the menace of Catholics, Arminians, Spaniards, and Hapsburgs? On these matters, Puritans in exile shared the concerns of many Dutch people. Stories about Catholic atrocities and "Spanish Tyranny" all around the world were in great demand. Among the English, the Reverend Thomas Scott, serving the English church at Utrecht (1622-26), had a great reputation for exposing Spanish plots in books printed both in England and the Netherlands.[105] Because of his brazen political meddling, he masked his publications in false title pages (Utrech, Goricom, The Hage, Helicon, Paradise); determining who did his printing and where it was done creates great problems for the historian. Scott's anti-Spanish, anti-Catholic campaign, directed from the Netherlands,

---

[104] Paget to David Calderwood, April 23, 1637, Wodrow MS, Folio XLII, fol. 253; Carter, *English Reformed Church*, p. 38.

[105] Sprunger, *Dutch Puritanism*, pp. 215-16.

inspired publication at the Dutch presses of many other books of similar spirit. These included Alexander Leighton, *Speculum belli sacri* (1624) and *Sions Plea* (1629), I. R., *The Spy* (1628), A. Ar., *The Practise of Princes* (1630), and *Tom Tell Troath* (c. 1629). Among Amsterdam Puritans, the guiding hand was Stephen Offwood. Like Scott, he was obsessed with Catholic conspiracies.

Stephen Offwood (1564-c. 1635) "fathered" several books for the Puritan reader through his activities in translating, editing, and financing of books. (See Appendix III, D.) A resident of Amsterdam since 1602, he made his living as a merchant and by running an inn, "At the White Hart", close to the Old Church. When he first came over, he was a Separatist, and after the schism of 1610, he went with the Ainsworthians. Not a model church member, his Separatist brethren lost patience and excommunicated him in 1617. The altercation which occasioned his excommunication arose when Thomas Stafford, a fellow church member, began courting and wooing Offwood's daughter, Susanna. The courtship events were not harmonious, and Offwood argued with Stafford, came to blows, and finally threw him out of the house. The wedding was called off, and the church excommunicated Offwood for anger and violence.[106] He never made his peace with his old church and instead went over to the Dutch Reformed Church, and later, April 18, 1629, transferred to the English Reformed Church.[107] His wife and children, however, continued in fellowship with the Separatists throughout, which caused further splintering of the household. Offwood went to press with his side of the church troubles in a sharp book, *An Advertisement to Ihon Deleclvse, and Henry May the Elder* (1632). There was a happy ending to the love story, however, when ten years after the Offwood-Stafford brawl, Thomas Stafford and Susanna Offwood were allowed to wed, making Thomas and Stephen at last father and son by marriage.[108] Both Offwood and Stafford for years pursued printing and publishing projects, but independently rather than as a team.

---

[106] Michael E. Moody, "Trials and Travels of a Nonconformist Layman: The Spiritual Odyssey of Stephen Offwood, 1564-*ca.* 1635", *Church History*, 51 (1982), pp. 157-63.

[107] CR, III, 4, 13.

[108] Van Eeghen, *AB*, IV, 101. The marriage with Susanna Offwood in 1627 was probably not Stafford's first; he had children born c. 1624 and c. 1627 (Inb. 27, fol. 84v).

The Offwood-produced books of the 1620s dealt with the Spanish, Catholic threat. Mostly these were new versions of previously printed works. For printing he commissioned Plater, Staresmore, and various "Successors of Thorp"; but as editor, he would create a preface or postscript, advertised with the label "Published by S.O." or simply the signature "S.O.". His first book was an English version of a Dutch pamphlet by Verheiden, *An Oration or Speech Appropriated vnto the Most Mightie and Illustrious Princes of Christendom* (1624), translated by Thomas Wood and edited by Offwood. The goal was to justify the "right and lawfulnesse" of the Dutch war against Spain and to reveal to the world the horror of Spanish cruelty.[109] Since the original work was not sufficiently fiery, Offwood added a supplement of his own, "An Adioynder of Svndry Other Particvlar Wicked Plots and Cruel, Inhumane, Perfidious; Yea Unnaturall Practices of the Spaniards." He relished telling about the blood and gore of Spanish actions; but to go into full detail would have been impossible, said Offwood, to "runne in infinitum".[110] Similar Offwood books followed. He became involved with Thomas Scott of Utrecht, the ringleader of publishing anti-Catholic, anti-Spanish propaganda. Offwood probably aided the printing of Scott's books, and some of Offwood's work was included in the 1624 edition of Scott's *Works* (A *Second Part of Spanish Practises*, STC 22078.5, containing a sampling of *The Oration* and of Offwood's *Adioynder*).

In 1630 Offwood came forth with *The Originall of Popish Idolatrie or the Birth of Heresies*, falsely attributed to the authorship of Isaac Casaubon; it was "Published by S.O.". Offwood's preface burned with the alarm and terror of the Protestants of the day. War and cruel enemies on every hand. The Antichrist loose in the world. England stood in as much danger as any nation, for the Lord would soon punish it for sin. "So except wee reforme our great and crying transgressions we shalbe ruinated and made an astonishment to all the world."[111]

---

[109] *An Oration*, STC 18837, a translation of Verheiden, *De jure belli Belgici* (Kn. 954). The Dutch ed. is Kn. 1490.

[110] *An Oration*, title page; *An Adioynder*, STC 18757 (1624), p. 12. No. 18757 has its own title page, but is paged continuously with *An Oration*, No. 18837. It was also printed as a separate pamphlet, *A Relation of Svndry Particvlar Wicked Plots...*, STC 18756. (n.p. 1624).

[111] *The Originall of Popish Idolatrie*, STC 4748 (n.p. 1630), "To the Christian Reader".

We may see the Angell of the Lord is executing of his wrath here, and all the world is in an uproare round about us. The whole frame of nature is out of order, yet wee do not lament as we should, therefore it doth prognosticate his plagues shall fall seven times heavier upon us. The gospell of Iesus Christ is departing from us, who can love his King and Country, and not lament and mourne and feare least his fiere wrath should consume us all in this troublesome, cruell, desperate and bloodie age in which wee live...[112]

Offwood could see no way out, except to combine political and military action with faith in God.

In the 1630s he put his printing efforts into financing and disseminating books against the Anglican hierarchy and Laudian ceremonialism, namely Ames' *Fresh Svit against Human Ceremonies* (1633, printed by Staresmore); *The Opinion...Concerning Bowing at the Name, or Naming of Jesus* (1634); and John Forbes' *Four Sermons* (1635). Offwood's books made his point pungently: Ceremonialists in religion are "Ceremoniall-astes or asses".[113] Although Offwood chose not to identify himself in every book passing through his hands, knowledgeable people regarded him as the master schemer behind the flood of Puritan "blew books" produced in the 1630s. The accusation was: "Stephen Offwood is certainly the man which procured the printing of all the blew books."[114] In Dutch parlance, scandalous pamphlets were "blew books". Offwood disappeared from the Amsterdam scene in 1635 and, consequently, must have died at about that point.

In the late 1630s, with Offwood out of the picture, Thomas Stafford (d. 1644), Offwood's son-in-law, and Thomas Crafford (fl. 1604-49) became the most active editors and publishers. Both Separatists in religion and merchants by trade, they collaborated on many publishing and bookselling projects. Stafford was the senior partner in the team; Crafford, a native of Reading, England, had ties to Offwood and took his meals at Offwood's inn (1633).[115]

Whenever the names of Stafford and Crafford were mentioned, one was reminded of unsavory scandals. Stafford had been excommuni-

---

[112] Ibid.

[113] *The Opinion, Judgement, and Determination of Two Reverend, Learned, and Conformable Divines of the Church of England, Concerning Bowing at the Name, or Naming of Jesus,* STC 14555 (n.p. 1634), p. 62 (publisher's note by H.D.).

[114] BP, I, 139v.

[115] Van Eeghen, *AB*, IV, 101; BP, I, 139v; Confessieboek, no. 303, p. 310v, Mar. 17, 1639 (on his age, about 35; from "Redding" in England).

cated from his church for cheating and Crafford, the dirty "vermyn", was notorious for going bankrupt and vicious, libelous talk.[116] The two men joined in 1639-40 to publish 1600 copies of the English Bible (printed for them by William Christiaensz of Leiden). Stafford was clearly the major investor and decision-maker for the deal, as stated by Christiaensz himself. Crafford conducted some of the business details at the Leiden print shop but declared himself to be only the underling; "I am only a servant in this business", (Ick bin maer een dienaar).[117] The result was the 1640 folio edition of the English Bible, "Printed by Thomas Stafford: And are to be sold at his house, at the signe of the Flight of Brabant, upon the Milk-market, over against the Deventer Wood-market. 1640" (STC 2344). This was a Genevan version which omitted the Apocrypha except for the Prayer of Manasses, one of the earliest English editions to deliberately omit the apocryphal books. Stafford produced a reprint edition in 1644.[118]

In addition to their joint publishing, Crafford ventured independently on his own books. Crafford in 1633 arranged with printer J.F. Stam for a Genevan edition, "Imprinted at Amsterdam, for Thomas Crafoorth. By Iohn Fredericksz Stam, dwelling by the South-Church at the signe of the Hope. 1633." In 1642 and 1644 he contracted with Stam for more Bibles.[119]

When not printing Bibles, Crafford delighted in producing books that were shockingly radical. He was responsible, likely with Stafford's backing in some cases, for a Dutch edition of the Scottish Covenanters' confession of faith, *De confessie des gheloofs vande Kerke van Schotlandt*, translated by Fredrick Willemsz Pennock, "gedruckt voor Thomas Craffort, 1638" (Kn. 4561); a Dutch translation of the Bastwick, Burton, and Prynne case in Star Chamber, *Een cort ende bondich verhael*, printed by Christiaensz, 1638 (Kn. 4599); *A Guide unto Sion*, "Printed for Thomas Crafford, 1639" (STC 26126), and for reprinting Poynet's *A Short Treatise of Politike Power* (original 1556, and now reprinted 1639, STC 20179). He had Joost Broers anonymously print the latter work. By concentrating efforts on translation, Crafford

---

[116] On Stafford, NA 1058 (Van de Ven), Feb. 16, 1641, fols. 56v-57v; on Crafford, SP 84/155/145.

[117] RA 79, V, 389 (pencil 238), GA Leiden; NA 1056 (Van de Ven), Dec. 16, 1639, fols. 81-82 (GA Amsterdam).

[118] Herbert, *Bible*, no. 545, pp. 180-81 and no. 579, p. 192.

[119] Ibid., no. 473, p. 166; Van Eeghen, *AB*, IV, 101. Kleerkooper and Van Stockum, pp. 1453-54.

showed his grasp of how to build up favorable Dutch support for the Puritan-Covenanter cause. In 1639 Crafford was arrested for publishing the Star Chamber book and the Poynet book but was released on bond, provided by Stafford, and fined 300 guilders.[120] Many Puritan "blew books" printed in the shops of Christiaensz, Canne, and Stam had the blessing and money of Stafford and Crafford behind them. Crafford, moreover, had some hands-on printing experience, being "practiced and knowledgeable in printing".[121]

The fiery Puritan book-team of Stafford and Crafford broke up in about 1641 over some financial details of Bible printing. Crafford refused to give way and libelously attacked Stafford for which he was sentenced in 1642 to six weeks in jail with only bread and beverage.[122] Crafford had gone around gathering up anti-Stafford statements and having them notarized. These documents, orchestrated by Crafford, provide some of the juiciest details available about Stafford.[123] In 1649, after another altercation with a Dutchman, he was banished from the city for being a libeller and "dirty vagabond".[124] Crafford had the unhappy distinction of being dragged into court, and sometimes to jail, probably more than any other Amsterdam Englishman of the time.

Mr. "T.L." was another English promoter of Puritan books, particularly those with an uplifting spiritual message. He financed three books in 1637-38, Thomas Hooker, *The Poore Doubting Christian*, STC 13726.4 (1637) and *The Sovles Hvmiliation*, STC 13728.5 (1638), and John Preston, *The Doctrine of the Saints Infirmities*, STC 20221.3 (c. 1638). These were published "for the benefit of our English nation". They were available for sale "at his chamber in Flowingburrow neare unto the English church". Who is this T.L. who lived on the Fluwelen Burgwal? One possibility is Thomas Loof, who was an investor in Bible printing in 1641.[125]

---

[120] Confessieboek, no. 303, p. 310v; Justitieboek, no. 578, p. 312v (GA Amsterdam).

[121] NA 1056 (Van de Ven), fols. 8lr, 8lv, 82r.

[122] Confessieboek, no. 305, p. 68v (August 26, 1642); Van Eeghen, *AB*, IV, 101.

[123] See the statements of Patrick Motley, John White, and others, "at the request of Thomas Craffort", Aug. 26, 30, 1642, NA 1062 (Van de Ven), fols. 297r, 297v, 304; also NA 1058, fols. 56v, 57r-v.

[124] Van Eeghen, *AB*, IV, 101.

[125] The publisher (T.L.) gave his address of Flowingburrow, i.e. *Fluwelen Burgwal*, on the title pages of the books; on Loof, the possible T.L., see Van Eeghen, *AB*, IV, 101.

There were other levels of involvement in the book business, less demanding than editing and publishing. Anonymity was often desired. Some pious men of financial means would pay for the work of printing without having the skills or time to edit or improve the text. They would be "at cost and charges for the printing of the booke" but their names were not revealed.[126] The profit motive also played its part. Many merchants of very respectable reputation invested in Dutch-printed English Bibles and shipped them to Britain for selling. "Manie merchantes bye great quantities...and bring them over."[127] Such buying and selling could be very profitable. Bibles were valuable merchandise. An English merchant Jeffry Tillis, handler of tobacco, in 1637 used a stock of 500 English Bibles in storage in Amsterdam—from his on-the-side dealings—as security for a loan of 415 guilders.[128] A large number of notarized contracts for English Bibles between merchant investors and printers are found in the archives. These deals involved large sums of money and many Bibles: 4000 Bibles and 2000 Psalms at Rotterdam in 1638;[129] 1600 Bibles at Leiden in 1639;[130] 1000 Bibles in 1641, 12000 Bibles in 1642, 6000 Bibles in 1644, the latter all at Amsterdam.[131]

More shadowy and hard to reconstruct were the deals for printing and financing controversial Puritan treatises. These books were most unlikely to produce a profit; moreover, such dealings could be dangerous on legal grounds. Under such circumstances, publishers and printers would not draw up notarized contracts. Printers like Thorp and Canne apparently carried much of the burden personally, sustained with contributions from their churches. Here and there, men of property and Puritan vision gave sufficiently to keep the Puritan presses moving. The zealous but impoverished John Canne commended certain financial backers—of which he could name three or four—who paid for books "printed for the common good of which there was neuer any returne of monie, but a spreading of them into all

---

[126] Fowler, *Shield of Defence*, p. 7.

[127] SP 84/387/79.

[128] NA 598 (Lamberti), fol. 186.

[129] NA 145, nos. 169-170 (GA Rotterdam); SP 84/387/79.

[130] NA 1056 (Van de Ven), fols. 81-82 (GA Amsterdam); Kleerkooper and Van Stockum, pp. 1244-46.

[131] Van Eeghen, *AB*, III, 48 (1641); NA 1062 (Van de Ven), fols. 58-59 (1642); Kleerkooper and Van Stockum, pp. 1453-54 (1644).

the parts of the land". Canne pled for more of these generous spirits to come forth.[132]

Scottish activities

Like the Puritans of England, the Scottish nonconformists extended their activities across the sea to Amsterdam. A good number of Scottish preachers lived abroad in Dutch exile and could be of help; prominent among these patriots-in-exile were John Forbes, preacher of the Merchant Adventures, Robert Dury, preacher of the English-Scottish church at Leiden 1610-16, Alexander Leighton, preacher at the English church at Utrecht in 1629, and William Spang, preacher at Veere 1630-50 (cousin of Robert Baillie). Most of the "English" churches were, in fact, a mixture of English and Scottish people, which often led to national rivalries within the "flock". Nonconformist Scots depended on Dutch-printed books to present the case for Presbyterian Scottish religion. The burning topic of these books was the forced intrusion of English episcopal religion into Scotland. We have a "dispute", said the Scottish zealots, we have a "quarrel". The Scottish cause, said George Gillespie, was a "Dispute" about "English-Popish Ceremonies *Obtrvded* vpon the Chvrch of Scotland".[133] According to Robert Baillie the Scottish national cause was resistance to Laud and his gang of "Canterburians". The "quarrel" was about "bookes, ceremonies, and Bishops".[134] Inasmuch as the Canterburians controlled the printing presses and books of Britain, the faithful remnant of Scots often had to produce their books abroad. Patrick Scot in 1625 reported about the extent of Scottish books printed at Amsterdam: "Behold, euery Bookesellers shop, and most Pedlers stalles, loaden with the nullitie"—"trumpets of *Sedition*". The discontented spirits of Scotland go "running to *Amsterdam*, make themselues *Libertines*".[135]

Some of the most powerful voices of Scottish religion depended upon the Puritan presses of Amsterdam. Dr. Alexander Leighton did

---

[132] Burrage, "Canne", p. 232.

[133] STC 11896, title page, italics added.

[134] Robert Baillie, *Ladensivm*, Part I, STC 1206 (n.p. 1640), sigs A3r, A4v.

[135] Patrick Scot, *Vox Vera: or Observations from Amsterdam*, STC 21863 (London, 1625), pp. 3-4, 56.

his publishing at Amsterdam; in 1624, while finishing the *Speculum belli sacri*, he "lodgeth at the printers house".[136] David Calderwood, working from Edinburgh, published more than a dozen books at Amsterdam; he had an agent who traveled frequently to Amsterdam, "the Scottsman whom the author...allways imployeth in his buy-sinesses".[137] Four of his books, along with the *Course of Conformitie* by William Scot, were on sale at Amsterdam in 1625, all bound into one volume, celebrated as if they were the "Oracles of Apollo".[138] Samuel Rutherford in 1636 had to arrange for publication of his anti-Arminian *Exercitationes* at Amsterdam, for which he was summoned before the High Commission.[139] Robert Baillie had various printing projects and published his own *Ladensivm* at Amsterdam (1640).

In the later 1630s Amsterdam, after the outbreak for the Bishops' Wars, served as *entrepôt* for weapons and war information. The Amsterdam arms merchants provided pikes, muskets, and bandoleers, for cash,[140] and the Amsterdam printers produced Scottish (anti-Royalist) propaganda in support of the war effort. Some of the earliest Covenanter books of 1637-38 from Amsterdam were Gillespie's *Dispvte against the English-Popish Ceremonies* (1637, STC 11896), *Newes from Scotland* (1638, STC 22013), and *The Beast is Wovnded. Or Infor-mation from Scotland concerning Their Reformation* ("printed in the yeare that the Bishops had their downefall in Scotland", 1638, STC 22032). The Netherlands was swarming with authors and their agents in search of printers for the pamphlets concerning "Scottish libertie" and "the persecution, and reformation of the Scottish church".[141] They had political books filled with "dangereuses maximes" belittling the power of kings.[142]

The Scots recruited John Canne of Amsterdam, the so-called "Cloppenburgh" printer, and Christiaensz from Leiden to produce the desired Scottish propaganda. The output of pamphlets was large,

---

[136] SP 84/117/157.
[137] Ibid.
[138] Scot, *Vox Vera*, p. 3.
[139] Samuel Rutherford, *Letters*, ed. Andrew A. Bonar (Edinburgh: Oliphant Anderson & Ferrier, 1891), pp. 12, 135.
[140] SP 84/154/25.
[141] SP 84/155/79; 84/155/260.
[142] SP 84/155/32v; Laud, *Works*, VII, 544. These sources report on the efforts in 1639 to reprint George Buchanan, *De iure regni apud Scotos* (1579). The efforts apparently failed; no edition of 1639-40 is known.

including many key works: a Dutch edition of "An Information to All Good Christians" (*Informatie aen alle oprechte christenen*, 1639, Kn. 4600), *The Remonstrance of the Nobility, Barrons, Burgesses, Ministers and Commons*, 1639, printed both in English and Dutch (STC 21908 and Kn. 4604), and *Een cort verhael van de misdaden ende crimen die de Schotse bisschoppen* (1639, Kn. 4601). There were also several printings of the Scottish Covenant, *Confession of Faith of the Kirk of Scotland* (1638) and *De confessie des gheloofs vande kerke van Schotlandt* (1638, Kn. 4561).

The translator of another book from Scotland, Thomas Abernathy's *Wonderlijcke historye vande paepsche regeringhe in Groot Bretaignen, insonderheyt in Schotlandt* (1639), laid out his translation goals: (1) To proclaim to all the world the audacious machinations and plots of the Papists who seek to establish their hierarchy and spiritual dominion in all lands, (2) To expose how the Pope, the Jesuits, and the Popish-minded are working in England and Scotland to bring in their religion, beginning with the introduction of various popish-like ceremonies in Scotland.[143] If the Anglican ceremonies were, in truth, papism in disguise, what choice did the Scots have except to revolt in the name of God? Latin books by William Spang of Veere, the *Brevis et fidelis narratio* (1640) and *Historia rerum nuper in regno scotiae gestarum* (1641), with the false imprint of "Dantisci", also helped to spread the Scottish word.[144]

The emphasis on getting the Scottish message into Dutch shows the significance attached to gaining support for the war in the Netherlands. The Scots were extremely aggressive in their Dutch publishing—"Machiavellian, Jesuitical, and diabolical".[145]

Hide and seek: the hunt for illegal Puritan books

Like the rest of the Netherlands, Amsterdam was bound by the press-control laws of the States General and the States of Holland, and in

---

[143] Thomas Abernathy, *Wonderlijcke historye vande paepsche regeringhe in Groote Bretaignen, insonderheyt in Schotlandt* (n.p. 1639), "tot den leser". This book was a translation of STC 72; Schoneveld no. 47. This translator was also responsible for *Een cort vernael* (1639, Kn. 4601).

[144] These were possibly printed by Stam; see Appendix I, H. On Spang, see William Steven, *The History of the Scottish Church, Rotterdam* (Edinburgh, 1932), p. 73n.

[145] SP 84/155/32.

addition, the Amsterdam magistrates passed a few edicts of their own
(1623, 1639, 1648, 1649). Nevertheless, the printing laws were so
loosely enforced, that Puritan books encountered few hindrances. The
basic printing laws of the Republic were contained in the Holland
edict of 1581, renewed and updated by the States General edicts of
1608, 1615, 1618, 1621, 1624, 1639, 1646, and 1651. The main point
of these regulations was to prohibit publication of libellous books and
to require each printer to print his name, place, year, the author, and
the translators. Anonymity was illegal. Punishment was a fine of 300
guilders.[146]

By the standards set forth by the States General, a large part of the
Puritan books printed at Amsterdam were illegal, because of the
omission of printer or author, or other essential data. Moreover, by
English standards of censorship, the Puritan books were clearly illegal,
and the English government treated them as such, subject to punishment if the author or printer could be seized. The city of Amsterdam
had its share of citizens who favored enforcement of the printing laws
for the sake of having an orderly city; the Dutch Reformed preachers
from time to time pushed for a strong system of preventive censorship
through ecclesiastical book inspectors (*visitatores librorum* or *censores
librorum*).[147] All of the earnest plans to establish a consistent regulatory policy at Amsterdam came to naught because of the prevailing
spirit of tolerance. To ban books, predicted the magistrates, would
simply make these *verboden* books more irresistible to curious readers.
One of the magistrates made this suggestion to the call for banning
bad books: "We live in a free land. He has written a book against you.
Well then, you should write a book against him."[148]

So long as the printing laws remained on the books, even though
largely unenforced, they were a threat to printers and authors. If
complaints about certain books became insistent enough, a hunt for
the books began, and all the parties involved would run for cover.
The government of England frequently asked for action against offensive Puritan authors and printers, and although the results were mea-

---

[146] J.T. Bodel Nyenhuis, *De wetgeving op drukpers en boekhandel in de Nederlanden tot
in het begin der XIXde eeuw* (Amsterdam: P.N. van Kampen & Zoon, 1892), pp. 99-
115; Nikolaas Wiltens, *Kerkelyk plakaatboek* (The Hague, 1772), pp. 385-461.

[147] R.B. Evenhuis, *Ook dat was Amsterdam* (Amsterdam: W. Ten Have, 1965-78),
II, 142-43; Acta Synod North Holland, 1638, art. 101 (no. 101, archief Classis
Amsterdam, GA Amsterdam).

[148] Van Eeghen, *AB*, V, 26.

ger, the commotion was frightening. In 1606, just after Giles Thorp had set up his shop, Ambassador Winwood, on orders from Archbishop Bancroft, requested control of the *"many dangerous Books and Pamphlets in English"*. The Amsterdam government and churchmen promised "to hinder the books", but little came of it.[149] An English printer of 1608, "on this side the seas", complained that "the Archbishop of Canterbury sent over two men to seeke me", but praise to God, the harassment came to naught.[150] In 1614 Winwood presented another complaint about political pamphlets that meddled with Parliamentary affairs. The burgomasters expressed total surprise and ignorance of the matter; but to make a show of cooperation, they passed a token proclamation against English printing done "without approbation" and raided the books in stock of the "English printer" (Giles Thorp?). They confiscated books and put them "in custody". Although the English printer's name was not mentioned in the documents, Thorp, the only English printer in town, was certainly the unlucky victim.[151] Moreover, because of the books seized, Thorp's corpus of printed books has a lacuna for the year 1614.

A sustained campaign against Puritan printing at Amsterdam occurred in the 1630s, when Laud became primate of the English Church. The English ambassador, Sir William Boswell, was in charge of seeing that the Puritan books were stopped once and for all. He appealed to the Amsterdam magistrates for the strict enforcement of the edicts of 1581, 1615, and 1621, especially about books "concerning other foreign kings and potentates, and ecclesiastical government".[152] His chief targets were John Canne of Amsterdam and William Christiaensz of Leiden.

Canne was on dangerous ground. He was "the master of libels".[153] His *Richt Right* books were "anonymous" and many of

---

[149] Winwood, *Memorials*, II, 195 (Feb. 9, 1605/06); Acta Kerkeraad Amsterdam, III, 146v, June 8, 1606; Hessels, *ELBA*, III, 1179, 1186-87.

[150] *Informations*, STC 14084, sig. *1r. This is one of the William Jones books, and there is debate about where the press was located, in Amsterdam or London. The present author leans to the Amsterdam hypothesis. See above nos. 22, 23.

[151] SP 84/69/177.

[152] SP 84/154/113-14; 84/154/148-49 (Plakkaat of 1621, Res. States General, no. 3180, fol. 17). See Harry Carter, "Archbishop Laud and Scandalous Books from Holland", in *Studia Bibliographica in Honorem Herman de la Fontaine Verwey* (Amsterdam, 1966), pp. 43-55.

[153] SP 84/154/312.

them harshly attacked the King of England and the bishops. Such books fell under the provisions of the printing laws, although they had not recently been enforced against English printers like Canne. In 1638 Boswell adopted a plan of action which succeeded in pulling Canne into court. Boswell's Amsterdam plan laid out the following steps:

1 To persuade the burgomasters of Amsterdam to take strong action.

2 "To presse the Schout (presently upon order) without any delay to search John Cann his houses, and sease upon all such scandalouse books, which he shall find there against the Church and State of England."

3 "To cause the said John Can to be examined upon oath concerning the Authors, Printers, Distributors, Abbettors, or furtherers of the said scandalouse books, and in particular concerning the booke, *A Dispute of English Popish Ceremonyes*."

4 "To make the said John Can produce his first Copies or originalls in manuscript or print..."

5 "To procure from the Schout and Magaistrats that the said Placarts be fully in every part executed against the said John Can, and other transgressors of the same and presse for arbitrary correction."

6 "To observe diligently where and by whom else in Amsterdam those or any other like scandalouse books are sould and procure suppression thereof."

7 "To proceed against any other whom he shall find delinquent as he proceedeth against Can in his Examinacion and otherwise."

8 "To entreat the Schouts, Burgomasters, and Schepens to be very vigilent and severe for preventing the like abuses and excesses hereafter."[154]

With Boswell in hot pursuit, the wheels of Amsterdam justice began turning against Canne. On July 3, 1638, the Amsterdam court condemned Canne for having "presumed to make, and consequently to put in print and publish" *A Necessitie of Separation* (1634, STC 4574) and for having "printed anew" *A Brief Relation of Certain Speciall and Most Materiall Passages, and Speeches in the Starre-Chamber*, concerning the June 14, 1637 case of Bastwick, Burton, and Prynne (1638, STC 1570.5). The said books were "scandalouse and touching his Royall Maiesty and the Church Gouernment of Great Brittain". The court

---

[154] SP 84/153/188-89.

fined him 300 guilders and confiscated all copies.[155] Two of the books originally charged against him were stricken from the final sentence (*Newes from Scotland* and Gillespie's *Dispvte*). Christiaensz of Leiden received an identical punishment for his books.

A larger account of Canne's legal troubles, with more information about his printing, is found in the records of the Schout of Amsterdam:

> Draught of the Demand and Conclusion of the Schout of Amsterdam against John Cann: Saith, that whereas he (the cited party) about fowre yeares past, hath made and caused to be printed and given out a certaine book intitaled *A necessity of Separation from the Church of England*; and that the cited hath since lately printed a certaine pamphlet named *A Brief Relation of Certaine Speciall and Most Materiall Passages in the Starr-Chambre &c.* That he also hath printed the Curranto called *Newes from Scotland*, and also a part of the book named *A Dispute against English Popish Ceremonies &c.* All which books and libells as being defamatory and scandalouse, and especially tending to the great prejudice and diminution of the honour and government of His Royall Maiesty of Great Brittaine; all which is contrary to the Placcart of the High and Mighty Lords...16 of January 1621. And for as much as the same concerneth His Majesty of Great Brittaine (A Potentat allyed unto these lands) and that it toucheth as well the Political as the Ecclesiastical to the perturbation of His Majesty's quiett reigne, the said officer...concludeth that the cited...shall be condemned by your Lordships, censured, above the forfeitture of all his said printed copies (which shall all be burned) to the summe of 300 guilders and moreover to arbitrary correction. 3 July 1638.[156]

With the punishment of John Canne, Boswell felt thoroughly victorious. "It is more then I can learne hath ever ben done before, much more then any man thought I could have gotten done at all. For it is the first tyme that the Placcarts have been executed." King Charles also felt "verie well satisfied".[157]

Much of the credit for repressing the Puritan books went to allies that Boswell and Laud recruited in Amsterdam. They received great aid from Reformed pastor Johannes le Maire (1567-1642).[158]

---

[155] SP 84/154/151v-152; Justitieboek, no. 578, p. 267v.
[156] SP 84/154/151r-v.
[157] SP 84/155/113-14; SP 84/154/146.
[158] *NNBW*, VII, 835; Evenhuis, *Amsterdam*, I, 193-95.

Unlike many Amsterdam citizens, Le Maire loved the notion of censorship and was disgusted by the viciousness of Puritan, especially Brownist, printing. He craved better law and order for the city, and he hated Brownism. A pastor of the Amsterdam church since 1601 and a zealous Calvinist, his anti-Brownist attitudes had been formed in the Johnson-Slade controversies of early century. He thoroughly believed that both Amsterdam and the Church of England would be better off without John Canne's printing. Moreover, Le Maire had a personal interest in the welfare of the English religion, having travelled in England and having met many of the churchmen, most likely including Laud himself. Consequently, when Archbishop Laud made known his displeasure about the Puritan books of Amsterdam, Le Maire volunteered to hunt down the printers and stop the books. "I thought with my selfe that it was my duty as the first and eldest minister of Amsterdam...to oppose and hinder the same as much as it were possible."[159] The anti-Laudian Amsterdam Puritans were "evil-doers", he declared.[160] For a good while, Le Maire was Laud's "constant Spie and Intelligencer".[161]

Le Maire was on duty every day: "I find daily by experience that there are a great many wicked spirits and bad affections toward His Majesty, your Grace, and the hierarchy of England among the English and Scots, and especially among the Brownists."[162] His intentions were to drive John Canne, whom he despised as a Brownist, out of the printing business, and to ruin Thomas Crafford, "that base and seditious fellow". The Amsterdam pastor judged Crafford to be Canne's chief assistant and financial supporter. Both must be silenced.[163] For that period 1638-40, Le Maire hunted down at least seventeen Puritan and Covenanter books at Amsterdam, Leiden, and Rotterdam, the majority being at Amsterdam. A few he headed off before publications. He attributed the pestiferous Amsterdam books to only two printers, Canne and Joost Broersz. The bitter, rebellious books offended his sense of decorum and decency. Le Maire, who did not understand the current English-Scottish ecclesiastical situation very

---

[159] SP 84/154/44; 84/155/93.
[160] SP 84/155/79.
[161] William Prynne, *Canterburies Doome*, Wing P3917 (London, 1646), p. 349.
[162] SP 84/155/32.
[163] SP 84/155/79.

well, was personally amazed that anyone should portray His Grace, the archbishop, in colors "charcoal black".[164]

Beginning in 1638, whenever Le Maire detected a new English or Scottish pamphlet, he dispatched the Amsterdam "praeter" (police officer) and demanded the full vigor of the printing laws. Many books were impounded, especially at Canne's shop (*de boutique de Canne*) and burned in the flames of justice.[165] This "hindered in the very birth" the printing of some books and caused Canne to be summoned to court a second time for illegal book printing in January 1639.[166] A few weeks later, also at Le Maire's instigation, Crafford was arrested and sentenced to a 300 guilder fine for procuring the printing of *Een cort ende bondich verhael* (Kn. 4559) by Christiaensz of Leiden and *A Short Treatise of Politike Power* (STC 20179) by Joost Broersz of Amsterdam. Broersz, who hid out for a while, was also brought to court. The magistrates caught the *Short Treatise* in press and stopped Broersz at chapter four; "neverthelesse, this venemous libell is printed againe, and perhaps in another place."[167]

With such printing disorder abounding, Le Maire attempted at this time to revive the church's *visitatores librorum* scheme, still unapproved by the burgomasters. In 1639 Le Maire proposed applying it exclusively to English and Scottish books. An Amsterdam proclamation should be drawn up, Le Maire urged, "that no English booke should bee printed, before it was seene and reade, by a learned man, that understands the tounge".[168] Pastor Le Maire, no doubt, saw himself as one of the censors or "learned men" to be employed. Although the proposal did not gain the support of the burgomasters, Le Maire could take some credit for helping to secure renewed printing proclamations of a more general nature: The States General resolution of October 3, 1639; the States of Holland resolution of May 24, 1639; and the Amsterdam resolution of April 16, 1639. These resolutions pleased Le Maire because they sounded severe and inserted the clause forbidding political pamphlets damaging to "the King of Great Britain and his principal ministers".[169]

---

[164] SP 84/155/6.

[165] SP 84/155/32.

[166] SP 84/154/256; 84/155/12.

[167] Confessieboek, no. 303, p. 310v; Justitieboek, no. 578, p. 312v; SP 84/155/79.

[168] SP 84/155/79.

[169] Wiltens, *Plakaatboek*, pp. 403-07; the phrase "King of Great Britain" was added to the States General res., Oct. 3, 1639; Res. States of Holland, May 24, 1639, no.

No arrangement about books was ever permanent at Amsterdam. While Boswell and Le Maire rejoiced, the presses of Canne quietly resumed their missionary work of producing Puritan-Separatist literature. In spite of his convictions in court, the Richt Right press produced many books throughout 1638, 1639, and 1640. It turned out that Canne was not so crippled in his printing work as first thought. The *maistre libelleuis* had "gotten wind" of the Schout's raids on his shop. "He hid some of the books" and saved part of the stock from the flames.[170] Moreover, when the printing doors closed temporarily at Amsterdam, they swung open at Leiden, Rotterdam, and other places. The authors and publishers, "seeing our Magistrates care to hinder them, doe goe to other cytties".[171] In 1639 the action temporarily shifted to Rotterdam, where such radical books as *The Beast is Wounded* and Bastwick's *Leteny* were everywhere available. These books "they dare, I say, hang before their dores".[172]

The laws multiplied and the burgomasters, at least, went through the motions of severely disciplining the printers of bad English-Scottish books. Political necessity required some public show of alliance with the governments of Britain. As always, the making of laws in 1639 and 1640 was a far different thing than consistently enforcing the laws. None of the Amsterdam printers, or the authors of the Puritan books, could be permanently silenced. Le Maire lamented to Laud that the ghostly printers and publishers dishonestly hid behind anonymity and the fake title page, *un nom feint*. The phantom books came from "Utopia"—nowhere.[173] Amsterdam's freedom of printing and its inefficient enforcement of the press laws served Puritanism very well. The Puritan and Covenanter printers sent forth the message produced in English, Dutch, French, and Latin, intent on "filling all of Europe with their books".[174]

1643, p. 119 (archief 5038, GA Amsterdam); SP 84/155/136 (res. States of Holland) gives the date of the Holland resolution as May 19, 1639; Willekeuren der stad Amsterdam, vol. L, p. 82v.

[170] SP 84/154/312.
[171] SP 84/155/79v.
[172] SP 84/155/93.
[173] SP 84/155/6.
[174] SP 84/155/32.

CHAPTER 5

PURITAN PRINTING AT LEIDEN

Leiden, like Amsterdam, excelled as a center of English-language printing in the seventeenth century. The city of more than 50,000 population had a sizeable English-Scottish community, some drawn by the university, the oldest and foremost in the Netherlands, others for commerce and for jobs in the textile workshops. The printing trade was an important economic boon to the city; and with its ties to university scholarship, it provided an intellectual stimulus which flavored the life of the city. In fine printing Leiden gained a world reputation. "There is no city in the entire world where so many people live off of the book trade. Whole streets are full of book-stores."[1]

The English-Scottish community: churches, university, and the book trade

The printing of English and Scottish books at Leiden grew steadily alongside the growth of the British churches. Several hundred English and Scots lived in seventeenth-century Leiden. Although economic motives were a large cause of settlement, religion also powerfully motivated many immigrants. The Separatists as a group sought religious sanctuary. Leiden had two seventeenth-century British churches, both with strong Puritan leadership but split over the theological issue of separation or non-separation from the Church of England. The first was the English Reformed Church, established in 1607, the other the Separatist church, which moved to Leiden in 1609. The non-Separatist English Reformed people were a group of 200 families (1609), served by pastors Robert Dury (1610-16) and Hugh Goodyear (1617-61). The Dury-Goodyear church, a *gereformeerde kerk* in communion with the Dutch Reformed Church, was supported by the Dutch govern-

---

[1] *Leids Jaarboekje* (1915), p. 73, from an account of the 1720s; P.J. Blok, *Geschiedenis eener Hollandsche stad* (The Hague: Nijhoff, 1910-18), III, 6-7, 210-11.

ment. The Separatists were headed by the Reverend John Robinson, and by 1620 the congregation of "Pilgrim Fathers" grew to about 300 persons. In 1620 a part of the group led by elder William Brewster emigrated to New England, but the larger part, including pastor Robertson himself, remained behind. After Robinson's death in 1625, the church had a downhill existence and faded out in the 1640s. The English Reformed Church was more durable, existing until 1807.[2] For several decades of the seventeenth century, the two churches co-existed without public controversy and vigorously served the English and Scottish settlers.

The Puritan leadership, through friendship and correspondence, linked up to the widespread network of English dissenters in the Netherlands, England, and America. Goodyear's Puritan contacts were well illustrated by his correspondence and personal papers (the "Goodyear Papers") preserved in the Leiden archives.[3] He corresponded on both sides of the Atlantic with such Puritan giants as John Cotton, John Paget, and Hugh Peter. From Goodyear's strategic position at Leiden, he could serve as a go-between for business and university affairs of friends in the New World and the Old. Goodyear entertained many travelling British preachers passing through Leiden, a situation which he found burdensome enough that he pleaded for a raise in salary in 1627, because of so many "foreign preachers and church members who ordinarily come addressed to him from other kingdoms, provinces, and towns, by virtue of his office".[4] He had long-standing university connections, having once been *theologiae studiosus*. Among Separatists, Robinson had even more prominent standing. Through his many publications he became one of the most-quoted Separatist theologians, and the church was a model of excellent Separatist practice. The Separatist churches of Amsterdam and Leiden, although differing somewhat on the nature of strict Separation, produced one large brotherhood of religion. Ainsworth of Amsterdam would consult with Robinson "in all matters of waight".[5]

---

[2] For the history of the English churches of Leiden, see K.L. Sprunger, *Dutch Puritanism* (Leiden: E.J. Brill, 1982), chap. 5.

[3] Goodyear Papers, Weeskamer archief 1355, GA Leiden. On Goodyear, see Greaves and Zaller, *BD*, II, 21-22.

[4] Reg. kerk. zaken, no. 2150, fol. 114v.

[5] William Bradford, "A Dialogue or the sume of a Conference...1648", *Publications of the Colonial Society of Massachusetts*, 22 (1920), p. 136; Walter H. Burgess, *John Robinson* (London: Williams and Norgate, 1920), pp. 192-200.

Other Puritans came to Leiden to consult with the churches. In 1610-11, William Ames, Henry Jacob, and Robert Parker "sojourned for a time in Leyden" to plan religious strategies and debate theology with Robinson.[6] When possible, the visitors enrolled at the university. The following students in particular should be noted: Robert Dury (1610), John Robinson (1615), Thomas Brewer (1615), Hugh Goodyear (1617), John Bastwick (1617), Alexander Leighton (1617), and William Ames (1619). About 950 English and Scottish students, 1575-1675, can be easily identified.[7] With membership in church and university, the British immigrants could more fully participate in the learned activities of the day. According to Pilgrim historian William Bradford, Robinson attended lectures by professor Simon Episcopius and forthrightly challenged his Arminian tenets, winning a "famous victory".[8] Another time, Goodyear debated Episcopius, "openly in ye face of ye whole Auditory". William Ames, "Hammer of the Arminians", lived in Leiden several times and earned an orthodox reputation through his books and teachings. In 1618 he was appointed at the Synod of Dort as advisor to president Johannes Bogerman.[9]

Outside of the university, William Brewster, elder of the Separatist church, "attained some learning", and taught classes in the English language for students. "For he fell into a way (by reason he had the Latin tongue) to teach many students who had a desire to learn the English tongue, to teach them English; and by his method they quickly attained it with great facility." This method in English grammar, although never published, was one of the early models of its kind in the Netherlands.[10] In the town and university, a little circle of English-Scottish intellectuals, centered around Robinson and Goodyear, was active in writing, publishing, and debating the issues.

---

[6] Bradford, "Dialogue", p. 131.

[7] Edward Peacock, *Index to English Speaking Students Who Have Graduated at Leiden University*, Index Society Publications, 13 (1883); John W. Stoye, *English Travellers Abroad 1604-1667*, (London: Jonathan Cape, 1952), p. 295.

[8] William Bradford, *Of Plymouth Plantation 1620-1647*, ed. Samuel Eliot Morison (New York: Alfred A. Knopf, 1970), p. 21.

[9] Quick, "Icones" (Life of Ames), fol. 13; K.L. Sprunger, *The Learned Doctor William Ames* (Urbana: Univ. of Illinois Press, 1972), pp. 48, 54.

[10] Bradford, *Plymouth Plantation*, pp. 325-26; G. Scheurweghs, "English Grammars in Dutch and Dutch Grammars in English in the Netherlands before 1800", *English Studies*, 41 (1960), pp. 129-30.

The bookish interests of the Leiden Puritans show up in the libraries they collected. Fortunately, a few book catalogues from Englishmen in Holland have survived, and they give insights into their publishing and collecting activities. These were printed as library auction or sale catalogues. Examples of these are the library catalogues of William Ames (1634) and Hugh Goodyear (1662). Also helpful for historians is the bookseller's auction catalogue of Govert Basson (1630), published when he went out of business. Basson, a Leiden printer and bookseller, was descended from an English family. Doctor Ames resided at Leiden for three years, 1619-22, and supported himself by running a tiny private house college or "burse", resembling the Staten College presided over by Festus Hommius, and the Walloon College. Theological students lived in the Ames house and had part of their instruction from Ames and part from the university professors. During this period, Ames collaborated with Brewster and Brewer in their press activities. In 1622 he received an appointment as professor of theology at the University of Franeker, and this took him north to Friesland.[11] Ames is the example *par excellence* of a Puritan theologian, who, in the service of the cause, taught, wrote books, published books for others, and in the process collected a large personal library. The Ames auction catalogue, *Catalogus librorum D. Guilielmi Amesii*, printed by Jansson at Amsterdam in 1634, contains 570 items.[12] It was printed the year following his death and preparative for selling his books. A library catalogue of this sort reveals the intellectual tastes of its Puritan owner, namely Reformed theology, Ramist philosophy, non-ceremonious worship, and Biblical ethics. For printing and bibliography, it shows the breadth of books available at the time and place.

Ames was in exile from England because of his Puritanism. Convinced of the power of books, from his Dutch sanctuary he produced several books much revered by Puritans; and when first arriving in 1610, he received financial support from "generous merchants" who

---

[11] Sprunger, *Doctor Ames*, pp. 68-70; Sprunger, "William Ames and the Franeker Link to English and American Puritanism", in G.Th. Jensma, F.R.H. Smit, and F. Westra, eds. *Universiteit te Franeker 1585-1811* (Leeuwarden: Fryske Akademy, 1985), pp. 265, 271; Matthias Nethenus, "Praefatio Introductoria" (on Ames), in Douglas Horton, ed., *William Ames by Matthew Nethenus, Hugo Visscher, and Karl Reuter* (Cambridge: Harvard Divinity School Library, 1965), pp. 13-14.

[12] *Catalogus*, STC 551.5 (Boston Public Library); reprinted in K.L. Sprunger, *The Auction Catalogue of the Library of William Ames*, vol. VI of *Catalogi Redivivi*, ed. R. Breugelmans (Utrecht: HES Publishers, 1988).

"sent him and Parker to Leyden to write against the English hier-archy".[13] He served the wider concerns of Puritan printing in the Netherlands by arranging for many of his Puritan friends to have books printed in Dutch print shops, the "iniquity" of the times in England not permitting "such *births* as those, a *kindly delivery*".[14] Ames was the mastermind behind the Dutch printing "births" of books by William Bradshaw, Paul Baynes, Robert Parker, and William Twisse, all appearing with prefaces by Ames or some notation like, "published by Dr. William Amis" (see Appendix III, A). Copies of several of these are listed in the library catalogue. These easily ident-ified Amesian books, however, are merely the top of the printing iceberg. Ames, certainly, was the hidden hand behind many of the most radical Puritan books anonymously printed in the Netherlands. Ambassador Sir Dudley Carleton in 1618 charged: "Mr. Amys hath his hand in many of these books."[15]

There were many suspicions that Ames collaborated with the Brewer-Brewster press at Leiden and the Thorp-Plater-Staresmore press at Amsterdam in their production of radical books, but proof was lacking. The Ames catalogue contains titles of many of these elusive books; but, in particular, clues about his involvement with the Puritan presses can be gleaned from the last section, "libri incompacta", fragments and unbound books. Where he possessed multiple copies of unbound works, or loose sheets and fragments, his role as author or editor is likely. Some of these unbound sheets were from his own writings ("diversa exemplaria" or "exemplaria 12"), leftovers from the print shop and author's honoraria. Some were by other authors. In this category, he had David Calderwood's *The Altar of Damascus*, "3 exemplaria", and single loose copies of other writings by Calder-wood.[16] Ames and Calderwood used the same printers at Leiden and Amsterdam (William Brewster, Richard Plater and the "Successors of Thorp"). The printers waited "dayly" for Ames' writings in honor of the "silenced ministers".[17] Sir Dudley's suspicions about Ames' "hand" in publishing the Calderwood books and similar books seems well founded.

---

[13] Nethenus, ed. Horton, p. 4.
[14] "Good Reader" in *The Works of Thomas Taylor*, Wing T560 (London, 1653).
[15] SP 84/92/45-46.
[16] Ames, *Catalogus*, p. 22.
[17] SP 84/127/157.

There is an old story told by Cotton Mather in the *Magnalia Christi Americana* that Mrs. Ames, after the death of the "Learned Doctor", shipped the library to Massachusetts when she immigrated in 1637. There is no documentary evidence for this. Since the book catalogue of 1634 was printed for sale purposes, the fine theological library must have been broken up and scattered. Some individual volumes bought by various persons, however, may have made the trip over to America.[18]

The Hugh Goodyear catalogue, *Catalogus librorum D. Hugonis Goodjeri*, printed at Leiden in 1662, is considerably larger than the Ames catalogue, containing over 1000 items.[19] Goodyear wrote no books of his own, but he was an avid collector. He collected many books by Puritan authors, a good number emanating from the Puritan presses of Leiden and Amsterdam. The letters and account books in the "Goodyear Papers" also record many of his book activities in buying for his personal library and helping his friends to print books in Leiden printeries. Goodyear aided Professor George Pasor of Franeker in publishing his *Manuale Graecarum vocum Novi Testamenti* at the Elseviers.[20] In 1661 Goodyear received book manuscripts on Sabbath observance by Daniel Cawdry, to be passed on to professor Johannes Hoornbeek, in hope that "a way might be open or directed unto for their publication".[21] Goodyear regularly bought books for his own use and spent generously on them. He was one of the subscribers for the great London Polyglot Bible of 1657 (6 vols.).[22] The full extent of his work in Puritan publishing can only be surmised.

The English Puritan circle, entrenched in church and university, made Leiden a capital of Puritan printing. The Leiden Puritans upheld strong Calvinist tenets against the Arminians through books by Bradshaw, Parker, Ames, and Robinson, "terrible to the Arminians".[23]

---

[18] Cotton Mather, *Magnalia Christi Americana*, ed. Thomas Robbins (1852-53 ed.; rpt. London: The Banner of Truth Trust, 1979), I, 236; Samuel Eliot Morison, *The Founding of Harvard College* (Cambridge: Harvard Univ. Press, 1935), p. 267.

[19] Copy in the Goodyear Papers, GA Leiden; reprinted in Jeremy D. Bangs, *The Auction Catalogue of the Library of Hugh Goodyear: English Reformed Minister at Leiden*, vol. II of *Catalogi Redivivi*, ed. R. Breugelmans (Utrecht: HES Publishers, 1985).

[20] Bangs, *Goodyear Auction Catalogue*, p. 16.

[21] Robert Paget to Goodyear, Feb. 3, 1661, Goodyear Papers, gg; Bangs, *Goodyear Auction Catalogue*, pp. 18-19.

[22] Bangs, *Goodyear Auction Catalogue*, pp. 16-17.

[23] Bradford, *Plymouth Plantation*, p. 21.

None of the English or Scots at Leiden dared to contradict Calvinist orthodoxy in printing or publishing, except for printers Thomas Basson and Govert Basson, who largely removed themselves from the English group and printed Arminian books. The Puritan books uniformly attacked English ceremonial worship; but on the issue of whether absolutely to separate from the Church of England, the Separatist Puritans and the non-Separatist Puritans divided, with books on both sides. Printing has an illustrious history at Leiden, highlighted by the great university printers, Willem Silvius, Christoffel Plantijn, Franciscus Raphelengius, and his grandsons Christoffel, Franciscus, and Joost Raphelengius, Jan Paets Jacobszoon, and the Elseviers. They constituted a printers and booksellers "aristocracy".[24] Puritans mostly relied upon the smaller shops and less eminent printers, or established their own print shop.

Thomas Basson

The "first English translator, publisher, and printer" at Leiden was Thomas Basson (1555-1613). J.A. van Dorsten has thoroughly presented Basson's history, so the story need not be extensively retold here, merely enough of it to fit him into the picture.[25] Born in England during the reign of Queen Mary, Basson emigrated and lived his life abroad, for reasons unknown, at one time in Cologne, then at Leiden. He first arrived at Leiden in about 1584, where he carried on a variety of book-related occupations, including printing, bookselling, bookbinding, translating, and the teaching of English.

Beginning in 1585 Basson had his own book shop and imprint. His own presses date back to about 1594, under the imprint, "Tot Leyden, By Thomas Basson teghen over de Universiteyt int Musieck-Boeck". His printer's device was a "music book". In 1595 he was admitted to the university: "Thomas Basson Anglus natus annos 40. typographus & Bibliopola."[26] Hereafter, he and his printery were very closely associated with the printing of student and professorial theses and orations.

[24] Blok, *Geschiedenis eener Hollandsche stad*, III, 211-212.

[25] J.A. van Dorsten, *Thomas Basson 1555-1613: English Printer at Leiden* (Leiden: Sir Thomas Browne Institute, 1961), p. 1; cf. J.A. van Dorsten, "Thomas Basson (1555-1613), English Printer at Leiden", *Quaerendo*, 15 (1985), 195-224.

[26] Van Dorsten, *Thomas Basson*, pp. 30-33, 76; Van Dorsten, "Thomas Basson" (1985), pp. 208-09.

He thoroughly valued having these connections to scholarship and the university. During 1586, when the Earl of Leicester was dominant, Basson stressed his English nationality, but thereafter he made much less of it.

Basson's book business had a certain English flavor throughout his career. He always stocked some English books for sale and printed a few as well. His facility in the English and Dutch languages led him into English teaching and English-Dutch translating. In a petition to Leicester in 1586, he announced his translating skills, having "understandinge in bothe the speches of Englishe & Duche". He pioneered in Dutch-English grammar by writing a book, *The Coniugations in Englishe and Netherdutche* (1586).[27] Basson's corpus of printed works was large, about 450, mostly in Dutch and Latin, and a few in English.[28] He avoided connections with the English Reformed and Separatist churches of Leiden, which were established in his later years, and he likewise ignored their doctrinal debates.

Basson's own religious views, undoubtedly, estranged him from the majority of English and Scottish settlers, who preferred Puritan religion. He showed a predilection for Arminian doctrines and lived by a liberal, tolerant spirit, which would hardly have recommended him to Robinson, Dury, or Ames. His press turned out a large quantity of Arminian treatises, a tradition carried on by his son Govert Basson. Thomas' translations from English into Dutch showed a similar taste for non-dogmatic "Anglican" works, rather than doctrinaire Puritanical works. Van Dorsten, moreover, has proposed that Basson had close associations with Hendric Niclaes' Family of Love, a mystical secret fellowship which taught love and devotion, rather than dogmatic orthodoxy.[29]

Thomas Basson's son, Govert Basson, carried on the Basson printing business after the death of his father, from 1612 to 1630. Thomas died while visiting in England about 1613. Like his father, Govert printed Arminian books, most notably in 1630 the first complete edition of the writings of Arminius. He printed at least one very significant Puritan book, Robert Parker's *De politeia ecclesiastica Christi* (1616), but such a book was the exception rather than the rule.[30] In

---

[27] *Thomas Basson*, p. 17; "Thomas Basson" (1985), pp. 202-03.
[28] "Thomas Basson" (1985), p. 195.
[29] Ibid., pp. 196-99.
[30] Theo Bögels, "Govert Basson, English Printer at Leiden", in Jeremy D. Bangs,

1630 Govert Basson closed his Leiden shop and moved to Amsterdam. At that point he printed an auction catalogue of his books, which listed a stock of many English books.[31] Thomas and Govert Basson were the only early seventeenth-century English printers anywhere in the Netherlands working from the non-Puritan side, at least until the time of Samuel Browne of The Hague and John Crosse of Amsterdam in the 1640s. The Bassons provided an alternative kind of English printing at Leiden.

The "Pilgrim Press" of Brewster and Brewer

After many years of uncoordinated English printing efforts at Leiden, the Separatists in 1617 began their own press. This "Pilgrim Press", as it has come to be known, functioned from 1617 to 1619.[32] William Brewster and Thomas Brewer of the John Robinson church ran the press. The relationship between the Separatist church and the press could hardly have been closer. Brewster was "Elder" of the church and chief printer, and Brewer was a heavy financial supporter of both church and press. Pastor John Robinson and nearly "the whole Company of Brownists" gave support.[33] The Leiden Separatists had printers among their ranks to help with the task.

The financial patron of the enterprise was Thomas Brewer, a well-to-do English gentleman, who settled at Leiden and a member of the Robinson congregation. "His partner" was William Brewster, who was in charge of the actual printing operation, although it is likely that Brewer himself developed some printing skills. One report referred to him as "Brewer the Printer".[34] Bradford's *History of Plymouth*

---

ed., *The Pilgrims in the Netherlands: Recent Research* (Leiden: Pilgrim Documents Center, 1985), pp. 18-23. Also see the forthcoming book by Theo Bögels, *Govert Basson, Printer, Bookseller, Publisher, Leiden 1612-30* (Nieuwkoop: De Graaf, 1992).

[31] Van Dorsten, *Thomas Basson*, pp. 115-20.

[32] The term "Pilgrim Press" was used by Edward Arber, *The Story of the Pilgrim Fathers, 1606-1623* (London: Ward and Downey, 1897), p. 195. The standard work on the press is Rendel Harris and Stephen K. Jones, *The Pilgrim Press, A Bibliographical & Historical Memorial of the Books Printed at Leyden by the Pilgrim Fathers* (Cambridge: W. Heffer and Sons, 1922); a new edition is available, ed. R. Breugelmans (Nieuwkoop: De Graaf Publishers, 1987).

[33] On Brewer, Brewster, and Robinson, see Greaves and Zaller, *BD*, I, 95-96, 97-98; III, 103-04; Arber, *Pilgrim Fathers*, p. 208.

[34] Arber, *Pilgrim Fathers*, pp. 203, 222, 223.

Planation described the high points of Brewster's life, including facts about his printing. The story of Brewer's life, however, was not so scrupulously recorded, perhaps because he did not take the immortal step of immigration to America. Bradford, in fact, barely mentioned him. A good number of details about Brewer, however, can be gleaned from English governmental reports and from Brewer's wills of 1617 and 1618. Notarial documents show that Brewer operated in both Amsterdam and Leiden and made money in trade, after coming to Holland. In 1617 he was "Tomas Breuwer, merchant of the English nation, living at Leiden", dealing in such products as saltpeter.[35]

Reports from ambassador Sir Dudley Carleton in 1619 described Thomas Brewer as a "man of meanes" and "a Gentleman of a good house, both of land and living", in contrast to the "inferior persons" making up the bulk of the Separatist congregation. He was a "professed Brownist".[36] Brewer had settled at Leiden by February 17, 1615, when he enrolled at the university (Thomas Braeber, Anglus). His "fantastical" Brownist religious zeal was notorious throughout Leiden, and the better sort regarded this Brownism as most regretable, because his gentlemanly stature might lead others astray.[37] Two wills drawn up by Brewer survive at Leiden, the first dated December 7, 1617, the second October 24, 1618. The earlier one speaks for Thomas Brewer and his wife, Anna Offley Brewer, with John Carver, Jonathan Brewster, and William Brewster as witnesses. All these Englishmen "understand Dutch fairly well".[38]

By the time of the second will, October 24, 1618, life for Brewer was grim. Sickness and death, apparently, had struck down Brewer's wife and two of his children in less than eleven months' time. Brewer himself was in hazardous health, being sickly but still able to walk. All that remained of his family was Mercie, a young daughter, who was to be the heiress to his considerable estate. John Carver, "his very good friend", was to serve as guardian. In the valley of the shadow, Brewer clung to his religion and designated a bequest of 200 guilders to the English Church of Leiden, to which he belonged (i.e. the Separatist

---

[35] NA 199 (Bruijningh), fols. 251v (Sept. 22, 1617), 276r (Oct. 5, 1617), GA Amsterdam. Brewer had dealings with Elias Trip.

[36] Arber, *Pilgrim Fathers*, pp. 206, 222.

[37] Ibid., p. 209; Leiden Univ. *Album*, col. 119.

[38] Brewer's wills in GA Leiden are: NA 179 (Paedts), fol. 94v, Dec. 7, 1617; NA 180 (Paedts), fols. 52-53, October 24, 1618. My thanks to Jeremy D. Bangs for help with these references and other items from the notarial archives.

church). In the event of Mercie's death or if she left no will or heirs
of her own, Brewer spelled out a detailed plan for the estate. After
providing bequests for various relatives, he gave his money to the
following worthy religious persons and causes: (1) the English Church
of Leiden, an additional bequest, (2) John Carver, an additional
bequest, (3) William Bruster (Brewster), (4) the poor of Leiden, (5)
the library here, (6) John Robbens (Robinson), (7) John Dodt (Dod),
(8) a fund for expelled, deprived English preachers, as designated by
John Carver, (9) Henry Jacob and Richard Lee, (10) Henry Aeynswart
(Ainsworth) of Amsterdam, (11) the English Church at Amsterdam
pastored by Ainsworth, and (12) a fund for distributing Puritan books
(more about this fund below).[39]

As revealed by this will and by other reports, Brewer was the
"speciall patrone" of Separatism in both Leiden and Amsterdam.[40]
Although Brewer's convictions were certainly tilted in favor of
Separatists, they were not rigidly so, with his generosity extending to
non-Separatists like John Dod and semi-Separatists like Henry Jacob.
He wanted to supply aid to needy deprived Puritan ministers, and
these would have included both Separatists and non-Separatists. These
wills, because they fill in several gaps in his biography, are some of the
best sources available on Brewer's life and activities in Leiden. However, the wills never functioned for dividing his estate, since Brewer
survived the illness, and most of the legatees, and he eventually moved
back to England.

The Brewster-Brewer venture in printing was undoubtedly inspired
by religion, although other factors entered in. The primary goal was to
produce wholesome religious books and to disseminate them to the
widest possible audience. In addition they hoped to make some
money. Their printing and book goals were set forth in writing in a
few places. Bradford's *History* has a short statement about Brewster's
printing activities. "Affter he came into Holland he suffered much
hardship after he had spent the most of his means..." Finally he found
employment in teaching English lessons. "He also had means to set up
printing by the help of some friends, and so had employment enough,
and by reason of many books which would not be allowed to be

---

[39] NA 180, fols. 52-53. There has long been a question about Brewer's church
membership. The will clearly indicates that he was a Separatist member of Robinson's
church.

[40] John Paget, *An Arrow against the Separation*, STC 19098 (Amsterdam, 1618), p. 7.

printed in England, they might have had more then they could do."[41] The Pilgrim goals, in this account, were mixed, economic to provide a livelihood, and religious to spread the Word of God.

Brewer's will of 1618 also has a clear statement about the importance of books as a Christian concern. He intended to establish a fund, under John Carver's administration, "to use for selling all the books that he can acquire, in this land or elsewhere, that have been published against the bishops and are forbidden by them".[42] Clearly, the printing partners were motivated by a solemn devotion to godly books, not books in general. Brewer always produced books "against the bishops". This kind of nonconformist printing could only be done safely and efficiently in the Netherlands. Brewster and Brewer saw themselves as grandly advancing the spread of the Gospel through publishing and printing, just as others served God by preaching and praying.

Several of the books printed by Brewster and Brewer contained timely statements about the precious ministry of printing. Although not their own writings, they chose to print books that corresponded with their convictions. Their printed books praised the invention and "benefit" of printing (in the words of Thomas Cartwright).[43] "Our bookes" reveal God's warning about the "deformities of our English reformation" (the words of Field and Wilcox).[44] Brewster and Brewer assumed that books were the chief weapons in the struggle "between the Saints and Antichrist" (the prelates of England being the agents of Antichrist). In the balance were England's printing presses, stationers, book shops, and the liberty to "invent and publish". In England the printing presses were not "open and free" to God's truth. "To us they are more then shut."[45]

The most explicit statement on Puritan printing from the Brewster-Brewer press was contained in their new edition of Thomas Whetenhall's *Discovrse of the Abuses Now in Question* (1617). The book begins with a printer's preface, "The Printer to the Christian Reader",

---

[41] Bradford, *Plymouth Plantation*, pp. 326-27.

[42] NA 180, fol. 53v.

[43] Thomas Cartwright, *A Confvtation of the Rhemists Translation*, STC 4709 (n.p., 1618), sigs. B2v, B3r.

[44] Field and Wilcox, *An Admonition to the Parliament*, STC 10849 (n.p., 1617), p. 33, "A Second Admonition".

[45] *A Trve, Modest, and Ivst Defence*, STC 6469 (n.p., 1618), "To the Christian Reader".

not by Brewster and Brewer but carried over from the original 1606 edition. In the text itself, Whetenhall in the spirit of John Foxe composed a marvelous rhapsody about "Printing the admirable gift of God":

> So now about the yeare of our Lord 1450...and a litle before the determinate Counsell of God had appoynted the light of the gospel by the preaching of *Luther* & *Zwinglius* should begin to shine againe; out of the middest of the palpable darknes wherwith the world was overwhelmed, he revealed unto men for the selfe same purpose, the admirable Art of *Printing*. By which the light of the Gospell flew abroad into all Nations, in despit of the *Emperours*, *Kings*, and all Princes and Potentats, which labored with all their might to staye the course thereof... This Divine and miraculous arte of *Printing* was given of God as an undoubted preparation to make the way for the flying of his Gospell over all Nations, though all Nations received it not. As in the Apostles time, by the gift of tongues their voyce went out into the end of the world... Yet in continuance of time doubtlesse by *Preaching* and *Printing*, the sincerity of the Gospell shall so prevaile that the great whore of Babell shall haue her fall.[46]

Although not thoroughly spelled out in their own words, it is clear from their work as a whole that Brewer and Brewster were guided by a theology of printing.

The Pilgrim printers were clandestine operators with no public book shop for selling the books. In their early period there were some exceptions; three of the books had their imprint. One of the Latin books, by William Ames, carried the offer that they were for sale at Brewster's shop in Choir Alley. Otherwise, their work was secret and anonymous. They distributed their books through underground channels and then awaited God's increase. Sir Dudley Carleton, charged with stamping out seditious English printing in the Low Countries at that time, labelled the Pilgrim secrecy as "underhand" and sneaky and their books as malicious, being "not for the use of the University of Leyden or these Provinces; but for His Majesty's disservice, and the trouble of his Kingdoms".[47] Because Brewer believed so strongly in the cause, he poured unstinted money into printing, until he "hath mortgaged and consumed a great part of his estate". By

---

[46] Thomas Whetenhall, *A Discovrse of the Abvses Now in Question*, STC 25332 (n.p., 1606), printed by William Jones?, pp. 64-65; STC 25333 (n.p., 1617), pp. 74-76.

[47] Arber, *Pilgrim Fathers*, pp. 201, 212, 217.

prudent standards such behavior was inexplicable. It was as if he had
lost his senses, betraying his class and nation. King James "doth so
much resent those Puritan pamphlets". Brewer was a "subject delinquent" and a "silly creature".[48]

Many details of the Brewster-Brewer press have been thoroughly
reported in the books by Harris, Jones, and Plooij, and they need not
all be repeated here. Some background, however, is needed to fill in
our picture. The press was located in the midst of the Pilgrim neighborhood of Leiden. Both Brewster and Brewer lived close to St.
Peter's Church. In the few books where Brewster gave a location for
his shop, he was in Vico Chorali (Choir Alley), which Harris and
Jones have identified as the garret of a house abutting on both Pieters-
kerkkoorsteeg and Stinksteeg. Brewer lived nearby in the Kloksteeg (a
little later he was recorded in the Nieuwsteeg).[49] There are many
unanswered questions about the equipment and supplies which they
used. Brewster and Brewer had type and ornaments and certainly did
their own letter setting. Little was ever said about having their own
press—only "printing type and papers"—even when they were examined by the magistrates; but many historians do assume that they did
have a press.

Altogether, the two printers turned out about nineteen books (see
Appendix II, A) in 1617, 1618, and 1619.[50] One of the questionable
books is Francis Johnson's *Christian Plea* (STC 14661), which is weak
on typographical grounds. This author believes it should be retained in
the Brewster-Brewer corpus based on a statement from John Paget. In
1617 he reported that one part of this book was "so imperfectly
published by Mr. B."[51] All were Puritanical books "against the
bishops" and against Arminians and Catholics. The press began by
printing some scholarly, rather noncontroversial books by William
Ames, Thomas Cartwright, and John Dod and Robert Cleaver, and
these carried a full title page with the name of author, printer, and
place: "Lugdvni Batavorvm, Apud Guiljelmum Brewsterum, In Vico
Chorali" or "Giliaem Brewster, Boeck-drucker". The rest of the
Brewster-Brewer books came out anonymously without any hint of

---

[48] Ibid., pp. 201, 222; SP 84/94/1, 84/94/49.
[49] Harris and Jones (ed. Breugelmans), chap. 1; Brewer in his will of Oct. 24, 1618
reported his house as being in the Nieuwsteeg.
[50] For a bibliographical analysis of the books by Brewster and Brewer, see Harris
and Jones (ed. Breugelmans).
[51] Paget, *Arrow*, p. 13.

the printer or place. The early imprinted books were intended as a screen of respectability for the little printing shop. However, by sending out samples of their printing style which could be identified with them, they left typographical tracks which allowed experts to trace the rest of the books back to them.

The Brewster and Brewer strategy of printing and publishing can be surmised by looking over their printing list. They reprinted Puritan classics from years past (eight of the books) as well as printing first-time books. They aided authors in exile in the Netherlands as well as Puritan authors unable to find printers at home in England or Scotland. In short, their enterprise was broadly conceived as a mission of books for Puritans of many shades of opinion, so long as they were against the bishops.

The reprinted books highlighted several Puritan authors of great reputation, such as William Ames, *Ad responsum Nic. Grevinchovii rescriptio contracta* (1617); *An Abridgement of That Booke* by the Lincoln-shire ministers (1617); Thomas Whetenhall, *Discovrse of the Abuses* (1617); John Field and Thomas Wilcox, *Admonition to the Parliament* (1617); Walter Travers, *A Fvll and Plaine Declaration* (1617); Robert Harrison, *A Little Treatise* (1618); and Laurence Chaderton *A Fruitfvll Sermon* (1618). These "out of print" books were considered whole-some and beneficial to Puritan Christians, but not the kind that could be printed in England those days. Of this group, Harrison was a dedicated Separatist, but several of the others were clearly "presby-terian" in belief (namely Travers, Chaderton, Field, and Wilcox). One reprint was in a class by itself, a Dutch translation of the John Dod and Robert Cleaver exposition of the Ten Commandments, *Een klare ende duydelijcke uytlegginghe over de thien gheboden*, 1617, (this was another issue, with changed imprint, of the edition by Hendrik Laurensz of Amsterdam). These translated and reprinted books had some potential for making a profit, which was one of Brewster's requirements for going into printing.

The remainder of the books were first editions and fall into two further groups. First, some were orthodox Puritanical books by signifi-cant authors published for the first time at Leiden. Of this type were two books by Thomas Cartwright, *Commentarii in Proverbia Salomonis* (1617) and *A Confvtation of the Rhemists Translation on the New Testa-ment* (1618), the latter an answer to the Catholic New Testament issued at Rheims. A similar type of book was *De vera religione* (1618) by anonymous English ministers. The new books of 1618-19 became ever more strident: two books by Thomas Dighton, *Certain Reasons against Kneeling* (1618) and a *Second Part* against kneeling (1619) and two fiery books by David Calderwood, *De regimine ecclesiae Scoticanae* (1618) and *Perth Assembly* (1619).

The next grouping of first edition books was a new supply of treatises in defense of Separatism. Earlier, Johnson's *Christian Plea* (1617) and Harrison's *Little Treatise* (1618) were produced, now Robinson's *The Peoples Plea* (1618) and William Eurings' *Answer to the Ten Covnter Demands* (1619). Taken as a whole, the Brewster-Brewer books were filled with the stories of evil bishops, idolatrous abuses in worship, and calls for a new reformation in England. The longer the press functioned, the more it retreated to its Brownist origins.

In view of the close connections between the Separatist churches of Leiden and Amsterdam, was there also a connection between the two printing houses? Brewer went back and forth between the two cities frequently. No evidence exists that the Separatist press of Giles Thorp and the Pilgrim press of Brewster and Brewer coordinated their activities; nevertheless, they did complement each other very well. During the period that the Pilgrim Press was functioning, 1617-19, the Thorp press was almost completely committed to an enormous project of printing Ainsworth's Bible commentaries; there was hardly time for anything else. In the meanwhile, the Leiden press produced many smaller works needful for the moment, and thus they kept the flow of Puritan books coming.

The printing of books, whether reprints or new books, exposed Brewster and Brewer to great risks. Reprinting the old books was as risky as publishing the new. When Wilcox and Field had first published their book in 1572, they landed in jail because such books were "too hote for this time".[52] In the judgment of king and bishops, who read them in 1617-19, such books were still "too hot". Throughout 1619 Ambassador Carleton spent much of his time tracing down the criminous printers and prosecuting them. The most offensive books were the Scottish ones, Calderwood's *Perth Assembly* and *De regimine ecclesiae Scoticanae*; and the rest of the printed works, being "Puritan books", were also not appreciated.

Sir Dudley Carleton first came into possession of the Calderwood books in January of 1619, and he was extremely annoyed about their

---

[52] Wilcox and Field, *Admonition* (1617), p. 35.

spirit of "scorn and reproach".[53] At first the English authorities thought these books might be the work of established printers. They wasted several weeks in searching at Edinburgh (James Cathkin) and at Middelburg (Richard Schilders) but nothing could be proved. Schilders gave a deposition and "solemn oath" that he was not the printer and did not know who the printer was. Up to this point, Carleton had never heard of the press of Brewster and Brewer.[54] Finally, in July of 1619 he picked up the trail to Leiden and roused up the entire town. By this time, Brewster and Brewer had nearly ceased all printing activities and hid from view. Nevertheless, Carleton intended to make public examples of them and insisted on full punishment for illegal printing (the anonymous title pages and subversive content). Brewster managed to slip out of town, lurking here and there. Brewer, a student of the university, took refuge in the academic community. From the summer of 1619 onward, the press was permanently silenced. Brewster went underground and did not surface again until he was safely overseas in Plymouth Plantation. William Ames, an author of books, also suffered from guilt by association. He lost a tempting professorship at the university, which had been nearly promised to him. Brewer dragged out the proceedings against himself a very long time, until he was finally allowed to withdraw from the scene.[55] Thus ended an important chapter in the history of English printing in the Netherlands.

Brewer returned to the Netherlands, after a trip to London, and lived unobtrusively for several years. Although he did not revive the press at Leiden, it seems to have had a small resurrection. The type and ornaments still served, although in other hands. The Puritan printers of Amsterdam in the 1620s, as A.F. Johnson has stated, used a supply of the Brewster-Brewer type and ornaments mixed in with their old type.[56] Brewer moved to Amsterdam, perhaps carrying the printing type with him.

At least two reports tell about Brewer at Amsterdam in the 1620s, still involved with books. One report calls him "Mr. Brewer of Amsterdam". Another report (1626) stated that Brewer "hath writ a

---

[53] Carleton, *Letters*, pp. 335, 351, 379; Arber, *Pilgrim Fathers*, p. 198.

[54] Deposition of Ric. Schilders, Mar. 26/April 5, 1619 (SP 84/89/84); Carleton, *Letters*, p. 351, 379.

[55] D. Plooij, *The Pilgrim Fathers from a Dutch Point of View* (New York: New York Univ. Press, 1932), chap. 3.

[56] Johnson (1951), pp. 230-31.

book" about prophecy—but seemingly never printed—in which he predicted the swift coming destruction of England within three years. If not publishing his own material, he was publishing for others. "The said Brewer coming, not long since, from Amsterdam...hath printed a most pestilent book beyond the seas: wherein he affirmeth, that King James would be the ruin of Religion. To the like purpose, he published a book or two more..."[57] These books produced by Brewer at Amsterdam (about 1625) cannot be definitely identified; however, quite a few books from the Amsterdam presses of the time fit the description of apocalyptic zeal and criticism of the episcopal religious policies of King James. Very likely the books referred to in the 1626 report included *Humble Petition to the Kings Most Excellent Majestie* (i.e. King James), STC 14425 (n.p., ca. 1625) and *Certaine Advertisements for the Good of the Chvrch and Commonwealth*, STC 10404 (n.p., ca. 1625). When Brewer returned to England in 1626—the house in Leiden was sold in 1630—the magistrates committed him to prison where he dropped from sight until released by Parliament in 1640. He died a month later. Such were the "persecutions endured under the Prelates".[58]

The smashing of the Pilgrim Press coincided with some wider events in England and the Netherlands, among them the repression of Dutch Arminians after the Synod of Dort and an anti-Puritan campaign directed by King James. The governments of England and the Netherlands, each for its own purposes, agreed that stricter press laws were needed at this time to control Arminians and Puritans. The States of Holland renewed the edict against seditious printing (Plakkaat of June 19, 1618), which Ambassador Carleton judged to be an excellent step in the right direction although primarily directed against Oldenbarnevelt and the Arminians.[59]

Next, as an aftermath to the Puritan printing commotions at Leiden, the States General published a new law against scandalous and seditious printing (Plakkaat of January 16, 1621), revising the 1615 plakkaat. England gave strong backing to the new law because it spoke more directly than ever before to the concern about English underground printing by prohibiting subversive books in English and Scottish. This 1621 law served as the basic plakkaat on printing for the next several decades. Sir Dudley Carleton proudly took credit for

---

[57] HMC, Salisbury XXII, 156-57 (ca. 1621); Arber, *Pilgrim Fathers*, p. 246 (1626).

[58] Arber, *Pilgrim Fathers*, p. 247; Burgess, *John Robinson*, p. 158.

[59] SP 84/84/July 1, 1618; Nikolaas Wiltens, *Kerkelyk plakaatboek* (The Hague, 1722), pp. 417-20.

moving the measure through the Dutch political channels. The Dutch obliged King James and him, Carleton claimed, "onely in his majesty's contemplation and at my pursuite, having caryed the same through divers colleages, as the States General, the States of Holland, and the high counsells...".[60] Sir Dudley glowed in the warmth of a job well done. In its own way, the little Pilgrim press at Leiden had helped to move Dutch history through its zealous books—although certainly not in the direction which Brewer and Brewster intended.

While Brewster and Brewer were the most famous printer-publishers at Leiden, theirs was not an isolated effort. One can name several other English printers, who for one reason or another worked at Leiden: (1) John Reynolds, printer from London; betrothed at Leiden July 28, 1617; moved to Amsterdam in 1619.[61] (2) Edward Winslow, printer, married at Leiden April 27, 1618; emigrated to Plymouth on the *Mayflower*.[62] (3) Sabine Staresmore, Separatist, lived at Leiden during the Robinson period and moved to Amsterdam about 1622; an active printer at Amsterdam.[63] Did he also print at Leiden? (4) Edward Raban, English printer, originally a soldier, worked at Leiden for several years prior to 1620; emigrated to Scotland in 1620.[64] (5) William Wilkinson, printer from Amsterdam, Anglus; at Leiden in 1627, 28 years old.[65] (6) Henricus Randulphus, Anglus; at Leiden in 1627, 26 years old.[66] (7) Matthew Simmons, English printer; worked with Willem Christiaensz in 1637-38.[67] (8) Benjamin Allen, English printer, worked with Christiaensz in 1638.[68] (9) Mr. Wheelers, printer working with Christiaensz in 1638.[69] (10)

---

[60] SP 84/99/51-53; 84/99/20-21.

[61] Harris and Jones (ed. Breugelmans), pp. 20-21; D. Plooij and J. Rendel Harris, *Leyden Documents Relating to the Pilgrim Fathers* (Leyden: E.J. Brill, 1920), fol. xxxii.

[62] Plooij and Harris, *Leyden Documents*, fol. xxxv.

[63] See above, chap. 4; Stephen Foster, *Notes from the Caroline Underground* (Hamden: Archon Books, 1978), p. 87.

[64] Gordon E. Duff, "The Early Career of Edward Raban, Afterwards First Printer at Aberdeen", *The Library*, ser. 4, 2 (1921-22), pp. 239-56.

[65] ERC Amsterdam, CR, II, 27 (member of Amsterdam ERC, Dec. 14, 1622); Leiden Univ. *Album*, col. 198, Feb. 12, 1627.

[66] Leiden Univ. *Album*, col. 198.

[67] SP 16/387/79; Plomer (1641-67), pp. 164.

[68] SP 84/153/187; Plomer (1641-67), pp. 1-2.

[69] Mr. Wheelers is mentioned in SP 84/153/187; but only as "Wheelers". A "Jacob Wheeler" was in Leiden at the time; see Leiden Univ. Volumen Inscriptionum, IX, 190 (Dec. 11, 1637), where he was landlord to a Scottish student.

Robert Wood, printer, working for Christiaensz in 1640.[70] (11) Michael Sparke, London printer who visited Leiden, most likely in the 1620s-1630s ("I remember when I was in *Leyden*").[71] Several of these Leiden printers later had printing careers in London (Simmons, Allen, Wood) or Aberdeen (Raban).

Some of the above persons, no doubt, assisted Brewster and Brewer in printing; the most likely Separatist collaborators were the first four on the list, Reynolds, Winslow, Staresmore, and Raban. Winslow and Staresmore were avowed Separatists. Although Raban might have been an assistant to Brewster, he also worked for a Dutch printer. Raban later recalled how his Dutch printing master died a horrible, fiery death, while boiling varnish on a Sabbath day. This unforgettable event converted Raban into a strict Sabbath keeper. After moving to Edinburgh in 1620 (Aberdeen, by 1622) he used ornaments and initials remarkably similar to Brewster's, including the famous "Brewster bear".[72] Raban either secured some of Brewster's type when the press was broken up, or, more likely, bought them from the same typefounder. Some of the English printers appear in a list of printers in 1627 (Wilkinson and Randulphus); they were a part of a group of eight who were enrolled at the university, February 12, 1627, at the expense of the city. Another member of the 1627 group was Willem Christiaensz, Middelburgensis, 44 years old.[73] Christiaensz was soon to play a very large part in Puritan printing at Leiden.

Willem Christiaensz van der Boxe

The 1620s was a low point in Puritanical activity at Leiden. The Puritan community experienced several blows: The ruin of the Brewer-Brewster press, Dr. Ames' failure to receive a professorship at Leiden University, the removal of a good number of the Pilgrims to New England in 1620, the death of pastor Robinson in 1625, and the splitting of the Separatist church into factions.

---

[70] RA 79, vol. V, fol. 389 (pencil 238), GA Leiden; Plomer (1641-67), p. 197.

[71] Michael Sparke, *A Second Beacon Fired by Scintilla*, Wing S2259 (London, 1652), p. 10; he reported that he saw the English church "Excommunicate all in that Meeting house to the last single man", which sounds like the Separatist situation in about 1630. See also Plomer (1641-67), p. 169.

[72] Duff, "Raban", pp. 243-48; Harris and Jones (ed. Breugelmans), pp. 58-61, 64.

[73] Volumen Inscriptionum, VIII, 232.

The result was shrinking and eventual death of the Separatist church. Only pastor Hugh Goodyear kept up a vigorous English-Scottish presence.[74] Finally, a ministry of English printing revived at Leiden under the leadership of Willem Christiaensz. There are many variations of the name, including W. Christiaens, W. Christianus, Guillielmus Christianus, Guillaume Chrestien, Ex Officina Wilhelmi Christiani, and in English publications, William Christian or Christienne.[75] In the 1640s he added the surname Van der Boxe to some of his imprints; thereafter he was Willem Christiaensz van der Boxe. The seventeenth century was a period of transition in Dutch nomenclature, as people moved away from simple patronymics, like Christiaensz or Christiaenszoon, to family names. In a similar move, printer Willem Jansz of Amsterdam adopted the surname of Blaeu to become Willem Jansz Blaeu.[76]

The story of Christiaensz' life is known in brief. He was born at Middelburg about 1583. He moved to Leiden around 1612 and established himself in some printing businesses, working in various shops as a letter setter or compositor. He became a citizen of the city in 1624.[77] In a preface written in 1631, he expressed gratitude to Thomas Erpenius (d. 1624), his past printing master, "whom he served for 12 years". Because Erpenius died in 1624, this places Christiaensz at Leiden as early as 1612.[78] The association with Erpenius was important to Christiaensz. Erpenius, in addition to printing and bookselling, was professor of oriental languages at the University of Leiden, having won out over Jan Theunisz for the position. Being with Erpenius opened doors for Christiaensz into the scholarly university circle. In 1627, in fact, he gained an entrance at the university as one of a group of eight printers inscribed in the student book at expense of the city.[79] By 1631 Christiaensz had his own print shop, and he

---

[74] For the later history of the Pilgrim church and the English Reformed church, see Sprunger, *Dutch Puritanism*, pp. 139-41.

[75] Briels, *ZB*, pp. 184-85; A.F. Johnson, (1955), pp. 121-23. J. Henselmans has done the most extensive work on Christiaensz, "Willem Christiaens: A Leyden Printer with an English Connection" (M.A. Scriptie, Leiden Univ., 1983).

[76] J. Keuning, *Willem Jansz. Blaeu* (Amsterdam: Theatrum Orbis Terrarum Ltd, 1973), pp. 10-11.

[77] Briels, *ZB*, p. 185.

[78] Preface to Erpenius, *De peregrinatione Gallica* (1631); *BWPG* II, 767-76; Henselmans, "Christiaensz", pp. 2-3.

[79] Volumen Inscriptionum, VIII, 232. On connections between printers and scholars, see Th.H. Lunsingh Scheurleer and G.H.M. Posthumus Meyjes, eds., *Leiden*

printed under his own imprint for the period of 1631 to 1658, the year of his death. All of his life, he aspired to be a "learned printer" of fine quality work and he, no doubt, prided himself on his ability to handle many languages. Nevertheless, alongside his fine printing, he did a great amount of polemical, cheap printing (the English, Puritan side of his career).

The Christiaensz printing shop was located "op't Rapenburgh" and "by de Universiteyt In den Gesonden Broeder".[80] This is at 35 Rapenburg (by today's numbering).[81] His various imprints also record some other locations, but all in the neighborhood of the university. His most common printer's symbol was a lively-looking ostrich and the motto "Nil penna sed usus".[82] However, these addresses and symbols were never used in his English printing.

From his Erpenius days onward, Christiaensz cultivated patronage and connections with the university professors; these included Petrus Scriverius and Marcus Zuerius Boxhorn. They provided manuscripts for printing and at times money for loans. Christiaensz's printing enterprise expanded in 1632 by a rental arrangement for 2000 pounds of type (parangon, text, augustijn, brevier and so on) from Arent Corsz van Hogenacker, typefounder of Leiden.[83] In this deal, or elsewhere about this time, he acquired a supply of Hebrew and Arabic type. In 1633 he asked professor Constantijn l'Empereur for scholarly printing work that would allow him to use his newly acquired Hebrew and Arabic types.[84] With such equipment and connections, Christiaensz advanced into the ranks of the established and senior printers of the city. He printed a steady stream of university-related scholarly publications in several languages, producing a corpus of printing that runs to several hundred items.[85] A glimpse of his print-

---

University in the Seventeenth Century: An Exchange of Learning (Leiden: E.J. Brill, 1975), especially the chapter by E. van Gulik, "Drukkers en Geleerden", pp. 367-93.

[80] Briels, ZB, pp. 184-85.

[81] Th.H. Lunsingh Scheurleer, et al., Het Rapenburg: Geschiedenis van een Leidse gracht, 5 dln. (Leiden, 1986-90), III, 444, 460, 504.

[82] Briels, ZB, p. 185.

[83] NA 366 (Oosterlingh), act 62, Aug. 3, 1632; the deal was renewed in NA 265 (Van Leeuwen) act. 69, fols. 67-72, September 17, 1636; Harry Carter, "Archbishop Laud and Scandalous Books from Holland", in Studia Bibliographica in Honorem Herman de la Fontaine Verwey (Amsterdam, 1966), p. 54.

[84] Peter T. van Rooden, Theology, Biblical Scholarship and Rabbinical Studies in the Seventeenth Century: Constantijn l'Empereur (Leiden: E.J. Brill, 1989), p. 155.

[85] See Henselmans, "Christiaensz".

ing activities appeared in a contract with an apprentice boy in 1635. Here he promised to teach the apprentice printing in "Dutch, Latin, also in Greek, in quarto, octavo, and duodecimo". Work in the shop would be from 6:00 a.m. to 8:00 p.m.[86]

The less visible side of his career was the English and Puritan part. (See Appendix II, B). Christiaensz knew the English language well, and he did many translations from English into Dutch. His press in the 1630s and 1640s was one of the two or three leading sources of English books in the Netherlands, along with John Canne and J.F. Stam. Many of these Christiaensz products had a fiery, religious flavor, and he personally sympathized with this cause. As a translator from English into Dutch, he produced translations of books by such authors as Thomas Adams, John Andrewes, Barnaby Rich, Arthur Dent, Henry Smith, Anthony Maxey, and William Prynne—books dear to the Puritan soul. Some he both translated and printed.[87]

Isaac Burchoorn, printer and bookseller, highly praised in poetry the translating skills of Christiaensz, especially of such works as Adams' *Den witten duyvel* and Andrewes' *Gouden Trompet*. Who brings these books into the Dutch mother tongue?

> ...'Tis William Christiaens.
> 'Tis the very same man, who found many English books,
> Lying here and there, in some dusty corners and hooks,
> And brought them to the light of day...
> He translated many books for us (such as Adams and Andrewes)
> ....
> Through his pen he set these before our eyes.[88]

Burchoorn's tribute to Christiaensz occurred in a Christiaensz book on the topic of women. In 1641 he took an English work by Joseph Swetnam about the "araignment of lewde, idle, froward, and unconstant women" and put it into Dutch, *Recht-Banck tegen de vrouwen* (3 parts).[89] This harsh, English attack upon women took Christiaensz' fancy, and to it he added a bit of his own Dutch wisdom, "Klinck-

---

[86] NA 468 (26 June, 1635).

[87] Cornelis W. Schoneveld, *Intertraffic of the Mind: Studies in Seventeenth-Century Anglo-Dutch Translation* (Leiden: Sir Thomas Browne Institute, 1983), pp. 246, 251.

[88] I. Burchoorn, in Joseph Swetnam, *Recht-banck* (Leiden: Willem Christiaensz, 1641), "Dagh-vaerdingh", sig. (aa 4).

[89] Joseph Swetnam, *The Araignment*, STC 23533. Christiaensz' translation of the Swetnam book appeared in 3 parts over a period of years.

Dicht, op de Vrouwen" by W.V.B.C.[90] Unless men asserted themselves quickly, the woman would soon be "Master of the House".[91]
Part III of *Recht-Banck* had a lauditory poem by M. Mat., which
extolled his translating skills and his courage in tackling such a prickly
topic. "Tell me, Willem Christiaens, how do you dare to stir up the
women—whose chief talent is scolding and complaining—by putting
out this Dutch-English book?" Can you hear their complaining and
abuse? Oh "Printer! Brave translator of so much English letters!"[92]
Christiaensz possessed a translating bravado in choosing topics, whether
chastising kings, archbishops, or wives—he would tell the world![93]

Where did Christiaensz gain his proficiency in English? Where did
he absorb the strict precisionist religion so compatible with the Puritan
militants? Living at Middelburg and Leiden meant he had ample
opportunities for associations with exiled English Puritans. Both cities
had English-Scottish churches with strong nonconformist leadership.
Perhaps, he might have lived for a few years in England. As a young
man he married Anna Perkins, who by name certainly was an English
woman; she died in 1624.[94] This connection to a Perkins family does
not lead very far, since a search of the records of the English church
at Middelburg and the incomplete records of the English Church at
Leiden do not reveal any information about Christiaensz or Perkins.
The papers of Hugh Goodyear, which are informative on many
aspects of Puritan affairs in Holland, also are silent about Christiaensz.
The student album for the university reveals that he took in several
English and Scottish students for lodging. Although he had an affec-
tion for England and its Puritan religion, there is a missing link in his
biography, the English link, that might fully explain it.

Somehow or other, the Puritan spirit moved Christiaensz; and
along with his Dutch printing, he became a printer for Puritan authors
of the 1630s. His print shop was a haven for refugee English printers,
and their many hands sped the work along. In 1637-38 he took in
Benjamin Allen, "lately fled out of England", as printer and lodger;
also working for him were Matthew Simmons, "lately come out of

---

[90] Joseph Swetnam, *Beeren-Iacht*, pt. III of *Recht-Banck* (Amsterdam, 1670), back of
title page, "Klinck-Dicht, op de Vrouwen".

[91] Burchoorn, "Dagh-vaerdingh".

[92] "Aen Willem Christiaens" by M. Mat., in *Recht-Banck*, pt. III (Amsterdam,
1670), sig A2v.

[93] His phrase was "to all nations", SP 16/387/79.

[94] Briels, *ZB*, p. 184.

England", and another man called "Wheelers".[95] Allen and Simmons were to become, on their return to England, very active printers of Puritan books. In 1640 his printing assistants included Robert Wood, Jan de Vechter, and Thomas Thymen.[96]

Nearly all of Christiaensz' Puritan printing of the period (1637-40) was anonymously issued and in the simplest, cheapest style, no fancy ornaments or fine craftsmanship. All the same, several were traced back to him. To get more information about Christiaensz, Ambassador Boswell in 1637 requested that the magistrates interrogate Matthew Simmons and compel him to reveal what he knew about Puritan printing. Simmons reported:

> William Christian [is] a master printer, and he was a translating the Newes from Ipswich into Duch [Kn. 4473]... Also the saide William was then in hand with a boocke called an Abridgement [STC 15648]... Another booke to goe to prese concerning the proceedinges of the last parlament in Scotland [STC 22013]... The saide William printeth much English.[97]

Also, reported Simmons, Christiaensz "printed Liles rules and cut the tree and hath bargained for to print the grammer" (this to be for Mr. Henry Tuthill in Rotterdam).[98] The polemical Puritan tracts would hardly have been very profitable, unless well subsidized, but the English grammars and English-language Bibles, which he sometimes printed, probably were good business ventures.

At certain times, Christiaensz showed that he was as much the true religious believer as the printing entrepreneur. Translating and printing William Prynne's *Nieuws uyt Ipswich* was his own project "at his own charge" with notes out "of his owne head", and he promised to put the book also into French. When asked "the reason why", Christiaensz harshly exclaimed: "He would make the Bishops crueltie knowne to all nationes."[99] English versions of Prynne's *News from Ipswich* were also circulating in Leiden in 1637, and there is a strong likelihood Christiaensz had his hand in the English editions as well as the Dutch and French ones. The intended French version seems to

---

[95] SP 84/153/187-90.

[96] RA 79, vol. V, fol. 389.

[97] SP 16/387/79. The interrogation took place either late 1637 or early 1638. The report was received in England April 14, 1638.

[98] Ibid.

[99] Ibid.

have vanished or, more likely, never saw the light of day. At Leiden
a furious, ranting "Mr. Daniel", an exile from Norwich but otherwise
not identified, had copies of the *Ipswich* book; he "had made a book,
which he saith, would make his Lordship and others scratche their
heads (these were his words) where it did not itche". He threatened
bloody vengeance against bishops Laud and Wren.[100] Leiden
abounded with Puritan fire and brimstone in those days.

In Puritan eyes the Christiaensz shop was a sanctified place for
God's service. On the contrary, Ambassador Boswell despised
Christiaensz as a dangerous menace to peace and good order, "a mean
fellow". He was a criminal, "coulpable and violatear" of laws.[101]
Armed with information from Matthew Simmons, Boswell in 1637
began action against Christiaensz on grounds that he had violated the
press laws of 1615 and 1621, disturbed the public tranquillity, and
defamed a friend of the Dutch state, namely the King of England and
Scotland. The ambassador sent a strong message to the magistrates of
Leiden, charging Christiaensz with "scandalous books" (December 17,
1637 and February 12, 1638). Secretary John Bouillon carried
Boswell's instructions to Leiden.[102]

In his instructions to Bouillon, Boswell laid out this plan of action:

> 1 First to go to the Schout "to presse him without any delay to search
> William Christian's house and sease upon all such other copies as
> remained with him of the scandalouse books against the state and
> church of England," especially the *Abridgement*.
> 2 To request the magistrates that Benjamin Allan, alias Allen or Allian,
> printer with Christians, "be apprehended and kept in safe custody untill
> further information against him". Matthew Simmons also "to be exam-
> ined".
> 3 To request of the Schout copies of the interrogation and answers of
> Christians, Wheelers, and Simmons.
> 4 The reward due to Bouillon as informant (fl. 100, which was 1/3 of
> the expected fine) to be donated to the poor people of Leiden.
> 5 "To press the Schout for arbitrary correction of the said William
> Christians."
> 6 Christians to be examined upon oath "concerning his printing, or
> furthering the printing and distributing of all former scandalouse

---

[100] SP 84/152/219, 221; on the thesis that *Newes from Ipswich* was printed in
Holland, see Foster, *Notes*, p. 74.
[101] SP 84/154/113; 84/153/189.
[102] The charges and documents on Christiaensz are in SP 84/153/183-87, 190.

bookes". Who are the authors, translators, printers, and suppliers of the money?

7 Finally, to entreat the Burgomasters and officials "to be very vigilant and severe for preventing the like herafter, it being otherwise impossible to prevent many unkind constructions and proceedings in England".[103]

The process of Leiden justice began its course, somewhat as Boswell had designed; after all, the royal wrath of England could not be forever flouted. Boswell reported "very good civility and respect" from the magistrates "promising mee Justice".[104] In April of 1638 the magistrates summoned Christiaensz to court and punished him for breach of the printing laws of 1615 and 1621. When the schout went to Christiaensz' shop to deliver the court summons, the printer responded meekly: "Tis well, I shall appear."[105]

The trial and sentencing took place April 13, 1638. "William Christiaensz, book printer, laying truely to his charge that he hath not only of late presumed and undertooke to print certain deffamatory and scandalouse books or pamphlets tending to the great prejudice and diminuation of the honor and government of his Royal Majesty of Great Brittaine." The criminous books in this court case were: *Wat Nieuws uyt Ipswich* (Kn. 4473), *The Answer of John Bastwick to the Information of Sir John Bancks* (STC 1568), part of *A Dispvte against the English Popish Ceremonies* (STC 11896, said to be done in collaboration with John Canne), and the translating from English into Dutch of *Newes from Ipswich* (i.e. *Wat Nieuws*) with his own marginal notes. The sentence continued: "Moreover that he among all of his said printed copies hath not set downe the name of the Author or Translator or the name of his residence, contrary to edict of the Estates General, January 16, 1621..., by the cited person's own confession. And these things touch his Royal Majesty of Great Britain, a potentate and ally of these lands. And that it touched as well the political and ecclesiatical matters, to the perturbation of his Majesty's peaceable government."[106]

The court declared that the printed copies of the illegal books must be forfeited and seized. In addition, the court condemned Christiaensz to a fine of 300 guilders, one-third going to informer Bouillon, as

---

[103] Ibid., fols 187, 189.

[104] SP 84/154/113.

[105] RA 4, Correctieboek, vol. L, fol. 146v (April 8, 1638).

[106] Ibid. fols. 145-46; cf. SP 84/154/150-51, 157.

demanded by Boswell.[107] The ambassador warmly savored these punitive actions against Christiaensz. His success against Puritan printing was "more then I can learne hath ever been done before", and from Leiden he went onward to Amsterdam to catch John Canne (achieved July 3, 1638).[108]

All of this chastisement, no doubt, caused Christiaensz a bit of inconvenience and embarrassment, but a few brushes with the law were a common part of doing seventeenth-century printing business. Christiaensz had been in court before, and he would have to appear there again in the future years on a variety of offenses.[109] His English and Puritan printing did not cease, in spite of condemnation in court, although he was thereafter more wary about it. In 1639 he produced more by Prynne, a Dutch translation in abridged form of *Histrio-Mastix*. The translation was by someone using the initials I.H., but the preface was by Christiaensz, telling about the latest outrageous cruelties against Prynne.[110]

Christiaensz' work must be seen in the wider Puritan book context. By undertaking such books, he became a link in the British-Netherlands Puritan printing and publishing network, along with Canne, Moxon, Stam, and various English and Scottish merchant financial backers. On certain projects, he collaborated with Canne of Amsterdam; one example was Gillespie's *Dispvte* (1637). At another time, Christiaensz was in league with James Moxon of Delft, later of Rotterdam, to bring out "Doctor Bastwicke thinges" (the *Answer* and *Leteny* in five parts, 1000 copies of each, also the *Flagellum pontificis*).[111] Christiaensz knew many Amsterdam merchants who had printing needs. Some of his best customers were Thomas Crafford and Thomas Stafford. He also accepted work from Mr. Hage (Wilham Haeke), "the fugitive Schotsman", a lawyer, who paid for *The Abridge-*

---

[107] SP 84/154/150-51.

[108] SP 84/154/113-14; on the campaign against Canne, see chap. 4.

[109] RA 45, Vonnisboek, vol. HH, fol. 152 (1629), for payment of debts; vol. PP, fol. 265v (1639), about payment for some tobacco.

[110] Prynne, *Histrio-Mastix* (Leiden: Ghedruckt by Willem Christiaens, 1639). J. Wille, *Literair-historische opstellen* (Zwolle: W.E.J. Tjeenk Willink, 1963), pp. 182-95. Two later works by Prynne in Dutch translation also appear to be Christiaensz' printing work; *De oodtmoedighe requesten van Willem Prynne, Burton, Bastwick, Wickins*, Kn. 4726 (n.p., 1641) and *Brief van Mr. Willem Prynne*, Kn. 6263 (n.p., 1649).

[111] SP 16/387/79, which reports that Moxon worked on five parts of Bastwick; however Christiaensz' own court conviction ties him to the *Answer* (STC 1568); Carter, "Laud," p. 52.

ment and other anti-prelatical books. Haeke was a sturdy champion of "Scottish libertie".[112]

The printing at Leiden, according to Johannes le Maire, the "Spie" of Amsterdam, was merely an extension of the Puritan printing in other cities, all one great conspiracy.[113] When the printing was temporarily thwarted at one place, the Puritan book printing shifted to another city. Christiaensz was willing to print the strongest which the Puritan authors could produce. Anything written by Bastwick or Prynne immediately caused great alarm among the authorities of England. The Star Chamber in 1637 condemned John Bastwick, Henry Burton, and William Prynne for illegal books and chopped off their ears. The Netherlands book Puritans counter-attacked by swiftly publishing several versions of a propaganda pamphlet about the trial, *A Brief Relation of Certain Speciall and Most Material Passages, in the Starre-Chamber, at the Censure of Dr. Bastwicke, Mr. Burton and Mr. Prynne.* Christiaensz printed one of these versions in 1638. This anti-Laudian blast was not enough. More blood-and-gore propaganda was required, and Christiaensz followed up with printing a Dutch version, and very likely was also doing the translating. This was *Een cort ende bondich verhael* (1638, Kn. 4559), once again proclaiming "the Bishops crultie...to all nationes". The Dutch version effectively fulfilled its mission of stirring up Holland "against the government of England, temporal and spiritual". The Christiaensz edition of the Bastwick-Burton-Prynne pamphlet went forth in very large quantities, 10,000 in English, 3000 in Dutch.[114] Thomas Crafford was the financial backer of these pamphlets.[115]

Crafford and Stafford were behind another large-scale printing project by Christiaensz, the printing of an English Bible in 1639-40 (contract December 16, 1639). The two Amsterdam merchants contracted with Christiaensz for 1250 English Bibles in folio (eventually, the deal was changed to 1600 Bibles, 500 for Crafford; 1000 for Stafford, and 100 for Stafford's children). These were to be printed according to a copy in the possession of Stafford, that is, the Junius-Beza Genevan edition, not "the Scottish Bible from Delft".[116] Although

---

[112] SP 84/155/146; 84/155/79; 16/387/79.

[113] SP 84/155/6v.

[114] Ibid.; Foster, *Notes*, chap. 5.

[115] On Crafford's role see SP 84/155/79 and Amsterdam RA 5061, Confessieboek, no. 303, fol. 310v.

[116] The contract with Christiaensz is recorded in Amsterdam NA 1056 (Van de Ven), fols. 81-82 (Dec. 16, 1639); Leiden NA 326 (Grotelande), Feb. 28, 1640; RA 79, vol.

Crafford made many of the on-the-spot arrangements with Christiaensz, Stafford was clearly the senior partner and major investor. When Craf-ford visited the print shop to check on progress, he found Christiaensz and his assistants Jan de Vechter, Robert Wood, and Thomas Thymen working on the Bible. The printers asked for *drinkgeld*, or drinks, for closing the contract. Crafford answered that they must talk to Stafford about this. "He will give you the drinkgeld. I am merely a servant in this." He refused to pay out of his own pocket.[117] According to the terms of the contract, Christiaensz went to Amsterdam to choose paper for the printing from the supplies of Peter Haeck, op't Water, and Crafford paid for it.[118] However, the printing was slow and often interrupted; meanwhile Stafford and Crafford fell to arguing among themselves. Whereupon, Stafford rewrote the contract with Christiaensz in his own name, and he removed Crafford's name. Stafford brushed Crafford aside as a mere servant or errand boy (*dienaar*), and he took away the old copy of the contract. The old document had no value "You can not thereby accomplish anything".[119]

A little later, probably still in 1640, Stafford returned to Leiden and removed the entire printing work from Christiaensz, and he salvaged the pages which were already printed. According to Christiaensz, Stafford "forced him to withdraw from the printing", and he packed up all the paper and letters connected with the Bible (which were later legally sequestered by Crafford).[120] In spite of all this commotion, a Bible finally was produced, carrying the imprint: "Amsterdam. Printed by Thomas Stafford: And are to be sold at his house..." (STC 2344 and 2344.5) Consistent with the documents of the time, the Bible does appear to be a composite work of two printers and presses.[121]

After 1640 Christiaensz' printing on behalf of Puritanism diminished. Christiaensz van der Boxe, as he now called himself, continued to do some translating into Dutch and occasional printing in English, but on

---

V, fol. 389. Cf. Van Eeghen *AB*, IV, 101; Kleerkooper and Van Stockum, pp. 1244-46. The edition was based on the "Copy printed at Edinburgh by Andro Hart, in the year 1610".

[117] RA 79, vol. V, fol. 389, Mar. 16, 1641, referring to "about a year ago".

[118] NA 326 (Grotelande), Feb. 28, 1640.

[119] Ibid. (1640); RA 79, vol. W, fol. 171 (pencil 321), which contains a copy of the revised contract produced Feb. 28, 1640.

[120] RA 79, vol. W, fol. 173 (pencil 233), May 6, 1644. Although the document is dated 1644, the action reported came much earlier, apparently in 1640.

[121] See entry for STC 2344; Herbert, *Historical Catalogue*, no. 545.

a smaller scale. Much Puritan printing could now be done in England. Christiaensz kept his printing shop going until the year of his death, 1658. After that the business continued under his son, Daniel Willemsz van der Boxe, and other members of the family.[122]

Freedom and restriction of printing at Leiden

As seen in this chapter, Leiden played a big role in Dutch-Puritan printing. The city of Leiden was hospitable to English and Scottish settlers and gave them much freedom to carry on their urgent Puritan activities. Whenever pressured severely, as with Brewer and Brewster in 1618, the magistrates moved against clandestine printing, but ever so slowly. When Brewer was in printing trouble, the university protected him. All of this commotion, however, must have produced uneasy feelings; and for a variety of reasons, the Leiden magistrates wished to control the book activities of outsiders. The city of Leiden in 1623 put forth a regulation forbidding foreigners, or anyone without Leiden citizenship, from selling books within the city, except during the regular yearly markets.[123] When pursuing Christiaensz in 1637-38, Boswell constantly struggled against governmental lethargy and delay, even when the legal facts against the printer were abundantly clear. At last the magistrates "accordingly performed" but not without exasperating delay, "by reason of sicknes in some of them, and the judges; small but frequent vacations; formalities of necessity observable in their courts; with other unavoydable diversions."[124] When it got too hot for the Puritans at Leiden, they shifted their printing to one of the other cities.

The Dutch Reformed Church of Leiden, like the church in Amsterdam, raised questions about disreputable printing. However, the churchmen seldom, if ever, directly attacked the books of the orthodox Puritan authors. Rather, the preachers express more concern about books tainted with Socinianism and Muslim doctrine.[125]

---

[122] Christiaensz' will is found in NA 635 (Doude), May 12, 1658; he was buried June 16, 1658; Gruys and De Wolf.

[123] J.T. Bodel Nijenhuis, *De wetgeving op drukpers en boekhandel in de Nederlanden tot in het begin der XIXde eeuw* (Amsterdam, 1892), p. 108.

[124] SP 84/154/113.

[125] Acta Kerkeraad Leiden, no. 002, May 29, 1626; 004, April 12, 1641.

CHAPTER 6

DISTRIBUTING THE BOOKS

After the writing and printing of the books, large obstacles remained until they reached their intended readers. Hugh Peter, most knowledgeable in such matters, reported in 1633 that a new book by Doctor Ames was printed at Amsterdam "but how the bookes will come into mens hands is a question".[1] Transporting and distributing Puritan books was a great challenge. In the circumstances, the Puritan book zealots were required to become agents of transporting, smuggling, and selling of books. A verse of Scripture inspired the book distributors, "*that the word of God might have free passage and be glorified*" (II Thessalonians 3:1). Puritans yearned for "free passage" for their books.[2]

The chief barrier against Puritanical books was the press and censorship laws of England. Were the prelatical censors simply book-hating "Vipers", venomously hindering the words of the Gospel? The annals of the Puritan book trade abound with stories about books being seized, "burnt or defaced", and "sealed vpp". Authors were whipped and mutilated, and booksellers suffered fines and pillory.[3] Some gave their lives for this cause; the Separatists revered the sacrificial service of John Coppin and Elias Thacker, hanged in England in 1583 "for dispersing of books".[4] Every archbishop complained about the flood of unlicensed books—*Amsterodami excusa*—flowing in from Holland. Laud professed to be "very sorry for the Publicke, which suffers much by them", and he personally suffered much abuse and wounded pride from the Puritan books.[5]

The usual means of book transportation and selling were closed to Puritan books from Holland. Consequently, almost the entire output

---

[1] SP 16/241/52.

[2] *Certaine Argvments and Motives of Speciall Moment*, STC 739.5 (n.p., 1635), p. 21.

[3] Ibid., pp. 20-21; W. W. Greg, *A Companion to Arber* (Oxford: Clarendon Press, 1967), pp. 31. 228, 314.

[4] William Bradford, "A Dialogue or the sume of a Conference...1648", *Publications of the Colonial Society of Massachusetts*, 22 (1920), p. 123.

[5] Tanner MS. 68, fol. 10r; Add. MS. C69 (Bod.).

of the Dutch-English Puritan book enterprise moved by secret networks of merchants, church congregations, and religiously inspired friends on both sides of the water. Believers at Rotterdam and London, at Amsterdam, Delft, Norwich, and Yarmouth, "have continual intercourse...and sundry schismatical books have thither been imported". "Holy friends" in Holland shipped books to "Holy friends" in England and Scotland.[6] The senders warned: Treasure these books, and be wary, lest they fall into the hands of the police. In "Rules for to Direct the Weake Reader" this advice was given: "I would intreat such, to craue the helpe of some judicious Minister, who is faithfull, not to betray him for hauing the booke..."[7]

The elements of the book distribution network were these: (1) merchants and sailors who travelled back and forth, (2) customs agents, some corrupt, who allowed the books to pass through, (3) English and Scottish booksellers who handled some of the books, (4) conventicles and cell groups, or philanthropic-minded individuals, who could sell or give the books away outside of the regular bookstore channels. Although one catches sight of some of these people at various stages of activity, or in court before the Star Chamber or High Commission, seldom can one see the process as a whole, so clandestine was the movement of the books. It is like tracking footsteps through the forest, or through patchy snow, here and there the footprints are clear, then they disappear. Ambassador Boswell referred to the Puritan conspiracy in Holland as a web of nearly invisible spider threads.[8]

Handling books in the Netherlands

The distribution of books went forward on several fronts. One was distribution to English-Scottish readers in the Netherlands. Some of the English language books were needed by the British communities close by. Several books, in fact, carried the advertisement on the title pages, "Printed (for the use and benefit of the English Churches) in the Netherlands".[9]

---

[6] Browne, *Congregationalism*, p. 78 (1626); Tanner MS. 68, fol. 10r (1638).

[7] William Ames, *Fresh Svit*, STC 555 (n.p., 1633), preface, sig. K1v.

[8] BP, I, 109.

[9] See Thomas Hooker, *The Sovles Preparation for Christ*, STC 13738 (n.p., 1638); Thomas Goodwin, *Aggravation of Sinne*, STC 12035 (n.p., 1639).

English refugee printers, like Thorp and Canne of Amsterdam and Brewster and Brewer of Leiden, kept their activity as quiet as possible. Giles Thorp may have had a small shop for selling books, but even so, most of his output was anonymous and disappeared into the usual Puritan book networks. Canne, Brewster, and Brewer did not keep an open shop, and relied upon clandestine distribution. Even though printed locally, certain English books were scarce and hard to find, "they being no where publiquely to bee sold". The Leiden Pilgrims wanted no public announcements about how "their pamphlets have been vented".[10] It was certainly prudent for printers and booksellers to keep their stock of books out of sight from prying eyes—under the counter—"sold only to such as are thought to like them".[11]

Dutch printers of Puritan books, for example Stam of Amsterdam and Christiaensz of Leiden, most likely sold some of the Puritan books in their own shops. However, even they chose to use anonymous title pages for a good many of the books; and then it was usually the responsibility of the Puritan author or financial backer to take delivery in bulk and proceed with their own distribution.

Availability of English books in the Netherlands rose and fell depending on the vigor of enforcement of the laws in the various Dutch cities. In 1625 many nonconformist books were on sale at Amsterdam, according to reports from Patrick Scot. He saw bookish "trumpets of *Sedition*" in "euery Booksellers shop, and most Peddlers stalles". The shops were "loaden" with them. However, he could not discover who wrote or printed them. Scot was pained to see buyers snatching up such books.[12] John Lilburne found the book shops very well stocked with Puritan books in 1637; Bastwick's books were in good supply. "You may buy an hundred of them at the booksellers, if you have a mind to them."[13] Then again, if investigations were afoot, the supply could rapidly disappear from the shelves. In 1639, when enforcement of book laws against Puritans was strict at Amsterdam, the sale of Puritan and Covenanter books moved to Rotterdam and such places. A mixture of sale in shops and hand-to-hand distribution among friends was the means of getting the books to the readers.

---

[10] SP 84/82/34v; Edward Arber, *The Story of the Pilgrim Fathers, 1606-1623* (London: Ward and Downey, 1897), p. 234.

[11] SP 84/155/145.

[12] Patrick Scot, *Vox Vera*, STC 21863 (London, 1625), pp. 3-4, 10, 21.

[13] M.A. Gibb, *John Lilburne, The Leveller* (London: Lindsay Drummond, 1947), p. 47.

When the Amsterdam Separatists wanted to communicate directly with Junius in 1599, they hand delivered the books to him.[14]

Transporting the books into England and Scotland

The transporting of books into Britain depended greatly upon the connivance of merchants and sailors who regularly travelled the North Sea. By tucking a few books into their shipments, the flow of Puritan books could proceed on a steady basis. The level of merchant participation in book transportation depended on the type of books that were to be moved. English-language Bibles, concordances, and similar fast-selling books were an investment that might be turned into a quick profit in England. However, the polemical pamphlets were not so profitable. The "convinced" Puritan carried them even if there was little likelihood of a profit.

A glimpse into the clandestine working of the transportation network comes from Matthew Simmons' "Information" (1637-38). According to his information, merchants and sailors were the indispensable agents of shipping and selling. He named many names. But to name them all was impossible. "Concerning the ship masteres they are all so giltie that I know not who to name... There is not one that I know but bring over anie prohibbeted goodes." They were so brazen and skillful, so "practised" in their cunning craft, that "nothing comes amisse".[15] Jan Fredericksz Stam of Amsterdam printed many Bibles with notes, in quarto, folio, and duodecimo, and he had 7000 in stock. "Manie merchantes bye great quantities of them here and packe them up in towe and other goodes and so bring them over." John Johnson (Johannes Janssonius), also of Amsterdam, printed Bayly's *Practice of Pietie* in batches of 10,000 copies at a time; "his vent is most by marchantes."[16] At Delft, James Moxon printed Doctor Bastwick's *Letany*—a five-part series—and similar radical books. His merchant collaborator was "Mr. John" (probably John Foote) who paid for the printing and then shipped away 1000 of each of the books along with copies of *Practice of Pietie* and Bibles in quarto. Mr. John sent them in

---

[14] Junius (Du Jon), *Certayne Letters*, STC 7298 (n.p., 1602), p. 31.

[15] SP 16/387/79. Simmons' information was written up either late 1637 or early 1638 (received April 24, 1638).

[16] Ibid.

a "large vessell" bound for Newcastle the last of November, 1637. He also had at Delft awaiting shipment many more books of all sorts which were against the prelates; "the like can scarse be seen together."[17] In another transaction, two merchants of Rotterdam commissioned a new edition of *A Justification of Separation* by John Robinson.[18]

In addition to the large shippers, who carried books by the hundreds, lesser persons also had their hands in book transportation. A cunning Brownist from Leiden, Robert Cockyn, alias Leonard Verse, successfully carried many books. "Frequenting England under pretence of a privat foot-post", he smuggled letters and pamphlets. He knew all the ports and skillfully "takes his passage at the port where he thinks to find least security for his person and papers he carieth".[19] The occasional travel-ler had opportunity to bring back a few books. "One Puckle" (Stephen Puckell), a "catterpiller to his cuntrie", sold books at the docks at Rotterdam, being a "great venter of them as passengers goe for Eng-land". In this way he helped spread Doctor Ames' *Fresh Svit*, and he had a book, *A True Table*, which he himself had written.[20]

When David Calderwood's book, *Perth Assembly*, was shipped to Scotland in 1619, the papers were stuffed into vats "as if they had been a mercantile consignment of French wines or strong waters". This method sent the pages over unfolded and unbound.[21] Shipping in unbound sheets, in addition to ease of smuggling, also offered a slight hope for contravening the British book laws, which originally forbade importation of "books" without mentioning "sheets".[22] It was also common, however, for Puritanical books to be bound in Holland, ready for the reader. Ames' *Fresh Svit* was ready for the reader at the Rotterdam docks. "There is a 100 or 200 bounde at this towne to sell" (another 300-400 copies were shipped over to London disguised as "white paper").[23]

---

[17] Ibid. At least one part of the *Letany* was printed by Christiaensz of Leiden, according to court records; see chap. 5. John Lilburne was charged with helping Foote of Delft; see Lilburne, *Worke of the Beast*, STC 15599 (n.p., 1638), pp. 10-12.

[18] SP 16/387/79.

[19] SP 84/153/30r and 30v.

[20] BP, I, 143; SP 16/246/56.

[21] Arber, *Pilgrim Fathers*, p. 240.

[22] Leona Rostenberg, *The Minority Press & the English Crown: A Study in Repression, 1558-1625* (Nieuwkoop: B. De Graaf, 1971), p. 192.

[23] BP, I, 143; SP 16/246/56.

It must be emphasized that many of these Dutch-printed books were not illegal in content; they were "prohibbited" because they were produced outside of the monopoly of the Stationers' Company. They were "Counterfeit...brought from beyond sea".[24] Regardless of the books, whether radical in content or without license, holy stealth and deception was the requirement of the day. The ship captains had many tricks of the trade to get books across. They could package the books like "white paper" addressed to stationers, "to be passed for white papers, and so never looked into, or let passe by negligence, or false-hood of the searchers".[25] Various customs searchers, apparently, were part of the smuggling scheme. If the ship was threatened by police, the ship captain might run upon the sand at Queensborough "and send away all there passengers and deliver all their prohibeted goodes in some small boote...". The ship masters boasted that they had ways "to cozen the devell".[26] Customs officers were warned to be always on guard about the "secrett and private wayes" of the book importers: "Seize all such bookes"![27]

Selling and giving away books in England and Scotland

If the books arrived safely, two options for book distribution were possible: Sell the books or give them away to worthy people. Selling radical Puritan books did not appeal to cautious booksellers because of danger of punishment. Nevertheless, numerous booksellers handled some of the books, especially the non-controversial Bibles, concord-ances, and devotional books, which were not in themselves illegal, except for infringement of monopoly patents. Since the Bibles usually had false title pages, they might pass as legitimate books, licensed by the censors, and disappear into the regular stock of the book store. Nevertheless, the possessor must always be very wary. Such was the situation of merchant William Cotton, who had possession of the entire printing of one of Hugh Broughton's "sharpe, and smart" pamphlets. Archbishop Bancroft moved to seize every book, except

---

[24] William A. Jackson, ed., *Records of the Court of the Stationers' Company 1602 to 1640* (New York: Bibliographical Society, 1957), pp. 304, 312, 487 (discussing "counterfeit Psalmes").

[25] SP 16/246/56.

[26] SP 16/387/79.

[27] Jackson, *Stationers' Company*, p. 387.

that Cotton, "foreseeing what would come to pass, had conveyed a trunk full of the Books out of the way, and so these escaped".[28]

Merchant speculators in books, looking for a profitable sideline, depended for a profit on having some English salesman or book dealer to handle their goods. Concerning Bibles and Bayly's *Pieties*, one merchant entrepreneur declared, "he had a chapman" in London. One of the London dealers in foreign books was Samuel Cartwright of Duck Lane.[29] Stocking the bitter "scandalous" kind of books, namely such as by Bastwick, Prynne, Burton, and Lilburne, was very risky for a bookseller. Only the hardiest Puritan believer would be willing to chance it. If caught with unlicensed books, the bookseller would attempt some lame excuses: The books were unordered. The books had been delivered by mistake. An unknown porter dropped them off. Two men dressed like sailors were delivering books, and so on.[30] Michael Sparke of London was a very resolute handler of Puritanical books from home and abroad. He defended the sale of all books by appealing to the rights of Magna Carta and the Petition of Right—freedoms of the press and of the citizen. He had to stand in the pillory.[31]

Other dealers in the shops and on the street also fared ill. The High Commission regularly dealt with smuggled Bible cases, involving legitimate printers and booksellers. Jail was the printer's and bookseller's purgatory.[32] One ship master with Bibles in 1637 had a severe business setback in selling; "he saide halfe the bookes are seased allredie."[33] Abraham Atfend, bookseller of Norwich, in 1640 was arrested and fined by the High Commission for receiving and selling "Holland Bibles and books in English printed beyond the seas".[34] Amateurs also paid the price for handling books. One Mr. Ash, a great clothier of Somersetshire, was arrested for "receauing and dispersing" 150 copies of *Newes from Ipswich*. The judge pronounced that he

---

[28] Hugh Broughton, *Works* (London, 1662), John Lightfoot preface, sig. C1r.

[29] SP 16/387/79. On Cartwright, see Plomer (1641-67), pp. 43-44.

[30] Greg, *Companion*, pp 78-79.

[31] Ibid., pp. 85-86; Susan A. Stussy, "Michael Sparke, Puritan and Printer", Diss. Univ. of Tennessee, 1983, pp. 30-35; Plomer (1641-67), p. 169.

[32] Michael Sparke, *Scintilla*, Wing S4818B (London, 1641), p. 3.

[33] SP 16/387/79; Greg, *Companion*, pp. 86, 91.

[34] David Stoker, "The Norwich Book Trades before 1800", *Transactions of the Cambridge Bibliographical Society*, 8 (1981), pp. 79-125. The above are just a few examples of booksellers' difficulties with the law.

would make "an example to the whole kingdome" of Ash because of his meddling in books.[35] Doubtless, these dealers were part of some larger plans for selling or giving out books, but the details are now lost.

In cases where the books were not vendible in the shops, then the books might be handed out free. This would truly be a mission in book evangelism. Samuel Hieron's book, *A Defence of the Ministers Reasons* (1607) had a difficult launching. Printed in Amsterdam, it was shipped back to England "packt up in ye goods of an eminent Marchant of Plymouth, old Mr. T. Sherwill". No bookseller would handle the book.

> So that ye Copys were dispersed abroad in ye kingdome after this manner. Some were sent superscribed to ye 26 Bishops, and unto other of his Antagonists, and to sundry Persons in ye Citty and Universitys. Some Copys were dropt on purpose in ye very streets, other left at the doors of Schollars and learned Ministers. Some were hung upon hedges in ye high way. And thus ye whole impression was freely and generously given away.

The book, of course, omitted the names of author and printer because it was not "safe" to print them. A tiny cell of friends carried out this plan, "few being privy to this Action".[36] In spite of such haphazard methods of publication, the Puritan word went forth. Several copies of Hieron's book survive to this day.

A more comprehensive scheme for dispersing books took shape at Yarmouth in 1637. This is but one example of what often occurred. The Yarmouth group tried to outwit Bishop Wren. Through a network of merchants in Holland and England, aided by ship captains, Puritan ministers, and conventiclers, the newly printed books moved from one country to the other. The shipments began at Rotterdam and Delft, and consisted of many copies of Doctor Bastwick's *Letany* ("Litany", parts 1-4) and his Latin book, *Flagellum pontificis*. This "diabolicall" scheme, involving "holy" Christians in Delft and Yarmouth, was masterminded by James Moxon, printer of the *Letany*, pastors Jeremiah Burroughes and William Greenhill, and merchants, "fit factors for venting such stuff". The ship, under master Robert

---

[35] *The Winthrop Papers*, in *Collections of the Massachusetts Historical Society*, 4th ser., 6 (1863), pp. 446-47.
[36] Quick, "Icones" (Life of Hieron), fols. 84-85.

Lewit (or Lovet), arrived at Yarmouth early in November 1637, loaded with letters and parcels of Bastwick's "very libellous Pamphletes". Also on board were Burroughes and Greenhill "disguised" like soldiers and sailors. The two "refractory" pastors, both suspended from their pulpits, were returning from Holland after scouting out the prospects for immigration.[37] The ship (early November) to Yarmouth was a very similar enterprise to the later ship to Newcastle, late November of 1637, also sent from Delft with a cargo of Bastwick's books and some for Scotland.[38] Through a mishap in the Yarmouth plans, government "searchers" found the books and seized the ministers. The captain and several other accomplices were also arrested. The unlucky captives included one John Robinson, a cordwinder, William Miller, and John England. Captain Lewit pleaded innocent, claiming that he was fooled because the books were packaged to look like blank, white paper.[39]

With the books and shippers stopped, the rest of the scheme soon came to light. Robinson, the "cordwinder", turned out to be actually a "schoolmaster" who worshipped with the Puritan conventicle which met in a barn at Somerleyton. The books from Holland were intended for these "barne conventiclers by whome they shouyld have been dispersed". Some of the parcels of books were directed to Puritans in surrounding towns, namely Mr. Toft at Fibridge and another Mr. Toft in Tombland, Norwich. A "silly weaver had some of the books".[40] An accomplice was Miles Corbett, recorder of Yarmouth, who entertained the two pastors shortly before their arrest. This event tells much about how conventicles and other Puritan circles could organize for book distribution without reliance on the booksellers. The Yarmouth revelations were tantalizing indeed, and Bishop Wren of Norwich and the Privy Council at London followed the case closely. What had begun as a small incident of contraband books at Yarmouth opened up to reveal a maze of people at Delft, Rotterdam, as well as several town and cities in England: "Holy friends" in Holland were in communion

---

[37] This story can be pieced together from Tanner MS. 68, fols. 9v, 10r, 90r, 277r, 281, 283, 285; see also PC 2/48/385 and 442; and SP 16/387/79. Christopher Wren, *Parentalia* (London, 1750), p. 95; Kenneth W. Shipps, "Lay Patronage of East Anglian Puritan Clerics in Pre-Revolutionary England", Diss. Yale Univ., 1971. My thanks also to Michael E. Moody for suggestions on this topic.

[38] SP 16/387/79.

[39] Tanner MS. 68, fol. 283.

[40] Tanner MS. 68, fols. 10, 283, 285; Shipps, "Lay Patronage", pp. 178, 241, 296.

with "holy meetings" in England.[41] The Delft-Rotterdam-Yarmouth connection, like other connections, silently moved books from the printing shops to the readers. Many hands carried the books.

Catalogues and book fairs

To reach a broader audience, Puritan writers and printers aimed some of their books at the international scholarly community. When appealing to the wider audience, the authors usually wrote in Latin, and they spread their message through the international fairs at Frankfurt and Leipzig. Their publishers and printers advertised their wares in the semi-annual books catalogues. Book fairs met twice yearly, spring and fall, and each fair produced catalogues. These catalogues provided a list of the publishers' best books of the year. Puritans saw this as the opportunity to address scholars at a wide range of universities in the Netherlands, Switzerland, and Germany, the "reverend and learned men", as well as readers in Britain. The Puritans designed books in Latin, it was surmised, "to perswade *forraigne aliens* to their faction".[42]

The first Puritan author who tapped the potential of the catalogues and book fairs was Hugh Broughton. Several times he arranged to have his Amsterdam Latin and Hebrew books advertised in the catalogues. "Franckfurt Mart" would speak for him, he proclaimed. The spring catalogue of 1606 carried one of Broughton's books; the autumn catalogues of 1606 for both Frankfurt and Leipzig listed six additional books by Broughton: "Amsteldami apud Commelin".[43] The house of Commelin, however, was not the printer of the books but only the distributor.

Before Broughton's venture, the officially sanctioned English writers, adversaries of the Puritans, had previously entered the catalogues. Writings of King James I and various bishops were listed in the

---

[41] Tanner MS. 68, fol. 90r.

[42] See the Separatist confession of faith (1602), STC 18434, with preface to the "reverend and learned men". The confession was put into Latin c. 1607 in order to reach its intended audience. Patrick Scot, *Vox Vera*, p. 4. On Dutch selling by catalogue, see B. van Selm, *Een menighte treffelijcke boecken: Nederlandse boekhandels-catalogi in het begin van de zeventiend eeuw* (Utrecht: HES Uitgevers, 1987).

[43] Broughton, *Works*, I, 350. See *Catalogvs Vniversalis*, spring 1606, Frankfurt, sig. B1v, Amsteldami, without publisher; autumn 1606, Frankfurt, sig. E4r; Leipzig, sig. B1r. I have used the catalogue collection at UB Leiden.

catalogues from at least 1604 onward. In addition, certain Latin orthodox scholarly works by erudite Puritans, including Thomas Cartwright, William Perkins, William Whitaker and Dudley Fenner,
printed on the Continent, appeared in early catalogues.

After Broughton's beginning, Puritan treatises from Dutch presses
began to appear in the catalogues on a more regular basis. These
advertisements included books from Amsterdam by Thomas
Brightman, starting in 1609, handled by publishers in Amsterdam and
Frankfurt.[44] Separatists tried to reach the larger audiences "of all
nations" with special Latin and French editions of Henry Ainsworth's
Communion of Saincts, advertised in the Frankfurt catalogue of 1608.
The 1608 Amsterdam catalogue of bookseller Cornelis Claesz also
listed the French edition. No copies of any French or Latin versions
from 1608, or thereabouts, are known. After very long delays, the
autumn 1618 catalogue listed the publication of the French version,
Communion des Saincts "par H. A. Amstero chez Giles Thorp".[45] The
Separatists, however, failed to get out their proposed Latin edition. A
Dutch edition came out in 1628. John Paget taunted Ainsworth and
Thorp for being so timid in finishing their translated books.
Ainsworth's *Communion* was only one of several Separatist books of
Thorp to "come forth" in this way at Frankfurt Mart.[46]

In 1610 *Quaestio de duabus epistolis tractata* by Francis Johnson and
John Carpenter appeared; this is a work commonly attributed to
Thorp. The title page carried the imprint, "Prostat apud viduam
Levini Hulsij, Francofurti, 1610"; however, the autumn catalogue
from Frankfurt states Amsterdam "apud Henricum Laurentium".[47] In
1611 Thorp printed the Sanford-Parker book, *De descensv domini nostri
Jesu Christi* (In aedibus Aegidij Thorpij); the book appeared in the

---

[44] Brightman's book on the *Apocalypsis* twice appeared in the spring 1609 Frankfurt
catalogue, sigs. B1v, B2r (offered "Prostat Francofurti apud Viduam Leuini Hulsii"
and "Ambstelrodami apud Cornelium Nicolai").
Apparently there were two versions with distinct title pages.
[45] Ainsworth's book, *Communion of Saincts*, was promised in French (spring 1608,
Leipzig edition, sig. G1v, chez Corneille Nicolas) and Latin (autumn 1608, Frankfurt,
sig. B1r, Cornelium Nicolai) but did not appear; the French version is also in the
autumn catalogue, 1618, sig. D4r, "chez Giles Thorp". The latter time, the book
actually did appear.
[46] John Paget, *An Arrow against the Separation*, STC 19098 (Amsterdam, 1618), p.
86. For the Dutch edition, see C.W. Schoneveld, *Intertraffic of the Mind* (Leiden: Sir
Thomas Browne Institute, 1983), no. 49.
[47] Johnson (1951), p. 226; autumn 1610 Frankfurt catalogue, sig. B2r.

spring 1612 catalogue by the name of its distributor, Hendrik Laurensz, not by its printer.[48] Thorp's books circulated rather widely, but not always under his own name.

As in the case of books by Thorp, many Puritanical works went into the international market through the services of large Amsterdam booksellers, like Laurensz, Commelin, and Cornelius Nicolai (Cornilis Claesz). Claesz' stock catalogues of 1608-10 advertised books by a good supply of English authors, such as William Perkins, John Rainolds, Hugh Broughton, William Whitaker, and Thomas Cartwright. He included some Brownist books, among them *Confessio fidei Anglorum*, the Ainsworth-Johnson confession of faith. (See Appendix I, O). Claesz died in 1609. The next year Widow Claesz put out an auction catalogue for selling the remaining stock. Claesz was one of the largest booksellers of the Netherlands. "If anyone has a great desire for reading books...you will find them in his catalogue"—in French, Spanish, Italian, Latin, and Dutch.[49]

An interesting publication was the William Bradshaw-William Ames Latin edition of *Puritanismus Anglicanus*, "Francofvrti. Prostat in Bibliopolio Aubriano, 1610", advertised in the spring 1612 catalogue.[50] This Latin edition carried no name of Dutch publisher. In light of Ames' exile to the Netherlands and his steady reliance on Dutch publishers, it seems very likely that *Puritanismus Anglicanus* was another of the Dutch-printed, Frankfurt-marketed books. Another significant Puritan book marketed at Frankfurt was Robert Parker's *De politeia ecclesiastica Christi* (autumn 1616 catalogue), published by Govert Basson of Leiden.[51] Janssonius, Elsevier, and Blaeu also used the Frankfurt catalogues to advertise Puritan, Calvinistic books; all of these, along with Laurensz, publicized many Latin books of William Ames.[52]

Brewster and Brewer of Leiden in 1617-18 aimed part of their output to the international reader. Three of their Latin books appeared

---

[48] Spring 1612 Frankfurt catalogue, sig. B2v.

[49] Cornelis Claesz, *Catalogvs*, (auction catalogue; Amsterdam: Weduwe Claesz, 1610), sig. A1v, "tot de coopers". Van Selm, *Boecken*, chap. 4.

[50] Autumn 1611 Frankfurt catalogue, sig. B1r.

[51] Autumn 1616 Frankfurt catalogue, sig. B2v. Parker's book was also offered spring 1628, STC 11331 (London, 1628).

[52] For a sampling of their work, see Johannes Janssonius (spring 1631, autumn 1633, autumn 1634); Gulielmus Blaeu (autumn 1633); Elsevier (spring 1618); Laurensz (autumn 1615).

in the Frankfurt and Leipzig catalogues. The spring 1617 catalogue had a book by William Ames, *Ad responsum Nic. Grevinchovij rescriptio contracta*, and Thomas Cartwright's *Succincti Commentarij in Prouerbia Salomonis*, both "Leidae apud Wilhelm Breusterum". In 1618, Brewster dropped the use of his own name and took his printing underground. The autumn 1618 catalogue again listed Cartwright's *Commentarij* and the anonymous *De vera religione*, both available "apud Joannem Orlers" (Jan Jansz Orlers) but, in fact, published by Brewster and Brewer.[53] William Bradshaw's *Dissertatio de justificationis* (apud Joannem Maire) appeared in the same catalogue of 1618.[54]

By occasionally advertising in the catalogues and exhibiting at the Frankfurt book fair, Puritan authors and printers extended the outreach of the books. Throughout the 1620s and 1630s, some Puritanical books continued to be listed.

Distributing books to America

Many of the Puritan books from Holland went on to America. There was no special system of shipping or selling. The American immigrants often took books along with them in their luggage, or later had them sent over. This is a larger topic than can be handled here; nevertheless, it would be worthwhile to study inventories of American libraries, which would give an indication of the dimensions of the Dutch-American book traffic.[55] Cotton Mather reported books coming over from Holland, even entire libraries.[56]

---

[53] R. Breugelmans, "The Pilgrim Press and How Its Books Were Sold", in Jeremy D. Bangs, ed., *The Pilgrims in the Netherlands: Recent Research* (Leiden: Pilgrim Documents Center, 1985), pp. 25-28. See spring catalogue, 1617, sig. B2r; also STC 11328 (London: Ex Off. Nortoniana, 1617), sig. B3v; autumn catalogue, 1618, Frankfurt, sig. B1r. Ames' *Ad responsum* and *De vera religione* were listed again, for example, in the spring 1628 catalogue, London, STC 11331, sigs. A2r, B4r.

[54] Autumn 1618, sig. A4v.

[55] Lawrence D. Geller and Peter J. Gomes, *The Books of the Pilgrims* (New York: Garland Publishing, Inc., 1975).

[56] *Magnalia Christi Americana* (1852-53 ed.), I, 236, referring to the library of William Ames. On this, I believe, Mather was mistaken about the entire Ames library being shipped over (see above, chap. 5) but correct on the flow of books into America from England and Holland.

Did the books get through?

Many a time the English ambassador would announce that the publication of Puritan books in Holland had been stopped. At Amsterdam or Leiden, all would be silent for a moment. "None dares to medle with any seditious kinde of libels more." The "watchfull eye" of repression would triumph.[57] Whether in Holland or Britain, the book controls according to John Lilburne, were "Clubb-Law"—the "infallible arguments" of the rod, irons, and jails.[58]

In spite of several well-publicized arrests of printers and authors in both Britain and the Netherlands, the Puritan books continued to flow through the clandestine channels and nearly every English Puritan or Scottish book published in the seventeenth-century Netherlands survives to this day, at least in a few copies. By comparing the lists of books reportedly published in the underground printing establishments and the entries of books in the *Short Title Catalogue*, the high survival rate can be seen. Only a handful of the hateful "libellous" books have totally disappeared. A few always seeped through the barriers to find their readers. The seventeenth-century authors and printers would be pleased. Just as the Lord had promised: He who sows the good seed will see the harvest, some an hundredfold, some sixtyfold, some thirtyfold. Even one book could produce a tiny harvest.

---

[57] SP 84/155/260; PC 2/50/421.
[58] John Lilburne, *Come out of Her My People*, STC 15596 (n.p., 1639), p. 32.

CHAPTER 7

THE WIDER FELLOWSHIP OF DUTCH-ENGLISH BOOK
PUBLISHING AND TRANSLATION

English and Scottish nonconformists in the Netherlands succeeded in producing books for the home countries in large quantities. Their tireless efforts paid off. Moreover, many sympathetic Dutch persons aided these enterprises of Puritanical books. These fellow travellers of the Puritans included printers, booksellers, politicians who did not rigorously apply the press laws, and many Dutch Reformed preachers supportive of Puritan religion.

The nonconformist English and Scots through the years shared in Dutch Reformed religion by establishing "English churches" in union with the Dutch Reformed church—*gereformeerde gemeenten*—and supporting the Reformed position against Arminianism. They excluded the high Anglican ceremonies. Still, the Puritans of the Netherlands desired a deeper, warmer religion than prevailed in their adopted republic, just as they desired a "purer" religion at home. Although much had been accomplished for God, the English and Scots preached that in all lands more was required: Much more reformation, "speedy Reformation". God demanded more from His people.[1] In the realm of church and nation the "Lord hath a *plumbline in his hand*" to judge "all Churches and people".[2] In the inner realm, Puritans called for personal conversion and the practice of a sincere, Spirit-filled life. These were "frozen times",[3] and God must warm the heart.

The pious English and Scots developed an especial fellowship with the strict, pietistic wing of the Dutch Reformed Church. There was a parallel Dutch movement to Puritanism, today called the *Nadere Reformatie*, the "further reformation", which linked many of the Dutch Reformed pietists into a spiritual brotherhood, and these had fellowship with the Puritan English and Presbyterian Scots. The Dutch

---

[1] William Prynne, *A Quench-Coale*, STC 20474 (n.p., 1637), p. 37.
[2] Francis Johnson, *A Christian Plea*, STC 14661 (n.p., 1617), pp. 83-84.
[3] John Robinson, *A Ivstification of Separation*, STC 21109 (n.p., 1610), p. 3.

pietists "opposed widespread abuses and fallacies and with prophetic inspiration not only urged the inner experience of Reformed doctrine and the sanctification of one's personal life, but also worked hard for the radical purification of all areas of life".[4] The conversion of national life was as much the concern as personal conversion, for how else would the Dutch become the people of Zion?[5] This pietistic movement was at first based in Zeeland, in the persons of such as Willem Teellinck, Eeuwout Teellinck, and G.C. Udemans, but spread out from there to other parts of the country. The confluence of English Puritans, Scottish Presbyterians (especially the Covenanters), and the Dutch pietists produced a wide and warm fellowship of pietistic action which shared many goals in religion.

This wider fellowship, which encompassed people from Holland, England, and Scotland, had an impact on the production of Puritan books. The *Nadere Reformatie* people, like the dissenters of Britain, believed in books as the way to get their message out; the Dutch launched a "book offensive" (*bibliocratisch offensief*) that spread the precise, pious word to families, schools, churches, and the nation.[6] The precise pious Dutch were sympathetic to the Netherlands-based publishing of English and Scottish books. The most obvious manifestation of cooperation occurred in book translations. A few of the popular and wholesome Dutch books were put into English (for example, books by Willem Teellinck and Johannes Bogerman). Conversely, a great many English and Scottish books were translated into Dutch. In this way, there was a sharing of religion.

A good example of this sharing of book concerns took place in the Teellinck circle of Middelburg. Core persons were pastor Willem Teellinck, his politician brothers, Eeuwout Teellinck and Cornelis Teellinck, pastor Godefridus Cornelisz Udemans, and schoolmaster

---

[4] W.J. op 't Hof, *Engelse pietistische geschriften in het Nederlands, 1598-1622* (Rotterdam: Lindenberg, 1987), pp. 23-37, 636, 643-45; L.F. Groenendijk, "De oorsprong van de uitdrukking 'Nadere Reformatie'", *DNR*, 9 (1985), pp. 128-32.

[5] L.F. Groenendijk, *De Nadere Reformatie van het gezin: De visie van Petrus Wittewrongel op de Christelijke huishouding* (Dordrecht: Uitgeverij J.P. van den Tol, 1984), pp. 18-24.

[6] F.A. van Lieburg, "Pietistische lectuur in de zeventiende en achttiende eeuw", *DNR*, 13 (1989), pp. 81, 86. See L.F. Groenendijk, "Kerk, school en gezin in dienst van het bibliocratische ideaal bij de gereformeerden tijdens ds 17e eeuw", in *Pedagogisch tijdschrift* 14 (1989), pp. 257-68.

Johannes de Swaef.[7] This group had contacts with many earnest Puritans: The pastors of the English churches of Middelburg and Flushing (John Drake and John Wing), Doctor William Ames, professor at Franeker, and others far and wide. An interesting associate was Thomas Brewer, colleague of William Brewster in the "Pilgrim Press" of Leiden. He stopped to visit on his way to England in 1619. Brewer "hath many friends in Middelburg; and those exceeding earnest in his Cause...".[8]

In 1620 Thomas Gataker of England visited Middelburg, and other places in the Netherlands, and although details are lacking, he apparently fellowshipped with the Teellincks. Gataker came with a high reputation and was friendly with many Dutch visitors to England.[9] Shortly after his visit, Gataker's book, *A Sparke toward the Kindling of Sorrow for Sion* (London, 1621) was translated into Dutch and printed, *Heylighe Voncke* (1622). Meanwhile, Gataker arranged for some of Teellinck's books to appear in England. *The Ballance of the Sanctuarie* (London, 1621), *Pauls Complaint against His Naturall Corruption* (London, 1621), and *The Resting Place of the Minde* (London, 1622) were soon available; Gataker provided prefaces for the first and third of these. A fourth translated book by Teellinck, *The Forceable Power of the Love of Christ*, was registered in the Stationers' Company register by publisher John Bellamy in 1621, but there is no sign that it ever appeared.[10] These visits and comradeship produced quite a flurry of activity.

Willem Teellinck was also an active translator from English, but it is not likely that he translated his own books of 1621-22 into English. One of the books has a translator's preface by Ch. Hamar, but who did the others? Teellinck had many personal contacts with England and Scotland, having visited on several occasions. The fellowship of believers in England gave impetus to his Christian conversion. He

---

[7] Op 't Hof, *Engelse piet. geschriften*, pp. 490-99.

[8] Edward Arber, *The Story of the Pilgrim Fathers, 1606-1623* (London: Ward and Downey, 1897), letter of Sir William Zouche to Carleton, Nov. 26/Dec. 6, 1619, p. 226; A.P. Bijl, "Teellinck en de Leidse Separatisten rond John Robinson", *DNR*, 10 (1986), 70-72.

[9] Op 't Hof, *Engelse piet. geschriften*, p. 507. Ole P. Grell, *Dutch Calvinists in Early Stuart London: The Dutch Church of Austin Friars 1603-1642* (Leiden: Sir Thomas Browne Institute, E.J. Brill, 1989), pp. 58-59.

[10] J.B.H. Alblas, "Een onbekende Engelse vertaling van W. Teellinck", *DNR*, 8 (1984), pp. 95-98.

married an English wife, Martha Grijns (Greenston or Greendon) of Derby. He translated into Dutch books by William Perkins and William Whately, one of Whately's directly from the manuscript.[11] Reverend Teellinck was also able to inspire friends to do further translations from English into Dutch.[12]

Other fellowship between Puritanism and the *Nadere Reformatie*, outside of Zeeland, took shape. At Leiden, the two English churches, the Separatist congregation (Robinson, Brewer, and Brewster) and the orthodox *Engelse gereformeerde kerk* (Goodyear), built up numerous Dutch, pietistic friendships. The Robinson-Brewer-Brewster connection reached out to the Teellincks of Middelburg. Hugh Goodyear championed a blend of Dutch Reformed orthodoxy and English heart religion, meanwhile opposing all Anglican ceremonies. Goodyear had university interests and cultivated contacts with English and Dutch students. One Dutch student friend was Jacobus Borstius, who learned the English language from Goodyear and had a taste for Puritan authors; he called Goodyear "a second father".[13] The Leiden Puritans had frequent connections with the Puritanical English churches of Amsterdam; unfortunately the Amsterdam Puritans, especially the Separatists, unlike the ones at Leiden, suffered from a very poor reputation because of factiousness. Separatist links to the Dutch Reformed church of Amsterdam were few and painful. Another strong center of *Nadere Reformatie* religion (the Voetius circle) grew up at Utrecht around mid-century, led by Professor Gisbertus Voetius (and assisted by Johannes Hoornbeek and others). Voetius' reputation for piety attracted many students from England and Scotland. This Utrecht group was often persuaded to aid Puritan publishing and the spread of Puritan ideas.[14]

The Separatist-Brownist issue was a troublesome one. Robinson of Leiden, in spite of his famous doctrine of separation, worked hard to build fellowship with the best part of the Dutch Reformed Church. Professor Antonius Walaeus of Leiden in 1628 wrote that Robinson (d.

---

[11] Willem J.M. Engelberts, *Willem Teellinck* (Amsterdam: Scheffer & Co., 1898), pp. 3-25; Op 't Hof, *Engelse piet. geschriften*, pp. 500-01.

[12] Op 't Hof, *Engelse piet. geschriften*, p. 508.

[13] Jacobus Borstius, *Vyftien predicatien* (Utrecht, 1696), "Kort verhaal van het leven"; W.J. op 't Hof, "Puriteinse invloed op J. Borstius", *DNR*, 11 (1987), pp. 13-15.

[14] BP, I, 335; Sprunger, *Dutch Puritanism* (Leiden: E.J. Brill, 1982), pp. 361-62, 367-68.

1625) had testified to wishing to end the "schism" between his church and other English and Dutch congregations; also he had favored a ministerial career for his son in the Dutch Reformed Church. In these efforts he had "the help of Domine Teellinck and myself" (Walaeus).[15] The Robinsonian Separatist-Reformed fellowship did not extend to translating Separatist books. No well-wishers facilitated the translation of any of Robinson's books into Dutch; and indeed, there was always a lingering Dutch suspicion of Brownism. Very few Separatist, Brownist books ever made it into the Dutch language. There must not have been much of a demand for them. The exception was books by Henry Ainsworth; his Bible commentaries, especially, had an appeal.

The translation of English and Scottish books into Dutch went on briskly across the Netherlands. Several studies help to document this activity. W.J. op 't Hof's book, *Engelse pietistische geschriften in het Nederlands*, on English pietistic writings, describes 60 translated books (1598-1622) into Dutch from such authors as Lewis Bayly, Paul Baynes, Thomas Brightman, William Cowper (10 titles), John Dod, Thomas Gataker, and William Perkins (29 titles), making a total altogether, with reprintings, of 114 editions. J. van der Haar's bibliography of English translations ("most Puritan works") cited at least 742 different translations for the period of the seventeenth century.[16] C.W. Schoneveld covered a broader scope, not exclusively Puritanical works, although many certainly were. His checklist of translations from English into Dutch published 1600-1700 amounts to 641 items.[17] A review of this flood of literature reveals that the main interest among Dutch translators and publishers was the pious, heart-warming Puritan books, seldom the hard-edged political, anti-prelatical books, also characteristic of Puritanism. Separatist-authored books, with their harsh spirit, had few translations.

The main initiative for the translation of Puritan pietistic writings came from the Dutch side. Nevertheless, there was a supply of politi-

---

[15] Dexter and Dexter, *England and Holland*, p. 592; Alice C. Carter, "John Robinson and the Dutch Reformed Church", *Studies in Church History*, vol. III, ed. G.J. Cuming (Leiden: E.J. Brill, 1966), pp. 232-41.

[16] J. van der Haar, *From Abbadie to Young: A Bibliography of English, Most Puritan Works, Translated i/t Dutch Language*, 2 vols. in 1 (Veenendaal: Uitgeverij Kool B.V., 1980).

[17] C.W. Schoneveld, *Intertraffic of the Mind: Studies in Seventeenth Century Anglo-Dutch Translation with a Checklist of Books Translated from English into Dutch, 1600-1700* (Leiden: Sir Thomas Browne Institute, 1983).

cal, polemical books put into Dutch in the 1630s. The initiative for these political books came from the English and Scottish side as a way of rallying support in Holland. As the struggles built up in Britain, having the good favor of Dutch churchmen and politicians was much valued. The Puritans wanted to darken the cause of Archbishop Laud and beautify their own. Consequently, books like *Wat nieuws uyt Ipswich* by Prynne (1637), *Een cort and bondich verhael* (1638, about Bastwick, Burton, and Prynne in the Star Chamber), and books about the Scottish Bishops' Wars became widely available. They were promoted by English and Scots, not for edification, but for arousing support. Translators were such men as William Christiaensz,[18] Fredrick Willemsz Pennock,[19] and Joseph Steyns (Amsterdam notary and member of the English Reformed Church).[20]

The Anglican party, organized by Ambassador Boswell, was also at work. Laud thought it was essential to get his side of the story to the Netherlands, so he offered to send over copies of his printed Star Chamber speech, "if you have any friends that read English".[21] A bit later he sent Boswell a dozen copies to pass out; meanwhile Boswell's party had arranged for a Dutch translation of Laud's speech, *Een oratie in de Ster-Camer* (1638, Kn. 4558).[22] Henry Hexham was the translator. In the 1640s, hoping to gain sympathy, Laudian supporters produced more pamphlets in Dutch about Laud and his painful trial before Parliament. Anglican adherents arranged for a Dutch translation of the Church of England liturgy and prayer book (Rotterdam, 1645).[23] English Puritans in the Netherlands had long resisted giving any foothold to the English liturgy and prayer book; now the hated book was in their midst, "for the use of such natives as chose to join". William Steven reported that the translation and propagation of the

---

[18] Christiaensz of Leiden was the translator of *Wat nieuws uyt Ipswich*, Kn. 4473 (n.p., 1637). He was also the printer.

[19] Fredrick Willemsz Pennock, Amsterdammer, was translator of *De confessie des gheloofs vande Kerke van Schotlandt*, Kn. 4561 (Gedruckt voor Thomas Craffort, 1638). Pennock (Pinnock) was a Separatist who joined the English Reformed Church of Amsterdam in 1621.

[20] Steyns was translator of *Translatie van twee requesten, soo door de edelen van Engelant, als de commissarisen van de jongstledene parlament der Schotten*, Kn. 4667 (Amsterdam, 1640).

[21] BP, I, 291.

[22] BP, I, 299.

[23] William H. Kynaston, *Catalogue of Foreign Books in the Chapter Library of Lincoln Cathedral* (London: Oxford Univ. Press, 1937), pp. 9-10, 12.

Anglican prayer book "excited much attention".[24] What began as a
battle of books in the Netherlands became a battle of arms in Britain.

   Translation broadened the effectiveness of a book. The translator
was, therefore, a significant link in the network of book activities.
With the right touch and devotion, the translator produces "a milde
style, to warme all to a good worke".[25] Johannes Lamotius saw his
translating work as a "gift of paper" to the people.[26] The translator of
Thomas Scott's *Vox Regis* declared his accomplishment as making the
English Scott "to speak Dutch" for the good of the Dutch nation.[27]
Translators were most often people who had first-hand experience
with the two languages. These were Dutchmen who had lived in
England, in many cases, or the reverse, Englishmen living in the
Netherlands or members of one of the English churches. Among the
English, the most active was Henry Hexham, a soldier with the
English troops. He claimed to lack all eloquence, "and bluntnesse
becomes a Souldier best".[28] Nevertheless, he could easily go from
language to language (English, Dutch, and French), and he eventually
produced a Dutch and English dictionary (1647).[29] Hexham rather
depreciated the work of translation; he was only a "pipe or conduit"
of other men's words. Taking his work as a whole, one can see that
he was a creator as much as a "pipe". Through his human "pipes",
words flowed back and forth between Britain and the Netherlands. As

---

[24] William Steven, *The History of the Scottish Church, Rotterdam* (Edinburgh, 1832),
p. 280.

[25] Hugh Broughton, *An Epistle to the Learned Nobilitie of England. Touching Translating the Bible*, STC 3862 (Middelburg, 1597), p. 43. Broughton's main concern was
Bible translation.

[26] Lamotius, dedication to States of Holland, in Dod and Cleaver, *Thien sermoonen*
(The Hague, 1614).

[27] L.G. van Renesse, dedication to magistrats of Utrecht, in Thomas Scott, *Vox
Regis of de stemme des Conincks van Enghelant* (Utrecht, 1624).

[28] Henry Hexham, *A Iovrnall of the Taking in of Venlo*, STC 13263 (Delft, 1633),
dedication.

[29] N.E. Osselton, *The Dumb Linguists: A Study of the Earliest English and Dutch
Dictionaries* (Leiden: Sir Thomas Browne Institute, 1973), chap. 3; Op 't Hof, *Engelse
piet. geschriften*, pp. 417-22. Schoneveld reported on 9 translations into Dutch by
Hexham. He also did translations from French into English. The Huntington Library
has a manuscript translation by Hexham, "A Justification of the course held by the
towns of Dort, Amsterdam, Schiedam..." (Kn. 2504), which was not printed. (MS.HM
41953).

the occasion demanded, or depending on his superior officers, his "pipes" spoke Puritan messages or Laudian ones.[30]

Puritan book printing in the Netherlands was a collaboration of Dutch and British efforts. However it was presented, whether printed and published in English or translated into Dutch, the Puritan book aimed to be an extension of the word preached and the life lived. "Thus we have written, professed and practised."[31] The books spoke words of salvation and comfort, but also, like the trumpets blasting from the tower, confrontation and action. Was there too much controversy and harshness of spirit? The Puritan author referred back to St. Jerome and asked the question: Why are we blamed for taking a stand with our writing? "Is the fault in us or in yourselves that provoke us? Are we not compelled to defend our selues in our just proceedings?"[32] Controversial Puritanism, as well as pious Puritanism, claimed its share of the books. Both were the voices of Puritanism.

---

[30] Sprunger, *Dutch Puritanism*, pp. 158-59.

[31] Francis Johnson, *A Short Treatise*, STC 14663 (n.p., 1611), sig. D3v.

[32] Mr. Sh., *An Answere to a Sermon*, STC 20605 (entered under the name of John Rainolds, n.p., 1609), p. 55.

SELECTED BIBLIOGRAPHY
ENGLISH AND SCOTTISH PURITAN PRINTING IN THE NETHERLANDS 1600-1640

I Manuscripts

Algemeen Rijksarchief, The Hague
  Res. States General 1576-1671 (nos. 3095-3242)
  Res. States of Holland (nos. 11-133)

Amsterdam Gemeente Archief
  Acta Classis Amsterdam (no. 379)
  Acta Kerkeraad Amsterdam (no. 376)
  Acta Synod North Holland (in no. 379)
  Doopsgezinde (Waterlander) Archive (no. 1120)
  English Reformed Church Archive (no. 318)
  Notarial Archives
  Rechterlijk Archive (no. 5061, Confessieboeken and Justitieboeken)

Bodleian Library, Oxford
  Add. MS. C. 69
  Tanner MSS.

British Library, London
  Add. MSS.
  Boswell Papers, Add. MSS. 6394, 6395

Doctor Williams's Library, London
  John Quick, "Icones Sacrae Anglicanae" (MS 38.34,35)

Leiden Gemeente Archief
  Acta Kerkeraad Leiden
  Hugh Goodyear Papers (Weeskamer 1355)
  Notarial Archives
  Oude Rechterlijke Archive (Correctieboeken and Vonnisboeken)
  Register van Kerkelijke Zaken (nos. 2148-2158)
  University Archive (Vol. Inscriptionum)

National Library of Scotland, Edinburgh
    Wodrow MSS.

Public Record Office, London
    SP 14, 16, 84
    Acts of the Privy Council

Rotterdam Gemeente Archief
    Hazewinkel, Rotterdamse boekverkopers (MS. 1686, 1687)
    Notarial Archives

Rotterdam Gemeente Bibliotheek
    Memoire...Thomas Leamer (MS. 519, Rem. Geref. Gemeente)

*

II Primary sources

For more extensive bibliography see Appendixes and items in List of Abbreviations, p. xiii). The books here contain commentary on book printing and distribution.

Bradford, William, "A Dialogue or the Sume of a Conference between Some Younge Men Borne in New England and Sundery Ancient Men that Came out of Holland and Old England Anno dom. 1648", *Publications of the Colonial Society of Massachusetts*, 22 (1920), pp. 115-41.
——, *Of Plymouth Plantation 1620-1647*, Ed. Samuel Eliot Morison, New York: Alfred A. Knopf, 1970.
Broughton, Hugh, *The Works*, Wing B4997, Ed. John Lightfoot, London, 1662.
Calvert, George (Lord Baltimore), *The Answer to Tom-Tell-Troth, The Practise of Princes and the Lamentation of the Kirke*, Wing B611, London, 1642.
Catalogvs Vniversalis, (Collectaneum Catalogorum, catalogues of the Frankfurt book fair), 1603-1638, UB Leiden.
Certaine Arguments and Motives, STC 739, n.p., 1634.
Claesz, Cornelis, *Catalogus librorvm* (5 stock and auction catalogues, 1608-10, Sammelbd. (1), (2), at the Herzog August Bibliothek, Wolfenbüttel).
Clapham, Henoch, *Errour on the Left Hand*, STC 5342, London, 1608.
——, *Errour on the Right Hand*, STC 5341, London, 1608.
F., L., *A Speedy Remedie against Spiritvall Incontinencie*, STC 10649, n.p., 1640.
Fowler, John, *A Shield of Defence*, STC 11212, Amsterdam, 1612.
Foxe, John, *Acts and Monuments*, 9th ed., 3 vols., Wing F2036, London, 1684.
Lawne, Christopher, *Brownisme Turned the In-Side Out-Ward*, STC 15323, London, 1613.

——, *The Prophane Schisme of the Brownists or Separatists*, STC 15324, n.p., 1612.

Lecluse, Jean de, *An Advertisement to Everie Godly Reader of Mr. Thomas Brightman His Book*, STC 15351.7, n.p., 1612.

Lilburne, John, *The Christian Mans Triall*, Wing L2089, 2nd ed., London, 1641.

——, *Come out of Her My People*, STC 15596, n.p., 1639.

——, *A Worke of the Beast*, STC 15599, n.p., 1638.

Paget, John, *An Answer to the Unjust Complaints of William Best*, STC 19097, Amsterdan, 1635.

——, *An Arrow against the Separation of the Brownists*, STC 19098, Amsterdam, 1618.

——, *A Defence of Chvrch-Government*, Wing P166, London, 1641.

Prynne, William, *Canterburies Doome*, Wing P3917, London, 1644.

Scot, Patrick, *Vox Vera*, STC 21863, London, 1625.

Scott, Thomas, *The Workes*, STC 22064, Utrecht, 1624.

Sparke, Michael, *Scintilla, or a Light Broken into Darke Warehouses*, Wing S4818B, London, 1641.

——, *A Second Beacon Fired by Scintilla*, Wing S2259, London, 1652.

T., A., *A Christian Reprofe against Contention*, STC 23605, n.p., 1631.

A Trve, Modest, and Ivst Defence of the Petition for Reformation, STC 6469, n.p., 1618.

Whetenhall, Thomas, *A Discovrse of the Abvses Now in Question in the Chvrches of Christ*, STC 25332, n.p., 1606 (also Leiden ed., 1617, STC 25333).

III Secondary sources

Adams, H.M., *Catalogue of Books Printed on the Continent of Europe, 1501-1600 in Cambridge Libraries*, 2 vols., Cambridge: Cambridge Univ. Press, 1967.

Adams, S.L., "Captain Thomas Gainsford, the 'Vox Spiritus' and the 'Vox Populi'", *Bulletin of the Institute of Historical Research*, 44 (1967), pp. 141-44.

——, "The Protestant Cause: Religious Alliance with the West European Calvinist Communities As a Political Issue in England, 1585-1630", D.Phil. thesis, Oxford University, 1973.

d'Ailly, A.E., (ed.), *Zeven eeuwen Amsterdam*, 7 vols., Amsterdam: N.V. Uitg. My. "Joost van den Vondel", n.d.

Alblas, J.B.H., "Een onbekende Engelse vertaling van W. Teellinck", *Documentatieblad Nadere Reformatie*, 8 (1984), pp. 95-98.

——, *Johannes Boekholt (1656-1693): The First Dutch Publisher of John Bunyan and Other English Authors*, Nieuwkoop: De Graaf Publishers, 1987.

Alphen, G. van, *Catalogus der pamfletten van de Bibliotheek der Rijksuniversiteit te Groningen 1542-1853*, Groningen: Wolters, 1944.

Allison, A.F. and V.F. Goldsmith, *Titles of English Books (and of Foreign Books Printed in England): An Alphabetical Finding List*, 2 vols., Hamden, CT: Archon Books, 1976-77.

Arber, Edward, *The Story of the Pilgrim Fathers, 1606-1623 A.D.*, London: Ward and Downey Limited, 1897.

——, *A Transcript of the Registers of the Company of Stationers of London; 1554-1640 A.D.*, 5 vols., Birmingham, 1875-94.

Baillie, Robert, *The Letters and Journals of Robert Baillie*, 3 vols., Edinburgh: The Bannatyne Club, 1841-42.

Bangs, Jeremy D., *The Auction Catalogue of the Library of Hugh Goodyear: English Reformed Minister at Leiden*, Vol. II of *Catalogi Redivivi*, ed. R. Breugelmans, Utrecht: HES Publishers, 1985.

—— (ed.), *The Pilgrims in the Netherlands: Recent Research*, Leiden: Leiden Pilgrim Documents Center, 1985.

Bennett, H.S., *English Books & Readers 1558 to 1603*, Cambridge: Cambridge Univ. Press, 1965.

——, *English Books & Readers 1603 to 1640*, Cambridge: Cambridge Univ. Press, 1970.

Blagden, Cyprian, *The Stationers Company: A History*, Stanford: Stanford Univ. Press, 1977.

Bodel Nijenhuis, J.T., *De wetgeving op drukpers en boekhandel in de Nederlanden tot in het begin der XIXde eeuw*, Amsterdam: P.N. van Kampen & Zoon, 1892.

Borst, H.M., "Joost Broersz: Biographie (1609-1647) en bibliographie (1634-1647) van een Amsterdamse drukker", doctoraalscriptie, Univ. of Amsterdam, 1988.

Breugelmans, R. (ed.), *The Pilgrim Press...by Rendel Harris & Stephen K. Jones*, partial reprint with new contributions, Nieuwkoop: De Graaf, 1987.

Briels, J.G.C.A., *Zuidnederlandse boekdrukkers en boekverkopers in de Republiek der Verenigde Nederlanden omstreeks 1570-1630*, Nieuwkoop: B. de Graaf, 1974.

Burger, C.P., Jr., "Amsterdamsche boeken op de Frankforter mis 1590-1609", *Het Boek*, 33 (1935-36), pp. 175-94.

——, "Een Metselaar-Latinist", *Het Boek*, 20 (1931), pp. 305-10.

——, "Jan Theunisz", *Het Boek*, 17 (1928), pp. 115-26.

Burgess, Walter H., *John Robinson: Pastor of the Pilgrim Fathers*, London: Williams and Norgate, 1920.

Burrage, Champlin, *The Early English Dissenters in the Light of Recent Research*, 2 vols., Cambridge: Cambridge Univ. Press, 1912.

——, "Was John Canne a Baptist? A Study of Contemporary Evidence", *Transactions of the Baptist Historical Society*, 3 (1913), pp. 212-46.

Bijl, A.P., "Teellinck en de Leidse separatisten rond John Robinson", *Documentatieblad Nadere Reformatie*, 10 (1986), pp. 70-72.

Carlson, Leland H., *Martin Marprelate, Gentleman*, San Marino: The Huntington Library, 1981.

Carlton, Charles, *Archbishop William Laud*, London: Routledge & Kegan Paul, 1987.

Carter, Alice C., *The English Reformed Church in Amsterdam in the Seventeenth Century*, Amsterdam: Scheltema & Holkema NV, 1964.

Carter, Harry, "Archbishop Laud and Scandalous Books from Holland", *Studia bibliographica in honorem Herman de la Fontaine Verwey*, Amsterdam, 1966, pp. 43-55.

—— and George Buday, "Stereotyping by Joseph Athias: The Evidence of Nicholas Kis", *Quaerendo*, 5 (1975), pp. 312-20.

Chrisman, Miriam U., *Lay Culture, Learned Culture: Books and Social Change in Strasbourg 1480-1599*, New Haven: Yale Univ. Press, 1982.

Christianson, Paul, *Reformers and Babylon: English Apocalyptic Visions from the Reformation to the Eve of the Civil War*, Toronto: Univ. of Toronto Press, 1978.

Clair, Colin, *A History of Printing in Britain*, New York: Oxford Univ. Press, 1966.

Cogswell, Thomas, *The Blessed Revolution: English Politics and the Coming of War, 1621-1624*, Cambridge: Cambridge Univ. Press, 1989.

Cole, Robert C. and Michael E. Moody (eds.), *The Dissenting Tradition; Essays for Leland H. Carlson*, Athens: Ohio Univ. Press, 1975.

Cressy, David, *Literacy and the Social Order: Reading and Writing in Tudor and Stuart England*, Cambridge: Cambridge Univ. Press, 1980.

Curtis, Mark H., "William Jones: Puritan Printer and Propagandist", *The Library*, 5th ser., 19 (1964), pp. 38-66.

Dahl, Folke, *Dutch Corantos 1618 1650: A Bibliography*, The Hague: Koninklijke Bibliotheek, 1946.

Davies, David W., *The World of the Elseviers 1580-1712*, The Hague: Martinus Nijhoff, 1954.

Dorsten, J.A. van, *Thomas Basson 1555-1613: English Printer at Leiden*, Leiden: Sir Thomas Browne Institute, 1961.

——, "Thomas Basson (1555-1613), English Printer at Leiden", *Quaerendo*, 15 (1985), pp. 195-224.

Duff, Gordon, "The Early Career of Edward Raban, Afterwards First Printer at Aberdeen", *The Library*, 4th ser., 2 (1922), pp. 238-56.

Eeghen, I.H. van, *De Amsterdamse boekhandel 1680-1725*, 5 vols., Amsterdam: Scheltema & Holkema, 1960-78.

——, "De befaamde drukkerij op de Herengracht over Plantage (1685-1755)", *Amstelodamum Jaarboek*, 58 (1966), pp. 82-100.

Eisenstein, Elizabeth, *The Printing Press As an Agent of Change*, 2 vols., Cambridge: Cambridge Univ. Press, 1982.

Enschedé, Charles, *Typefoundries in the Netherlands from the Fifteenth to the Nineteenth Century. A History Based Mainly on Material in the Collection of Joh. Enschedé en Zonen at Haarlem First Published in French in 1908. An English Translation with Revisions and Notes by Harry Carter with the Assistance of Netty Hoeflake. Edited by Lotte Hellinga*, Haarlem: Stichting Museum Enschede, 1978.

Evenhuis, R.B., *Ook dat was Amsterdam*, 5 vols., Amsterdam: W. Ten Have, 1965-78.

Fincham, Kenneth, *Prelate as Pastor: The Episcopate of James I*, Oxford: Clarendon Press, 1990.

Foster, Stephen, "The Faith of a Separatist Layman: The Authorship, Context, and Significance of *The Cry of a Stone*", *William and Mary Quarterly*, 34 (1977), pp. 375-403.

——, *Notes from the Caroline Underground: Alexander Leighton, the Puritan Triumvirate, and the Laudian Reaction to Nonconformity*, Hamden, CT: Archon Books, 1978.

Fuks, L. and R.G. Fuks-Mansfeld, *Hebrew Typography in the Northern Netherlands 1585-1815: Historical Evaluation and Descriptive Bibliography*, 2 vols., Leiden: E.J. Brill, 1984-87.

Fuks-Mansfeld, R.G., *De Sefardim in Amsterdam tot 1795: Aspecten van een joodse minderheid in een Hollandse stad*, Hilversum: Historische Vereniging Holland, 1989.

Gaskell, Philip, *A New Introduction to Bibliography*, New York: Oxford Univ. Press, 1978.

Gedrukt in Dordrecht: Vier eeuwen boek en prent (catalogus), Dordrecht: Gemeentelijke Archiefdienst, 1976.

Gelder, H.A. Enno van, *Getemperde vrijheid*, Groningen: Wolters-Noordhoff, 1972.

Geller, Lawrence D. and Peter J. Gomes, *The Books of the Pilgrims*, New York: Garland Publishing, Inc., 1975.

Gent, W. van, *Bibliotheek van oude schrijvers*, 2nd ed., Rotterdam: Lindenbergs Boekhandel, 1979.

Gibb, M.A., *John Lilburne, the Leveller*, London: Lindsay Drummond, 1947.

Greenslade, S.L. (ed.), *The West from the Reformation to the Present Day*, Vol. III of *The Cambridge History of the Bible*, Cambridge: Cambridge Univ. Press, 1963.

Greg, W.W. (ed.), *A Companion to Arber: Being a Calendar of Documents in Edward Arber's Transcript*, Oxford: Clarendon Press, 1967.

—— and E. Boswell, *Records of the Stationers' Company 1576 to 1602*, London: Bibliographical Society, 1930.

Grell, Ole P., *Dutch Calvinists in Early Stuart London: The Dutch Church of Austin Friars 1603-1642*, Leiden: Sir Thomas Browne Institute, E.J. Brill, 1989.

Groenendijk, L.F., *De Nadere Reformatie van het gezin: Die visie van Petrus Wittewrongel op de christelijke huishouding*, Dordrecht: Uitgeverij J.P. van den Tol, 1984.

——, "De oorsprong van de uitdrukking 'Nadere Reformatie'", *Documentatieblad Nadere Reformatie*, 9 (1985), pp. 128-34.

Gruys, J.A., and C. de Wolf, *Thesaurus 1473-1800. Nederlandse boekdrukkers en boekverkopers*, Nieuwkoop: De Graaf, 1989.

Haar, J. van der, *From Abbadie to Young: A Bibliography of English, Most Puritan Works, translated i/t Dutch Language*, Veenendaal: Uitgeverij Kool B.V., 1980.

——, *Schatkamer van de Gereformeerde theologie in Nederland (c. 1600-c.1800): Bibliografisch onderzoek*, Veenendaal: Antiquariaat Kool B.V., 1987.

Hamilton, Alastair, *William Bedwell: The Arabist 1563-1632*, Leiden: Sir Thomas Browne Institute, 1985.

Harris Rendel and Stephen Jones, *The Pilgrim Press, a Bibliographical & Historical Memorial*, Cambridge: W. Heffer and Sons, 1922.

Hellinga, Wytze Gs., *Copy and Print in the Netherlands*, Amsterdam: North Holland Publishing Co., 1962.

Henselmans, Jos, "Willem Christiaens: A Leyden Printer with an English Connection", doctoraalscriptie, Leiden Univ., 1983.

Herbert, A.S., *Historical Catalogue of Printed Editions of the English Bible 1525-1961*, London: British & Foreign Bible Society, 1968.

Hirschel, L., "Een godsdienstdisput te Amsterdam in het begin der 17e eeuw", *De Vrijdagavond*, 6 (1929), pp. 178-80.

——, "Jodocus Hondius en Hugh Broughton: Bijdrage tot de kennis der eerste Hebreeuwsche uitgaven in Amsterdam", *Het Boek*, 17 (1928), pp. 199-208.

——, "Uit de voorgeschiedenis der Hebreeuwsche typographie te Amsterdam", *Amstelodamum Jaarboek*, 31 (1934), pp. 65-79.

Hof, W.J. op 't, *Engelse pietistische geschriften in het Nederlands, 1598-1622*, Rotterdam: Lindenberg, 1987.

——, *De visie op de Joden in de Nadere Reformatie tijdens het eerste kwart van de zeventiende eeuw*, Amsterdam: Uitgeverij Ton Bolland, 1984.

Hoftijzer, P.G., *Engelse boekverkopers bij de beurs: De geschiedenis van de Amsterdamse boekhandels Bruyning en Swart, 1637-1724*, Amsterdam/Maarssen: APA-Holland University Press, 1987.

——, "Het Elixir Salutis: Verkoop en bereiding van een Engels medicijn in Amsterdam", *Amstelodamum Maandblad*, 72 (1985), pp. 73-78.

Hurst, Clive, *Catalogue of the Wren Library of Lincoln Cathedral: Books Printed before 1801*, Cambridge: Cambridge Univ. Press, 1982.

Jackson, William A, *Records of the Court of the Stationers' Company 1602 to 1640*, London: Bibliographical Society, 1957.

Johnson, A.F., "The Exiled English Church at Amsterdam and its Press", *The Library*, 5th ser., 5 (1951), pp. 219-42.

——, "J.F. Stam, Amsterdam, and English Bibles", *The Library*, 5th ser., 9 (1954), pp. 185-93.

——, "Willem Christiaans, Leyden, and His English Books", *The Library*, 5th ser., 10 (1955), 121-23.

Jong, C.G.F. de, *John Forbes (ca. 1568-1634)*, Proefschrift Rijksuniversiteit te Groningen, 1987.

——, "John Forbes (c. 1568-1634), Scottish Minister and Exile in the Netherlands", *Nederlands Archief voor Kerkgeschiedenis*, 69 (1989), pp. 17-53.

Juynboll, W.M.C., *Zeventiende-eeuwsche beoefenaars van het Arabisch in Nederland*, Utrecht: Kemink en Zoon, 1931.

Katchen, Aaron L, *Christian Hebraists and Dutch Rabbis: Seventeenth-Century Apologetics and the Study of Maimonides Mishneh Torah*, Cambridge: Harvard Univ, Center for Jewish Studies, 1984.

Katz, David S., *Philo-Semitism and the Readmission of the Jews to England 1603-1655*, Oxford: Clarendon Press, 1982.

——, *Sabbath and Sectarianism in Seventeenth-Century England*, Leiden: E.J. Brill, 1988.

Keblusek, Marika, "Boekverkoper/drukker in ballingschap: Samuel Browne, boekverkoper/drukker te London, 's-Gravenhage en Heidelberg 1633-1665", doctoraalscriptie, Leiden Univ., 1989.

Keuning, J., *Willem Jansz. Blaeu. A Biography and History of His Work as a Cartographer and Publisher*, Amsterdam: Theatrum Orbis Terrarum Ltd, 1973.

Kleerkooper, M.M., and W.P. van Stockum Jr., *De boekhandel te Amsterdam voornamelijk in de 17e eeuw*, 2 vols., 's-Gravenhage: Nijhoff, 1914-16.

Knuttel, W.P.C., *Verboden boeken in de Republiek der Vereenigde Nederlanden*, The Hague: Nijhoff, 1914.

Koeman, Ir. C., *Joan Blaeu and His Grand Atlas*, Amsterdam: Theatrum Orbis Terrarum Ltd, 1970.

Kogel, J.C. van der, "Barent Otsz. 1585-1647 boeckdrucker 1609-1631 t'Amstelredam, inde nieuwe druckery", doctoraalscriptie, Univ. of Amsterdam, 1987.

Kossmann, E.F., *De boekhandel te 's-Gravenhage tot het eind van de 18de eeuw*, The Hague: Nijhoff, 1937.

Kronenberg, M.E. and W.H. Kynaston, "Nederlandsche uitgaven, door Michael Honywood in ons land gekocht (midden 17e eeuw) en thans nog te Lincoln bewaard", *Het Boek*, 21 (1932), pp. 131-48.

Kühler, W.J., *Geschiedenis der Nederlandsche Doopsgezinden*, 3 vols., Haarlem: H.D. Tjeenk Willink & Zoon N.V. 1932-56.

Kynaston, William Herbert, *Catalogue of Foreign Books in the Chapter Library of Lincoln Cathedral*, London: Oxford Univ. Press, 1937.

Laceulle-Van de Kerk, J.J., *De Haarlemse drukkers en boekverkopers van 1540-1600*, The Hague: Nijhoff, 1951.

Lambert, Sheila, "Richard Montagu, Arminianism and Censorship", *Past and Present*, no. 124 (1989), pp. 36-68.

Lieburg, F.A., van, "Pietistische lectuur in de zeventiende en achttiende eeuw", *Documentatieblad Nadere Reformatie*, 13 (1989), pp. 73-87.

Lunsingh Scheurleer, Th.H. and G.H.M. Posthumus Meyjes (eds.), *Leiden University in the Seventeenth Century: An Exchange of Learning*, Leiden: E.J. Brill, 1975.

Lunsingh Scheurleer, Th.H., C. Willemijn Fock, and A.J. van Dissel, *Het Rapenburg: Geschiedenis van een Leidse gracht*, 6 vols., Leiden: Afdeling Geschiedenis van de Kunstnijverheid Rijksuniversiteit Leiden, 1986-92.

McKenzie, D.F., "Milton's Printers: Matthew, Mary and Samuel Simmons", *Milton Quarterly*, 14 (1980), pp. 87-91.

——, *Stationers' Company Apprentices 1605-1640*, Charlottesville: Bibliographical Society of the Univ. of Virginia, 1961.

Meeter, Daniel J., "The Puritan and Presbyterian Versions of the Netherlands Liturgy", *Netherlands Archief voor Kerkgeschiedenis*, 70 (1990), pp. 52-74.

Milward, Peter, *Religious Controversies of the Jacobean Age: A Survey of Printed Sources*, Lincoln: Univ. of Nebraska Press, 1978.

Moes, E.W. and C.P. Burger, *De Amsterdamsche boekdrukkers and uitgevers in de zestiende eeuw*, 4 parts, Amsterdam: C.L. van Langenhuysen, 1900-15.

Moody, Michael E., "The Apostacy of Henry Ainsworth: A Case Study in Early Separatist Historiography", *Proceedings of the American Philosophical Society*, 131 (1987), pp. 15-31.

——, "A Critical Edition of George Johnson's *Discourse of Some Troubles* 1603", Ph. D. Diss., Claremont Graduate School, 1979.

——, "'A Man of a Thousand': The Reputation and Character of Henry Ainsworth, 1569/70-1622", *Huntington Library Quarterly*, 45 (1982), pp. 200-14.

——, "Trials and Travels of a Nonconformist Layman: The Spiritual Odyssey of Stephen Offwood, 1564-ca. 1635", *Church History* (1982), pp. 157-171.

Morgan, John, *Godly Learning: Puritan Attitudes towards Reason, Learning, and Education, 1560-1640*, Cambridge: Cambridge Univ. Press, 1988.

Morison, Stanley, *John Fell: The University Press and the "Fell" Types*, Oxford: Clarendon Press, 1967.

Morrish, P.S., *Dr. Higgs and Merton College Library: A Study in Seventeenth-Century Book-Collecting and Librarianship*, Leeds: Proceedings of the Philosophical and Literary Society, vol. 21, 1988.

Moxon, Joseph, *Mechanick Exercises on the Whole Art of Printing 1683-4*, Ed. Herbert Davis and Harry Carter, 2nd ed., London: Oxford Univ. Press, 1962.

Myers, Robin and Michael Harris, *Aspects of Printing from 1600*, Oxford: Oxford Polytechnic Press, 1987.

Nijenhuis, Willem, *Matthew Slade 1569-1628: Letters to the English Ambassador*, Leiden: Sir Thomas Browne Institute, 1986.

Oastler, C. L., *John Day, the Elizabethan Printer*, Oxford: Oxford Bibliographical Society, 1975.

Osselton, N. E., *The Dumb Linguists: A Study of the Earliest English and Dutch Dictionaries*, Leiden: Sir Thomas Browne Institute, 1973.

Patterson, Annabel, *Censorship and Interpretation: The Conditions of Writing and Reading in Early Modern England*, Madison: Univ. of Wisconsin, 1984.

Plooij, D., *The Pilgrim Fathers from a Dutch Point of View*, New York: New York Univ. Press, 1932.

Rooden, Peter T. van, *Theology, Biblical Scholarship and Rabbinical Studies in the Seventeenth Century: Constantijn L'Empereur (1591-1648) Professor of Hebrew and Theology at Leiden*, Leiden: E.J. Brill, 1989.

Roodenburg, Herman, *Onder censuur: De kerkelijke tucht in de gereformeerde gemeente van Amsterdam, 1578-1700*, Hilversum: Verloren, 1990.

Rostenberg, Leona, *Literary, Political, Scientific, Religious & Legal Publishing, Printing & Bookselling in England, 1551-1700: Twelve Studies*, New York: Burt Franklin, 1965.

——, *The Minority Press & the English Crown: A Study in Repression, 1558-1625*, Nieuwkoop: B. de Graaf, 1971.

Schoneveld, Cornelis W., *Intertraffic of the Mind: Studies in Seventeenth-Century Anglo-Dutch Translation with a Checklist of Books Translated from English into Dutch, 1600-1700*, Leiden: Sir Thomas Browne Institute, 1983.

Seaver, Paul S., *Wallington's World: A Puritan Artisan in Seventeenth-Century London*, Stanford: Stanford Univ. Press, 1985.

Sellin, Paul R., *So Doth, So Is Religion: John Donne and Diplomatic Contexts in the Reformed Netherlands, 1619-1620*, Columbia: Univ. of Missouri Press, 1988.

Selm, Bert van, *Een menighte treffelijcke boeken: Nederlandse boekhandels catalogi in het begin van de zeventiende eeuw*, Utrecht: HES Uitgevers, 1987.

Siebert, Fredrick S., *Freedom of the Press in England 1476-1776: The Rise and Decline of Government Controls*, Urbana: Univ. of Illinois Press, 1952.

Simoni, Anna E.C., *Catalogue of Books from the Low Countries 1601-1621 in the British Library*, London: The British Library, 1990.

Smith, Nigel, *Perfection Proclaimed: Language and Literature in English Radical Religion 1640-1660*, Oxford: Clarendon Press, 1989.

Sprunger, Keith L., *The Auction Catalogue of the Library of William Ames*, Vol. VI of *Catalogi Redivivi*, ed. R. Breugelmans, Utrecht: HES Publishers, 1988.

——, *Dutch Puritanism: A History of English and Scottish Churches of the Netherlands in the Sixteenth and Seventeenth Centuries*, Leiden: E.J. Brill, 1982.

——, *The Learned Doctor William Ames: Dutch Backgrounds of English and American Puritanism*, Urbana: Univ. of Illinois Press, 1972.

——, "William Ames and the Franeker Link to English and American Puritanism", In G.Th. Jensma, F.R.H. Smit, and F. Westra (eds.), *Universiteit te Franeker 1585-1811*, Leeuwarden: Fryske Akademy, 1985.

Steinberg, S.H., *Five Hundred Years of Printing*, 3rd ed., Harmondsworth: Penguin Books, 1979.

Stockum, W.P. van, Jr., *The First Newspapers of England Printed in Holland 1620-1621*, The Hague, 1914.

Stoker, David, "The Norwich Book Trades before 1800", *Transactions of the Cambridge Bibliographical Society*, 8 (1981), pp. 79-125.

Stussy, Susan A., "Michael Sparke, Puritan and Printer", Diss. Univ. of Tennessee, 1983.

Temperley, Nicholas, "Middelburg Psalms", *Studies in Bibliography*, 30 (1977), pp. 162-70.

Trevor-Roper, H.R., *Archbishop Laud 1573-1645*, 2nd ed., London: Macmillan & Co., 1963.

Tyacke, Nicholas, *Anti-Calvinists: The Rise of English Arminianism c. 1590-1640*, Oxford: Clarendon Press, 1987.

Tyson, Gerald P. and Sylvia S. Wagonheim, *Print and Culture in the Renaissance: Essays on the Advent of Printing in Europe*, Newark: Univ. of Delaware Press, 1986.

Van Eerde, Katherine S., "Robert Waldegrave: The Printer as Agent and Link between Sixteenth-Century England and Scotland", *Renaissance Quarterly*, 34 (1981), pp. 40-78.

Vervliet, H.D.L., "Gutenberg or Diderot? Printing as a Factor in World History", *Quaerendo*, 8 (1978), pp. 3-28.

——, *Sixteenth-Century Printing Types of the Low Countries*, Amsterdam: Menno Hertzberger & Co., 1968.

Verwey, H. de la Fontaine, *Uit de wereld van het boek*, 3 vols., Amsterdam: Nico Israel, 1975-79.

Voet, Leon, *The Golden Compasses: A History and Evaluation of the Printing and Publishing Activities of the Officiana Plantiniana at Antwerp*, 2 vols., Amsterdam: Vangendt & Co., 1969.

Voorn, H., *De geschiedenis der Nederlandse papierindustrie*, 2 vols., Haarlem: Stichting voor het onderzoek van de geschiedenis der Ned. papierindustrie, 1960-73.

White, B.R., *The English Separatist Tradition from the Marian Martyrs to the Pilgrim Fathers*, Oxford: Oxford Univ. Press, 1971.

Wijnman, H.F., "De Hebraïcus Jan Theunisz, Barbarossius alias Johannes Antonides als lector in het Arabisch aan de Leidse Universiteit (1612/1613)", *Studia Rosenthaliana*, 2 (1968), pp. 1-29; 149-77.

——, "Jan Theunisz alias Joannes Antonides (1569-1637) boekverkooper en waard in het musiekhuis 'D'Os in de Bruyloft' te Amsterdam", *Amstelodamum Jaarboek*, 25 (1928), pp. 29-123.

——, "Jodocus Hondius en de drukker van de Amsterdamsche Ptolemaeus-uitgave van 1605", *Het Boek*, 28 (1944-46), pp. 1-49.

——, "Moet Jodocus Hondius of Jan Theunisz beschouwd worden als de eerste drukker van Hebreeuwsche boeken te Amsterdam?", *Het Boek*, 17 (1928), pp. 301-13.

Wille, J., *Literair-historische opstellen*, Zwolle: W.E.J. Tjeenk Willink, 1963.

Wilson, J. Dover, "Richard Schilders and the English Puritans", *Transactions of the Bibliographical Society*, 11 (1909-11), pp. 65-134.

Wilson, John F., "Another Look at John Canne", *Church History*, 33 (1964), pp. 34-48.

Woodfield, Denis B., *Surreptitious Printing in England 1550-1640*, New York: Bibliographical Society of America, 1973.

Wulp, J.K. van der, *Catalogus van de tractaten, pamfletten, enz. over de geschiedenis van Nederland, aanwezig in de bibliotheek van Isaac Meulman*, 3 vols., Amsterdam: H. van Munster & Zoon, 1866-68.

CHECKLIST OF BOOKS

These appendixes are a checklist of English language Puritan-related books, plus a few relevant Dutch language books, produced in Amsterdam and Leiden in the years approximately 1600-1640. The books are arranged as follows: Appendix I, Amsterdam printers; Appendix II, Leiden printers; Appendix III, editors and publishers; and Appendix IV, selected anonymous books. Books are attributed to printers and booksellers according to documentary and typographical "evidence". Where other sources are lacking, the *STC* attribution is generally used. Because a large number of these books were published anonymously, a full and definitive list is impossible. The checklist is not definitive, and many problems regarding printers and authors are unresolved. Nevertheless, the list will help to indicate current scholarship on the topic and will give information about the size and scope of Puritan printing done by various printers. I have examined many of the books personally at the libraries. Where that was not possible, I used the University Microfilms series of "Early English Books, 1475-1640" or other microfilm copies.

Within each appendix and sub-category, books are listed chronologically, and within years, according to STC numbers. Notes appear after most entries. Under "Literature" (Lit.), I listed some of the printed sources of information. Under "Comment", I have added notes of my own.

I made special use of the following sources for the "Literature" notes: *STC*, Wing, Simoni, Knuttel, Sayle, Hoftijzer, and articles by Johnson; for full bibliographical data on these, see the abbreviations sections at the front of the book. For other short bibliographical references (Foster, Moody, Wilson, Carter, Schoneveld, etc.), see the bibliography section.

AMSTERDAM PRINTERS AND BOOKSELLERS

A Giles Thorp (Amsterdam 1604-22)

Thorp's imprints appear in 10 books: STC 209, 228, 235, 2407, 5450, 12857.8, 12858, 18553, Sanford, *De descensv*, and Ainsworth, *La Communion des saincts*.

1604-1610

Ainsworth, Henry and Francis Johnson, *An apologie or Defence of Such True Christians*, n.p., 1604, STC 238.
>   Lit.: Johnson, 1951; Simoni, A41; *STC*. Comment: STC 239 seems to be from a different press.

Barrow, Henry, *A True Description out of the Word of God*, n.p., n.d., STC 1527.
>   Lit.: *STC*. Comment: Text dated 1589; printed about 1604. According to Henoch Clapham, *Error on the Right Hand*, pp. 10-12, this 2nd ed. was printed at Amsterdam after 1589.

Broughton, Hugh, *Declaration of General Corruption of Religion*, n.p., 1604, STC 3856.5.
>   Lit.: *STC* with a ?, regarding printer; Simoni, B285.

Broughton, Hugh and Henry Ainsworth, *Certayne Questions*, n.p., 1605, STC 3848.
>   Lit.: *STC* with a ?; Simoni, B282; Johnson, 1951. Comment: Published by F.B., i.e. Francis Blackwell.

Barrow, Henry, *A Plaine Refvtation of M. Giffards Booke*, n.p., n.d., STC 1524.
>   Comment: Advertisement is dated 1605. According to Bradford's "Dialogue", it was published at Amsterdam by Francis Johnson.

Johnson, Francis, *An Inqvirie and Answer of Thomas White*, n.p., 1606, STC 14662.
>   Lit.: *STC* with a ?; Johnson, 1951.

Broughton, Hugh, *Two Epistles unto Great Men of Britanie*, n.p., 1606, STC 3891.
>   Lit.: *STC* with a ?; Simoni B299.

Ainsworth, Henry, *The Commvnion of Saincts*, Imprinted at Amsterdam by Giles Thorp, 1607, STC 228.
>   Lit.: Johnson, 1951; *STC*; Simoni A44.

Netherlands, *The Confession of Faith of Certayn English People*, Living in Exile, in the Low Countreyes, n.p., 1607, STC 18435.
> Lit.: Johnson, 1951; *STC*; Simoni C152.

Confessio fidei Anglorum, n.p., n.d.
> Lit.: Johnson, 1951, *STC*; Simoni C153; Shaaber E186, E187. Comment: Publ. 1607; trans. of STC 18433.7, 18434. It was available for sale from Cornelis Claesz.

Ainsworth, Henry, *Counterpoyson*, n.p., 1608, STC 234.
> Lit.: Johnson, 1951; Simoni A47.

Johnson, Francis, *Certayne Reasons and Arguments*, n.p., 1608, STC 14660.
> Lit.: Johnson, 1951; *STC*; Simoni J77.

Niclas, Hendrik; *An Epistle sent vnto Two Daughters of Warwick from H.N.*, ed. by H. Ainsworth, Imprinted at Amsterdam by Giles Thorp, 1608, STC 18553.
> Lit.: Johnson, 1951; *STC*; Simoni N195.

Broughton, Hugh, *A Petition to the Lords to Examine the Religion*, n.p., 1608, STC 3878.
> Lit.: *STC* with a ?.

Ainsworth, Henry, *A Defence of the Holy Scriptures*, Imprinted at Amsterdam by Giles Thorp, 1609, STC 235.
> Lit.: Johnson, 1951; *STC*; Simoni B48.

Broughton, Hugh, *Principal Positions for Groundes of the Holy Bible*, n.p., 1609, STC 3879.5.
> Lit.: *STC*.

Johnson, Francis, *A Brief Treatise against Two Errours of the Anabaptists*, n.p., 1609, STC 14659.
> Lit.: Johnson, 1951; *STC* with a ?.

Rainolds, John (?), *An Answere to a Sermon Preached the 17 of April Anno D. 1608, by George Downame*, n.p., 1609, STC 20605.
> Lit.: Johnson, 1951; *STC*; Simoni A104. Comment: Not by Rainolds but by "Mr. Sh.". See notes for STC 20620, 1613. Pt. 2 of book by Thorp; Pt. 1 perhaps by J. Hondius.

Ainsworth, Henry, *An Arrow against Idolatrie*, n.p. 1610, STC 220.5.
> Lit.: Johnson, 1951; *STC*.

Broughton, Hugh, *Job. To the King*, n.p., 1610, STC 3868.
> Lit.: Johnson, 1951; *STC*; Simoni B143.

Broughton, Hugh, *A Revelation of the Apocalyps*, n.p., 1610, STC 3883.
> Lit.: Johnson, 1951; *STC*; Simoni B298.

Clyfton, Richard, *A Plea for Infants*, printed at Amsterdam by Gyles Thorp, 1610, STC 5450.
> Lit.: Johnson, 1951; *STC*; Simoni C130.

Robinson, John, *A Ivstification of Separation*, n.p., 1610, STC 21109.
  Lit.: Johnson, 1951; *STC*; Simoni R74. Comment: Fowler, *Shield of Defence*, p. 8, states that Thorp had a hand in printing the book.
Carpenter, John and Francis Johnson, *Quaestio de duabus epistolis*. Prostat apud viduam Levini Hulsij, Francofurti, 1610.
  Lit.: Johnson, 1951; Shaaber C126; Simoni C33. Comment: Sold by H. Laurensz in Frankfurt fair catalogue, autumn 1610.

1611-1615

Ainsworth, Henry, *An Arrow against Idolatrie*, n.p., 1611, STC 221.
  Lit.: Johnson, 1951; *STC*; Simoni A43.
Broughton, Hugh, *A Petition to the King*, n.p., 1611, STC 3876.
  Lit.: Johnson, 1951; *STC*; Simoni B292.
A Record of Some Worthy Proceedings; in the Howse of Commons, n.p., 1611, STC 7751.
  Lit.: *STC* with a ?. Comment: Another ed., STC 7751.2, also likely by Thorp.
Penry, John, *Mr. John Penry, His Apologie*, n.p., 1611, STC 19608.5.
  Lit.: *STC*.
Sanford, Hugh, *De descensv domini nostri Iesv Christi ad inferos. Libri quatvor*, Amstelrodami: In aedibus Aegidij Thorpij, 1611.
  Lit.: Johnson, 1951; Shaaber S31; Simoni S31. Comment: The book was completed by Robert Parker; in the autumn 1612 Frankfurt catalogue it had the imprint of H. Laurensz.
Ainsworth, Henry, *The Book of Psalmes: Englished Both in Prose and Metre*, Imprinted at Amsterdam by Giles Thorp, 1612, STC 2407.
  Lit.: Johnson, 1951; *STC*; Simoni B148.
Clyfton, Richard, *An Advertisement concerning a Book*, n.p., 1612, STC 5449.
  Lit.: *STC*.
Lescluse (Ecluse), Jean de, *An Advertisement to Everie Godly Reader of Mr. Thomas Brightman His book*, n.p., 1612, STC 15351.7.
  Lit.: Johnson, 1951; *STC*. Comment: Epistle is signed Iean de Lescluse.
Ainsworth, Henry, *An Animadversion to Mr. Richard Clyftons Advertisement*, Imprinted at Amsterdam by Giles Thorp, 1613, STC 209.
  Lit.: Johnson, 1951; *STC*; Simoni A38.
Harrison, John, *The Messiah Alreadie Come*, Amsterdam: Imprinted by Giles Thorp, 1613, STC 12857.8.
  Lit.: *STC*.
Rainolds, John (?), *A Replye Answering a Defence of the Sermon*, n.p., 1613, STC 20620.
  Lit.: *STC*; Johnson, 1951, Simoni R31. Comment: On the authorship by "Mr. Sh.", rather than Rainolds, and the printing at Amsterdam, see Paget, *Defence*, "Publisher to the Christian Reader". The book is a follow-up to no. 20605. Part 2 is dated 1614.

1614: no books surviving, except for part 2 of no. 20620.

Ainsworth, Henry, *The Commvnion of Saincts*, n.p., 1615, STC 229.
  Lit.: Johnson, 1951; *STC*; Simoni A45.

Ainsworth, John and Henry Ainsworth, *The Trying ovt of the Truth*, pub. by E.P., n.p., 1615, STC 240.
  Lit.: Johnson, 1951; *STC*; Simoni A50.

Robinson, John, *A Manvmission to a Manvdvction*, n.p., 1615, STC 21111.
  Lit.: Johnson, 1951; *STC*. Simoni R75.

1616-1620

Ainsworth, Henry, *Annotations upon Genesis*, n.p., 1616, STC 210.
  Lit.: Johnson, 1951; *STC*; Simoni A39.

A Collection of Sundry Matters, n.p., 1616, STC 5556.
  Lit.: Johnson, 1951; *STC*.

Jacob, Henry, *Anno domini 1616. A Confession and Protestation of the Faith of Certaine Christians*, n.p., n.d., STC 14330.
  Lit.: Johnson, 1951; *STC*; Simoni J26.

Ainsworth, Henry, *Annotations upon Exodvs*, n.p., 1617, STC 212.
  Lit.: Johnson, 1951; *STC*; Simoni A39.

Ainsworth, Henry, *Annotations upon the Book of Psalmes*, 2nd ed., n.p., 1617, STC 2411.
  Lit.: Johnson, 1951; *STC*; Simoni B149.

Ainsworth, Henry, *Annotations upon Leviticvs*, n.p., 1618, STC 214.
  Lit.: Johnson, 1951; *STC*; Simoni A39.

Ainsworth, Henry, *La communion des saincts*, trans into French by Jean de Lescluse, n.p., n.d.
  Lit.: Johnson, 1951. Comment: Appeared in 1618; listed in autumn 1618 Frankfurt catalogue with imprint of Giles Thorp. There was an earlier advertisement by Cornelis Claesz in his catalogue of French books, 1608, but no copies are known.

Ainsworth, Henry, *Annotations upon Numbers*, n.p., 1619, STC 215.
  Lit.: Johnson, 1951; *STC*; Simoni A39.

Ainsworth, Henry, *Annotations upon Devteronomie*, n.p., 1619, STC 216.
  Lit.: Johnson, 1951; *STC*; Simoni A39.

Harrison, John, *The Messiah Already Come*, Amsterdam: Imprinted by Giles Thorp, 1619, STC 12858.
  Lit.: Johnson, 1951; *STC*; Simoni H22. Comment: *STC* describes as anr. issue of 1613 ed. with prelim. pages done in London.

Staresmore, Sabine, *The Vnlawfulnes of Reading in Prayer*, n.p., 1619, STC 23235.
  Lit. Johnson, 1951; *STC*.

Wilkinson, John, *An Exposition of the 13. Chapter of the Revelation of Iesus Christ*, n.p., 1619, STC 25647.
  Lit.: Johnson, 1951; *STC*.

Ainsworth, Henry, *A Reply to a Pretended Christian Plea*, n.p., 1620, STC 236.
  Lit.: Johnson, 1951; *STC*; Simoni A49.
Calderwood, David, *A Defence of Our Arguments against Kneeling*, n.p., 1620,
  STC 4354.
  Lit.: Johnson, 1951; *STC*.
Calderwood, David, *A Dialogve betwixt Cosmophilus and Theophilus*, n.p., 1620,
  STC 4355.
  Lit.: Johnson, 1951; *STC*. Comment: According to Scot, *Vox Vera*,
  1625, the book was widely on sale at Amsterdam.
Calderwood, David, *The Speach of the Kirk of Scotland*, n.p., 1620, STC 4365.
  Lit.: Johnson, 1951; *STC*; Simoni C12. Comment: See Scot, *Vox Vera*,
  p. 3.

1621-1622
Ainsworth, Henry, *Annotations upon Genesis*, n.p., 1621, STC 211.
  Lit.: Johnson, 1951; *STC*; Simoni A40.
Baynes, Paul, *The Diocesans Tryall*, n.p., 1621, STC 1640.
  Lit.: Johnson, 1951; *STC*. Comment: According to a later ed., Wing
  B1546, it was "published" by William Ames, who also wrote the pref-
  ace.
Calderwood, David, *The Altar of Damascus*, n.p., 1621, STC 4352.
  Lit.: Johnson, 1951; *STC*. Comment: See Scot, *Vox Vera*, p. 3.
Calderwood, David, *Quaeries concerning the State of the Church of Scotland*, n.p.,
  1621, STC 4361.5.
  Lit.: *STC*.
Proctor, Thomas, *The Right of Kings*, n.p., 1621, STC 20410.
  Lit.: Johnson, 1951; *STC*.
Proctor, Thomas, *The Righteous Mans Way*, n.p., 1621, STC 20411.
  Lit.: Johnson, 1951; *STC*.
Scotland, Church of, *The First and Second Booke of Discipline*, n.p., 1621, STC
  22015.
  Lit.: Johnson, 1951; *STC*; Simoni S92.
Ames, William, *A Reply to Dr. Mortons Generall Defence*, n.p., 1622, STC 559.
  Lit.: Johnson, 1951; *STC*.
Calderwood, David, *Scoti paraclesis*, n.p., 1622.
  Lit.: Johnson, 1951; Shaaber C12.
Scot, William, *The Course of Conformitie*, n.p., 1622, STC 21874.
  Lit.: Johnson, 1951; *STC*. Comment: See Scot, *Vox Vera*, pp. 3, 10.

B Richard Plater (Successors of Thorp)

Bachiler, Samuel, *Miles Christianvs, or the Campe Royal*, Amsterdam: Printed by R. P., 1625, STC 1106.
  Lit.: Johnson, 1951; *STC*.
Forbes, John, *A Frvitfvll Sermon*, Amsterdam: Printed by Richard Plater, 1626, STC 11130.
  Lit.: Johnson, 1951; *STC*.
Een generael en waerachtigh verhael, trans. from French into Dutch, Amsterdam: Ghedruckt by Richard Plater, n.d., Kn. 3732.
  Lit.: Kn.; Johnson, 1951. Comment: c. 1627; The original French tract was dated Nov. 1627.
Ainsworth, Henry, *The Communion of Saincts*, Amsterdam: Printed by Richard Plater, dwelling by the Long Bridge, 1628, STC 231.5.
  Lit.: Johnson, 1951; *STC*; Simoni A46. Comment: Nos. 230 (misdated 1618) and 231 also by Plater.
Bachiler, Samuel, *The Campe Royal*, Amsterdam: Printed by R.P., 1629, STC 1106.5.
  Lit.: Johnson, 1951; *STC*. Comment: There is a strong likelihood that most English books printed at Amsterdam between 1625-29 were the work of Plater.

C Sabine Staresmore (Successors of Thorp)

Staresmore, Sabine, *The Loving Tender* (the 16 Questions), 1623.
  Comment: No copies known; see A.T., *Christian Reprofe*, p. 3.
Ainsworth, Henry, *Certain Notes of M. Henry Ainsworth His Last Sermon*, n.p., 1630, STC 227.
  Lit.: *STC*; A.T., *Christian Reprofe*, p. 3; Johnson, 1951.
Ames, William, *A Fresh Svit against Human Cermonies in God's Worship*, n.p., 1633, STC 555.
  Lit.: Johnson, 1951; *STC*, which states that it is the work of more than one press. Comment: Sir William Boswell identified Staresmore in SP 16/246/56.
Davenport, John, *A Ivst Complaint against an vnivst Doer*, n.p., 1634, STC 6311.
  Lit.: *STC*; Paget, *Answer*, preface.

D Richard Raven (Successors of Thorp)

Speed, Joshua, *Loves Revenge*, Amsterdam: Printed by Richard Raven, 1631, STC 23050.
  Lit.: *STC*.

E   Other (Anonymous) Successors of Thorp

These books cover the period 1623-35. Many may have been done by Plater or Staresmore, but they lack imprint or other specific evidence. Johnson, 1951, first used the phrase "Thorp's Successors".

1623-1625

Ainsworth, Henry, *A Censvre upon a Dialogve of the Anabaptists*, n.p., 1623, STC 226.
   Lit.: Johnson, 1951; *STC*.

Ainsworth, Henry, *Solomons Song of Songs. In English Metre*, n.p., 1623, STC 2775.
   Lit.: Johnson, 1951; *STC*.

Ames, William, *A Reply to Dr. Mortons Particvlar Defence*, n.p., 1623, STC 560.
   Lit.: Johnson, 1951; *STC*.

Calderwood, David, *Altare Damascenvm*, n.p., 1623, STC 4353.
   Lit.: Johnson, 1951; Shaaber C10; Scot, *Vox Vera*, p. 4.

Ainsworth, Henry, *An Arrow against Idolatrie*, n.p., 1624, STC 222.
   Lit.: Johnson, 1951; *STC*.

Calderwood, David, *A Dispvte vpon Communicating*, n.p., 1624, STC 4356.
   Lit.: Johnson, 1951; *STC*.

Calderwood, David, *An Epistle of a Christian Brother*, n.p., 1624, STC 4357.
   Lit.: Johnson, 1951; *STC*.

Calderwood, David, *An Exhortation of the Particular Kirks of Christ in Scotland*, n.p., 1624, STC 4358.
   Lit.: Johnson, 1951; *STC*.

Certaine Advertisements for the Good of the Chvrch and Common-wealth, n.p., n.d., STC 10404.
   Lit.: Johnson, 1951; *STC*. Comment: c. 1624 or a little later.

Hitching, John, *The Church Estate from the Worlds Creation*, n.p., 1624, STC 13531.5.
   Lit.: *STC*.

Leighton, Alexander, *Speculum Belli Sacri: Or the Lookingglasse of the Holy War*, n.p., 1624, STC 15432.
   Lit.: Johnson, 1951; *STC*; Scot, *Vox Vera*, p.4.

Leighton, Alexander, *A Friendly Tryall of Some Passages*, n.p., 1624, STC 15431.
   Lit.: Johnson, 1951; *STC*.

Offwood, Stephen, *An Adioynder of Svndry Other Particvlar Wicked Plots*, n.p., 1624, STC 18757.
   Lit.: *STC*. Comment: A part of STC 18837 but with its own title page; also separately printed as STC 18756.

Offwood, Stephen, ed., *An Oration or Speech Appropriated vnto the Most Mightie and Illustrious Princes of Christendom*, n.p., 1624, STC 18837.
Lit.: Johnson, 1951; *STC*; Kn. 954; Kn. 1490. Comment: A trans. by Thomas Wood of a book by W. Verheiden.

Robinson, John, *An Appeale on Truths Behalf*, n.p., 1624, STC 21107.
Lit.: Johnson, 1951; *STC*. Comment: No title page; it is a letter dated Sept. 18, 1624, but actually a part of STC 227 from 1630.

Robinson, John, *A Defence of the Doctrine Propovnded by the Synode at Dort*, n.p., 1624, STC 21107a.
Lit.: Johnson, 1951; *STC*.

Bate, Randal, *Certain Observations*, n.p., n.d., STC 1580.
Lit.: Johnson, 1951; *STC*. Comment: No title page.

James I, *An Humble Petition to the Kings Most Excellent Majestie*, n.p., n.d., STC 14425.
Lit.: Johnson, 1951; *STC*. Comment: No title page; about 1625.

Leighton, Alexander, *A Short Treatise against Stage-Playes*, n.p., 1625, STC 15431.5.
Lit.: Johnson, 1951; *STC*.

Philadelphos, Theophilos, *Ad reverendissimos patres*, n.p., 1625, STC 19829.
Lit.: Johnson, 1951; *STC*.

Robinson, John, *A Iust and Necessarie Apologie of Certain Christians*, n.p., 1625, STC 21108.
Lit.: Johnson, 1951; *STC*.

Robinson, John, *Observations Divine and Morall*, n.p., 1625, STC 21112.
Lit.: Johnson, 1951; *STC*.

S., G., *Sacrae Heptades, or Seaven Problems concerning Antichrist*, n.p., 1625, STC 21492.
Lit.: Johnson, 1951; *STC*.

Tuke, Thomas, *Concerning the Holy Evcharist*, n.p., 1625, STC 24305.
Lit.: *STC*. Comment: Another ed, 1636, STC 24306, also apparently from Amsterdam.

1626-1630

R., I., *The Spy*, Printed at Strasburgh, 1628, STC 20577.
Lit.: Johnson, 1951; *STC*.

Robinson, John, *New Essayes or Observations Divine and Morall*, n.p., 1628, STC 21112a.
Lit.: Johnson, 1951; *STC*, which states it is a reissue with opening pages reprinted elsewhere. Comment: See STC 21113, a reissue dated 1629.

Leighton, Alexander, *An Appeal to the Parliament; or Sions Plea*, n.p., n.d., STC 15428.5.
Lit.: Johnson, 1951; *STC*. Comment: About 1629.

Burton, Henry, *A Reply of Henry Burton*, n.p., 1629, STC 4153.7.
    Lit.: *STC*.
Ar., A. (publisher), *The Practice of Princes*, n.p., 1630, STC 722.
    Lit.: Johnson, 1951; *STC*.
Casaubon, Isaac, *The Originall of Popish Idolatrie, or the Birth of Heresies*, Pub.
    by Stephen Offwood, n.p., 1630, STC 4748.
    Lit.: Johnson, 1951; *STC*. Comment: Not actually written by Casaubon
    and repudiated by his family.
Peters, Hugh, *Milk for Babes, and Meat for Men*, n.p., 1630, STC 19798.5.
    Lit.: *STC*.

1631-1635
Forbes, John (captain), *A Letter Sent to His Reverend Father Mr. Iohn Forbes*,
    n.p., n.d., STC 11128.5.
    Lit.: *STC*. Comment: Deals with a battle of Sept. 7, 1631.
Puckle, Stephen, *A Trve Table of All Such Fees*, n.p., 1631, STC 20484.
    Lit.: *STC*.
T., A., *A Christian Reprofe against Contention*, n.p., 1631, STC 23605.
    Lit.: Johnson, 1951; *STC*.
Twisse, William, *A Discovery of D. Iacksons Vanitie*, n.p., 1631, STC 24402.
    Lit.: Johnson, 1951; *STC*.
Twisse, William, *The Doctrine of the Synod of Dort and Arles*, n.p., n.d., STC
    24403.
    Lit.: Johnson, 1951, which dates it at about 1631; *STC*.
Ainsworth, Henry, *The Booke of Psalmes in English Metre*, n.p., 1632, STC
    2734.5.
    Lit.: *STC*; Johnson, 1951. Comment: It makes the first use of the "Right
    Right" device, later used by Canne's Richt Right Press.
Canne, John, *The Right Way to Peace: or Good Covnsell for It*, Amsterdam,
    1632, STC 4574.5.
    Lit.: *STC*.
Henric, James, *The Curtaine of Chvrch-Power*, n.p. 1632, STC 13071.
    Lit.: *STC*.
Offwood, Stephen, *An Advertisement to Ihon Deleclvse, and Henry May the
    Elder*, n.p., date uncertain, STC 18789.
    Lit.: *STC*; Moody, "Stephen Offwood". Comment: 1632 or 1633.
Canne, John, *A Necessitie of Separation from the Church of England*, n.p., 1634,
    STC 4574.
    Lit.: Johnson, 1951; *STC*. Comment: Canne was convicted in 1638 of
    having "made" and "caused" the book "to be printed", but not of per-
    sonally doing the printing; SP 84/154/151.
Emanuel, Don, *A Declaration of the Reasons*, n.p. 1634, STC 7678.
    Lit.: Johnson, 1951; *STC*.

The Opinion, Judgement, and Determination of Two Reverend, Learned, and Conformable Divines Concerning Bowing at the Name, or Naming of Jesus, Printed at Hambourgh, 1632, Reprinted 1634, STC 14555.
   Lit.: *STC.*

Robinson, John, *A Treatise of the Lawfvlnes of Hearing, of the Ministers in the church of England,* n.p., 1634, STC 21116.
   Lit.: *STC;* L.F., *Speedy Remedie,* pp. 3-5. Comment: May be the work of Staresmore; see Foster, "Faith of a Separatist Layman", pp. 380-81.

Brightman, Thomas, *A Most Confortable Exposition of the Prophecie of Daniel,* n.p., 1635, STC 3753.
   Lit.: *STC.*

Cotton, Clement, *A Complete Condordance to the Bible,* n.p., 1635, STC 5846.4.
   Lit.: *STC.*

Forbes, John, *Fovr Sermons,* published by Stephen Offwood, n.p., 1635, STC 11129.
   Lit.: Johnson, 1951; *STC.*

Robinson, John, *An Appendix to Mr. Perkins,* n.p., 1635, STC 21107.5.
   Lit.: *STC.* Comment: Also another ed., no. 21107.7, 1636.

F John Canne and the Richt Right Press

This press was active from 1637 into the 1640s. Its most distinctive typographical marks are a title page device with the words "Richt Right" (earlier "Right Right") and a headpiece with the motto "Cor unum via una". The "Cor unum" headpiece was not absolutely unique to Canne, similar ones being used in England; see, for example, STC 4235. However, I am not aware of its being used in the Netherlands for English printing by anyone other than Canne. The "Right Right" device was first used in a book of 1632 (STC 2734.5) before Canne personally took up printing. On Canne's printing, also see John F. Wilson, "Annother Look at John Canne", *Church History,* 33 (1964), pp. 34-48.

1637

Gillespie, George, *A Dispvte against the English-Popish Ceremonies Obtrvded vpon the Chvrch of Scotland,* n.p., 1637, STC 11896.
   Lit.: *STC.* Comment: Canne collaborated with Christiaensz of Leiden on this book; SP 84/153/271; SP 84/154/153.

Prynne, William, *A Quench-Coale,* n.p., 1637, STC 20474.
   Lit.: *STC;* Sayle 6365. Comment: See Simmons, SP 16/387/79.

Hooker, Thomas, *The Poore Doubting Christian,* 4th ed., Amsterdam, for T. L., 1637, STC 13726.4.
   Lit.: *STC.* Comment: See SP 16/387/79.

1638

During 1638, the "Right Right" device was damaged or altered. Thereafter, it read "Richt Right".

Bastwick, John, *A Breife Relation of Certaine Speciall, and Most Materiall Passages, and Speeches in the Starre-Chamber*, n.p., 1638, STC 1570.5.

Lit.: *STC*. Comment: See Canne's court conviction, SP 84/153/271.

Hooker, Thomas, *The Sovles Hvmiliation*, Amsterdam, Printed for T.L., 1638, STC 13728.5.

Lit.: *STC*. Comment: See Simmons, SP 16/387/79.

Laud, William, *Divine and Politicke Observations Newly Translated Out of the Dutch Language*, n.p., 1638, STC 15309.

Lit.: *STC*; Sayle 6368.

A Light for the Ignorant, n.p., 1638, STC 15591.

Lit.: *STC*; Sayle 6369. Comment: Le Maire in SP 84/155/32.

Lilburne, John, *A Worke of the Beast*, n.p., 1638, STC 15599.

Lit.: Kn. 4560; *STC*; Sayle 6370. Comment: See Le Maire in SP 84/154/256.

Preston, John, *The Doctrine of the Saints Infirmities*, Amsterdam, Printed for T.L., n.d., STC 20221.3.

Lit.: *STC*. Comment: c. 1638.

Newes from Scotland, n.d., n.p., STC 22013.

Lit.: *STC*. Comment: No title page; Canne was charged in court in 1638 for printing this book, SP 84/153/271.

Scotland, Church of, *The Confession of Faith of the Kirk of Scotland*, n.p., 1638, STC 22026.6.

Lit.: *STC*; Sayle 6367. Comment: Another ed., no. 22026.8, apparently also by the same press.

Scotland, Church of, *The Beast is Wovnded*, n.d., n.p., STC 22032.

Lit.: *STC*; Sayle 6366. Comment: Le Maire in SP 84/154/25; printed in 1638.

Sibbes, Richard, *A Fountain Sealed*, Amsterdam, 1638, STC 22496.5.

Lit.: *STC*. Comment: Simmons in SP 16/387/79.

Walker, George, *The Doctrine of the Sabbath*, Amsterdam, 1638, STC 24957.

Lit.: *STC*; Sayle 6371.

Wickins, Nathaniel, *Woodstreet-Compters-Plea, for its Prisoner*, n.p., 1638, STC 25587.

Lit.: *STC*. Comment: Le Maire in SP 84/154/256.

A Guide unto Sion, Amstelredam, 1638, STC 26125.

Lit.: *STC*. Comment: Simmons in SP 16/387/79.

In addition to the above items for 1637-38, Matthew Simmons reported that Canne had printed other books in this period; he referred to books by Dr.

John Preston (*The New Covenant* and *The Saints Spiritual Strength*), *The Coal from the Altar*, presumably by Samuel Ward, and "2 greatbookes on and against the altar".

1639

Canne, John, *A Stay against Straying*, n.p., 1639, STC 4575.
    Lit.: *STC*. Comment: Le Maire in SP 84/155/32.
Dury (Durie), John, *Motives to Induce the Protestant Princes*, n.p., 1639, STC 7367.5.
    Lit.: *STC*.
Goodwin, Thomas, *Aggravation of Sinne and Sinning*, Amsterdam: Printed for the benefit of the English Churches in the Netherlands, 1639, STC 12035.
    Lit.: *STC*.
Lilburne, John, *Come Out of Her My People*, n.p., 1639, STC 15596.
    Lit.: *STC*.
Lilburne, John, *The Poore Mans Cry*, n.p., 1639, STC 15598.
    Lit.: *STC*.
The Repayring of the Breach, n.p., 1639, STC 20889.3.
    Lit.: *STC*. Comment: Written by John Dury.
Robinson, John, *A Ivstification of Separation*, n.p., 1639, STC 21110.
    Lit.: *STC*; Sayle 6372. Comment: According to Simmons in his report of 1637-38, "2 merchants of Rotterdam" were in charge of the book, SP 16/387/79.
Vertves Reward wherein the Living Are Incouraged unto Good Workes, n.p., 1639, STC 24844a.3.
    Lit.: *STC*. Comment: By John Dury.
Walker, George, *The Doctrine of the Sabbath*, Amsterdam, 1639, STC 24958.
    Lit.: *STC*.
A Wel-wisher. Wherein Is Briefly Shewed, a Ready Way and Meanes To Procure the Publike Good, n.p., 1639, STC 25229.5.
    Lit.: *STC*. Comment: By John Dury.
A Guide unto Sion, 2nd. ed. Amsterdam, 1639. STC 26125.5.
    Lit.: *STC*.

Books on Scotland (1639)

Copye van eenen brief, ghesonden door seeckere hooghe graven ende heeren van Schotland, Edindburgh: Gedruckt by James Bryson, 1639, STC 21904.7.
    Lit.: Kn. 4607; *STC*. Comment: Fictitious title page.
The Remonstrance of the Nobility, Barrons, Burgesses, Ministers and Commons, of Scotland, Edinburgh: Imprinted by James Bryson, 1639, STC 21908.
    Lit.: *STC*. Comment: Fictitious title page.
Remonstrantie vande edelen, baronnen, staten, kercken-dienaers, ende gemeente van Schotlandt, Edinburgh: Gedruckt by James Bryson, 1639, STC 21908.5.

Lit.: Kn. 4604; *STC*. Comment: Fictitious title page; Le Maire in SP 84/155/119; a trans. of STC 21908.

Een cort verhael van de misdaden en crimen die de Schotse bisschoppen te laste gheleyt werden, Edinburgh: Gedruckt by James Bryson, 1639, STC 22057.
  Lit.: Kn. 4601; *STC*. Comment: Fictitious title page.

Informatie, aen alle oprechte christenen in Engelandt, na de copye gedruckt tot Edinburgh, in Februarij, 1639, Kn. 4600.
  Lit.: *STC*, trans. of no. 21905; Kn.

1640

Ainsworth, Henry, *An Arrow against Idolatrie*, n.p., 1640, STC 222.5.
  Lit.: *STC*.

Ainsworth, Henry, *The Commvnion of Saincts*, Amsterdam, 1640, STC 232.
  Lit.: *STC*.

Baillie, Robert, *Ladensium*, n.p., 1640, STC 1206.
  Lit.: *STC*; Sayle 6373.

Franck, Sabastian, *The Forbidden Fruit*, n.p., 1640, STC 11324.
  Lit.: *STC*. Comment: Author listed as August. Eluthenius.

Greenwood, John, *More Worke for Priests*, n.p., 1640, STC 12341.
  Lit.: *STC*.

The Confession of Faith of Certaine English People, Living in Exile, in the Low Countries, n.p., 1640, STC 18436.
  Lit.: *STC*.

Scotland, *Vertoog van de wettelyckheyt van onsen tocht in Engelant*, na de copye, gedruckt tot Edinburgh by Robbert Brison, 1640, STC 21925.
  Lit.: Kn. 4664; *STC*. Comment: Trans. of STC 21923.

A Guide unto Sion, 3rd ed., Amstelredam, 1640, STC 26127.
  Lit.: *STC*.

The 1640s

After 1640 Canne continued to print some Puritan pamphlets, using the Richt Right device and other designs. His main efforts at this time went into Bible printing.

Baynes, Paul, *The Diocesans Trial*, n.p., 1641, Wing B1547.
  Lit.: Wing.

Robinson, John, *The Peoples Plea for the Exercise of Prophesie*, n.p., 1641, Wing R1696.
  Lit.: Wing; Wilson, "Canne".

Syons Prerogatyve Royal, Amsterdam, 1641. Wing S3871.
  Lit.: Wilson, "Canne". Comment: According to Paget's *Defence*, publisher's preface, it was written by Canne.

Ainsworth, Henry, *Covnterpoyson*, n.p., 1642, Wing A809.
Lit.: Wing.
Bibles: Canne printed Bibles for the English market, including Wing B2207 (1644), B2211 (1645), and B2220A (1647).
Lit.: Wing; Herbert, *Historical Catalogue*, no. 601; Wilson, "Canne".
Comment: See chap. 4.

G Joris Veseler and Widow Veseler

Paget, John, *An Arrow against the Separation of the Brownists*, Amsterdam: George Veseler, 1618, STC 19098.
Lit.: Johnson, 1954; *STC*.
Calderwood, David, *A Solvtion of Doctor Resolvtvs*, n.p., 1619, STC 4364.
Lit.: Johnson, 1954; *STC*; Simoni C11.
Corantos in English (1620-21), Amsterdam: G. Veseler, soulde by Petrus Keerius, STC 18507.1-18507.17.
Lit.: Johnson, 1954; *STC*; Simoni.
Louis XIII, *Certaine Articles or Ordinances Made by the French Kinge*, Amsterdam: George Veseler, 1621, STC 16839.
Lit.: Johnson, 1954; *STC*.
A Notable and Wonderfull Sea-Fight, Amsterdam: George Veseler, 1621, STC 22131.
Lit.: Johnson, 1954; *STC*.
Proctor, Thomas, *Englands Pvrginge Fire*, n.p., 1621, STC 20408.5.
Lit.: *STC*.
Proctor, Thomas, *Religions Crowne*, Amsterdam: George Veseler, 1621, STC 20409.
Lit.: Johnson, 1954; *STC*.
Heidelberg Catechism, *A Catechisme of Christian Religion*, Amsterdam: By the Widowe of George Veseler, 1626, STC 13031.7.
Lit.: Johnson, 1954; *STC*.
W., Ez., *The Answere of a Mother vnto Hir Sedvced Sonnes Letter*, n.p., 1627, STC 24903.
Lit.: *STC*. Comment: The *STC* assigns to Stam, but it seems too early for Stam; perhaps by Widow Veseler, who married Stam in 1628.

H Jan Fredericksz Stam

Stam married the Widow Veseler in 1628 and took over the Veseler printing business. His imprint is found 1628-1664; this appendix concentrates on his English work up to 1640.

1629-1630

Top, Alexander, *The Book of Prayses, Called the Psalmes*, Amstelredam: Jan
Fredericksz Stam, 1629, STC 2415.
Lit.: Johnson, 1954; *STC*. Comment: Also a variant with imprint, STC
2415.2, 1629.

Leighton, Alexander, *An Appeal to the Parliament; or Sions Plea*, n.p., n.d., STC
15429.
Lit.: Johnson, 1954; *STC*. Comment: About 1629; another ed., STC
15428.5, done by Thorp's successors the same year.

Prempart, James, *A Historicall Relation of the Famous Siege of the Citie Called the
Bvsse*, Amsterdam: For Henrico Hondio, Colophon: Printed at Amster-
dam, By Ian Frederickz Stam, 1630, STC 20202.
Lit.: Johnson, 1954; *STC*.

1631-1635

Brabourne, Theophilus, *A Defence of That Most Ancient, and Sacred Ordinance
of Gods, the Sabbath Day*, 2nd ed., n.p., 1632, STC 3473.
Lit.: *STC*.

Audley, Eleanor, *Given to the Elector Prince Charls of the Rhyne from the Lady
Eleanor, Anno 1633*, Amsterdam: Frederick Stam, 1633, STC 903.5.
Lit.: *STC*.

The Bible. London: By the Deputies of Christopher Barker, 1599. STC 2309,
STC 2177.
Lit.: *STC*; Johnson, 1954. Comment: No. 2309, a variant of no. 2177,
has this New Testament imprint: "Imprinted at Amsterdam, for Thomas
Crafoorth. By John Fredericksz Stam, dwelling by the South-Church, at
the signe of the Hope. 1633." Another variant of STC 2177 at the Univ.
of Illinois has Stam's name on a colophon instead of on the New Testament title page.

Best, William, *The Chvrches Plea for Her Right*, Amsterdam: John Fredericksz
Stam, 1635, STC 1974.
Lit.: *STC*; Johnson, 1954. Comment: A variant, no. 1973.5, lacks Stam's
imprint.

Boye, Rice, *The Importvnate Begger for Things Necessary*, n.p., 1635, STC 3450.
Lit.: Johnson, 1954; *STC*.

Burton, Henry, *A Brief Answer to a Late Treatise of the Sabbath Day*, n.p., n.d.,
STC 4137.7.
Lit.: *STC*. Comment: Text is dated Oct. 2, 1635.

Odell, Thomas, *A Brief and Short Treatise, Called the Christians Pilgrimage*,
Amsterdam: John Fredericksz Stam, 1635, STC 18780.
Lit.: Johnson, 1954; *STC*.

Odell, Thomas, *Isaacks Pilgrimage*, Amsterdam: John Fredericksz Stam, 1635, STC 18781.
    Lit.: Johnson, 1954; *STC*.
Paget, John, *An Answer to the Unjust Compaints of William Best*, Amsterdam: John Fredericksz Stam, 1635, STC 19097.
    Lit.: Johnson, 1954; *STC*.
Scott, Thomas, *Josephs Flight out of Aegypt*, Amsterdam: John Frederick Stam, 1635, STC 22079.5.

1636–1640
Burton, Henry, *An Apology of an Appeale*, n.p., 1636, STC 4134.
    Lit.: Johnson, 1954; *STC*.
Burton, Henry, *The Lords Day, the Sabbath Day*, 2nd ed., n.p., 1636, STC 4137.9.
    Lit.: Johnson, 1954; *STC*.
Burton, Henry, *A Divine Tragedie Lately Acted*, n.p., 1636, STC 4140.7.
    Lit.: Johnson, 1954; *STC*.
Burton, Henry, *For God, and the King*, n.p., 1636, STC 4142.
    Lit.: Johnson, 1954; *STC*.
Prynne, William, *Certaine Quaeres Propounded*, 4th ed., n.p., 1636, STC 20456.
    Lit.: Johnson, 1954; *STC*.
Prynne, William, *The Vnbishoping of Timothy and Titvs*, n.p., 1636, STC 20476.
    Lit.: Johnson, 1954; *STC*. Comment: A John Paget letter of 1637 identified Stam as the Printer, Wodrow MS, Folio XLII, fol. 253; another issue also by Stam, no. 20476.5.
Bastwick, John, *A Briefe Relation of Certain Speciall and Most Materiall Passages, and Speeches in the Starre-Chamber*, n.p., 1637, STC 1569.
    Lit.: *STC*.
Morton, Thomas, *New English Canaan or New Canaan*, Amsterdam: Jacob Frederick Stam, 1637, STC 18202.
    Lit.: Johnson, 1954; *STC*.
Prynne, William, *A Breviate of the Prelates Intollerable Usurpations*, n.p., 1637, STC 20454.
    Lit.: Johnson, 1654; *STC*. Comment: Like Prynne's *Vnbishoping* above, no. 20476, the 1637 Paget letter identified Stam as the printer.
Prynne, William, *XVI. New Qvaeres*, n.p., 1637, STC 20475.
    Lit.: Johnson, 1954; *STC*.
Heidelberg Catechism, *A Catechism of Christian Religion*, Amsterdam: John Fredericksz Stam, 1639, STC 13031.8.
    Lit.: Johnson, 1954. Comment: Stam produced another ed. in 1652, Wing C1475.

Spang, William, *Brevis et fidelis narratio motuum in regno et ecclesia scotica*, Dantisci, 1640.

Lit.: Shaaber S285; Carter, "Archbishop Laud". Comment: Le Maire on Dec. 20, 1639 reported that a Scotsman named Haick had a manuscript in Latin about the sufferings and reformation of the Scottish church. He had offered it to several stationers for printing, but none so far would touch it. Haick's book sounds a good deal like Spang's book; SP 84/ 155/260.

Bibles. Stam was very active in printing English Bibles, for example, STC 2174-2179, all with false imprints, and *The Booke of Psalmes*, STC 2499; no doubt many others. Only two had Stam imprints, no. 2309, or colophons, no. 2177, Univ. of Illinois copy. In the Matthew Simmons report of 1637-38, he said that Stam was printing "Bibles in 4to with notes, Bibles in follio with notes, and Bibles in 12 now in hand" (SP 16/387/79).

Lit.: see Johnson, 1954; *STC*.

I Jodocus Hondius (1563-1612)

Hondius was more of a publisher than a printer. He was involved with several Puritan books, including non-English works of Hugh Broughton. See chap. 3.

Bradshaw, William, *A Shorte Treatise, of the Crosse in Baptisme*, Amsterdam: Printed by I. H., 1604, STC 3526.

Lit.: Curtis, "William Jones"; *STC*; Simoni B251. Comment: Hondius could be the I.H. of the imprint in connection with another printer, perhaps William Jones.

Brightman, Thomas, *A Revelation of the Apocalyps*, Amsterdam: Printed by Iudocus Hondius & Hendrick Laurenss, 1611, STC 3754.

Lit.: *STC*.

Hieron, Samuel, *A Defence of the Ministers Reasons, for Refvsall of Svbscription*, n.p., 1607, STC 13395.

Lit.: *STC*; Curtis, "William Jones"; Simoni H111. Comment: A part possibly by Hondius.

Rainolds, John (?), *An Answere to a Sermon Preached the 17 of April Anno D. 1608, by George Downame*, n.p., 1609, STC 20605.

Lit.: *STC*. Comment: Possibly by Hondius; part also by Thorp. Rainolds was not, in fact, the author.

J Johannes Janssonius (Johnson)

Ames, William: Janssonius was the chief printer for Ames' Latin works, including the significant *Omnia Opera* (1658). See Shaaber A265-306. Janssonius advertised many Amesian books in the Frankfurt fair catalogues.

Bastwick, John, *Elenchus religionis papisticae*, 3rd ed., Amsterdam: Apud Joannem Janssonium, 1634, STC 1571.5.

Lit.: Shaaber B318; *STC*.

Bayly, Lewis, *The Practice of Pietie*.

Comment: Janssonius used false imprints. According to Matthew Simmons, in 1637-38 he printed *Pieties* "by tenn thousand at a time"; SP 16/387/79. The autumn 1638 Frankfurt catalogue listed an ed. by Jacob Williams of Amsterdam, STC 1614.5; who is Jacob Williams?

Marolois, Samuel, *The Art of Fortification*, trans. Henry Hexham, Amsterdam: For M.J. Johnson, 1638, STC 17451.

Lit.: *STC*.

Slade, Matthew, *Cum C. Vorstio*, pars altera, Amsterdam: Janssonius, 1614.

Lit.: Simoni S168; Shaaber S239. Comment: The autumn 1614 Frankfurt catalogue listed Janssonius as publisher.

Twisse, William, *Ad Jacobi Arminii collationem*, Amsterdam: Apud Joannem Janssonium, 1649.

Lit.: Shaaber T187.

Twisse, William, *Vindiciae gratiae*, preface by William Ames, Amsterdam: Apud Joannem Janssonium, 1632.

Lit.: Shaaber T189.

Atlases: Janssonius was much involved in printing English editions of Blaeu's *Light of Navigation* and, in collaboration with Henricus Hondius, *Mercator's Atlas*.

K Hendrik Laurensz

Laurensz was a bookseller and publisher. There is a question that he ever had his own printing presses. Some of his publishing was in English and he did considerable in Latin for Puritan authors. He also served as distributor of Latin Puritan books, which he had not printed or published. Several significant Puritan books appeared in the Frankfurt fair catalogues under his name. These Frankfurt books included: Carpenter and Johnson, *Quaestio de duabus epistolis* (autumn 1610 cat., sig. B2r; printed by Thorp); Sanford and Parker, *De descensv* (autumn 1612 cat., sig. B2v; printed by Thorp with the Thorp imprint); Slade, *Cum Conrado Vorstio, pars prima* (spring 1612 cat., sig. B3r).

Ames, William, *Aenhangael van de Haegsche conferentie*, Amsterdam: Voor Hendrick Laurentsz, 1630.
Lit.: Shaaber A276.

Ames, William, *Rescriptio scholastica & brevis*, Amsterdam: Apud Henricum Laurentium, 1615.
Lit.: Shaaber A297.

Brightman, Thomas, *A Revelation of the Apocalyps*. Amsterdam: Printed by Iudocus Hondius & Hendrick Laurenss, 1611, STC 3754.
Lit.: *STC*.

Brightman, Thomas, *Apocalypsis apocalypseos*, Frankfurt: Prostat apud Viduam Leuini Hulsii, 1609.
Lit.: Shaaber B673. Comment: A trans. of STC 3754, or vice versa. The printer is uncertain, but by the same printer as the English version. Fowler wrote in *Shield*, p. 7, that the Latin was printed at Amsterdam by the same printer as the English ed. i.e. by Laurensz and Hondius? The spring 1609 Frankfurt cat. entered the book twice, once for Widow Levini Hulsii of Frankfurt and once for Cornelius Nicolai of Amsterdam.

Cartwright, Thomas, *Commentarii in Proverbia Salonomis*, Amsterdam: Sumptibus Henrici Laurentii, 1632.
Lit.: Shaaber C133; also see C134.

Cartwright, Thomas, *Metaphrasis et homiliae in librum Salomonis...Ecclesiastes*, Amsterdam: Sumptibus Henrici Laurentii, 1632.
Lit.: Shaaber C137.

Charles I, *A Petition to the King*, Amsterdam: Hendrick Lawrentz, 1628, STC 5028.
Lit.: *STC*.

Dod, John and Robert Cleaver, *Een klare ende duydelijcke uytlegginghe over de thien gheboden des Heeren*, Tot Amstelredam, Voor Hendrick Laurensz. Boeck-verkooper, 1617.
Lit.: Harris and Jones, ed. Breugelmans, pp. 154-55, which points out that this edition, with a changed title page, was also used by Brewster of Leiden; Shaaber D86.

Fenner, Dudley, *Sacra theologia*, Amsterdam: Sumptibus Henrici Laurentii, 1632.
Lit.: Shaaber F35.

Fowler, John, *A Shield of Defence against the Arrowes of Schisme*, Amsterdam: Henry Lawrenson, 1612, STC 11212.
Lit.: *STC*.

Rainolds, John, *Censura librorum apocryphorum Veteris Testamenti*, Sumptibus Viduae Levini Hulsii & Henrici Laurentii, 1611
Lit.: Shaaber R1. Comment: Entered in the spring 1612 Frankfurt cat., sig. B2v.

Rutherford, Samuel, *Exercitationes apologeticae pro divina gratia*, Amsterdam: Apud Henricum Laurentii, 1636
Lit.: Shaaber R160. Comment: Entered in the spring 1637 Frankfurt cat., sig. A3.

L *Joost Broersz*

Poynet, John, *A Short Treatise of Politike Power*, Printed in the year 1556 and now reprinted, 1639, STC 20179.
Comment: Broers was the printer of at least the first four chapters; see Amsterdam confessieboek, no. 303, fol. 310v.
The Holy Bible, Amsterdam: Printed by Joost Broersz, 1642, Wing B2207.
Lit.: Wing; Herbert, *Historical Catalogue*, nos. 564, 571; for more on Bibles by Joost Broersz, see H.M. Borst, "Joost Broersz". Comment: Has notes by J.C., i.e. John Canne; printed for John Tracy; a reissue came out in 1643 (Borst nos. 1116, 1116a, 1140).
Dutch translations: Broesz printed a large number of English works put into Dutch 1639-43.
Lit.: Kn.; Borst.

M *Cloppenburgh (Cloppenburg) Press*

The STC refers to a group of books from 1640 as coming from "Amsterdam, Cloppenburg Press". Perhaps some of these are the work of the successors of Jan Evertsz Cloppenburgh (1598-1636); Sayle tied one of these books to Cloppenburg. He was a publisher and bookseller; he may not have had his own press. None of these books has the Cloppenburgh imprint. Two books (STC 4148 and 21921) have an editor's mark or device earlier used by Cloppenburgh; cf., for example, Menno Simons, *Een Fondament* (Cloppenburgh, 1613) and Beza, *Een cort begrijp* (Cloppenburgh, 1611). The other 12 books, although similar to each other, are rather different from the books mentioned above. See chap. 4. That all 14 books were done by Cloppenburgh, or even at Amsterdam, is questionable.

Burton, Henry, *Jesu-Worship Confuted*, n.p., 1640, STC 4148.
Lit.: *STC*.
Burton, Henry, *A Replie to a Relation, of the Conference between William Laude and Mr. Fisher the Jesuite*, n.p., 1640, STC 4154.
Lit.: *STC*.

A Dialogve Wherin Is Plainly Layd Open the Tyrannicall Dealing of Lord Bishops,
Published by Dr. Martin Mar-Prelat, n.p., 1640, STC 6805.3.
Lit.: *STC*.

E., N., *Information for the Ignorant*, n.p., 1640, STC 7435.5.
Lit.: *STC*.

Englands Complaint to Iesvs Christ against the Bishops Canons, n.p., 1640, STC 10008.
Lit.: *STC*.

F., L., *A Speedy Remedie against Spiritvall Incontinencie*, n.p., 1640, STC 10649.
Lit.: *STC*. Comment: Part II is dated 1641.

How, Samuel, *The Svfficiencie of the Spirits Teaching, without Hvmane Learning*, n.p., 1640, STC 13855.
Lit.: *STC*.

Hughes, Lewis, *Certaine Grievances Well Worthy the Serious Consideration of Parliament*, n.p., 1640, STC 13917.
Lit.: *STC*.

Prynne, William, *Lord Bishops, None of the Lords Bishops*, n.p., 1640, STC 20467.
Lit.: *STC*.

Books on Scotland

An Information from the States of the Kingdome of Scotland, to the Kingdome of England, n.p., 1640, STC 21916.5.
Lit.: *STC*.

The Intentions of the Armie of the Kingdome of Scotland Declared to Their Brethren of England, n.p., 1640, STC 21921.
Lit.: *STC*; Sayle. Comment: STC 21921.5 another ed. also from the same press.

The Lawfvlnesse of ovr Expedition into England Manifested, Reprinted in England by Margery Mar-Prelat, 1640, STC 21924.
Lit.: *STC*.

Ovr Demands of the English Lords Manifested, Being at Rippon Octob. 8, 1640, Printed by Margery Mar Prelat, 1640, STC 21926.
Lit.: *STC*.

A Remonstrance concerning the Present Troubles, n.p., 1640, STC 21928.
Lit.: *STC*.

N Joseph Bruyning (Bruyningh, Browning)

Bruyning was active in the business of selling English books, but he did not print English books, at least with his own imprint. He put out several English books in Dutch translation, beginning in 1639, using the imprint "Joseph

Bruyning te Amsterdam aen de Beurs in 't Serpent ende Duyf' or a similar
one. He died in 1672. The Widow Bruyning continued selling English books
and publishing Dutch translations of English books; her imprint on English
related books appeared 1673-89. For Bruyning's publishing, see Hoftijzer,
Engelse boekverkopers, "Fondslijst Bruyning", pp. 223-45.

O *Cornelis Claesz*

Cornelis Claesz (also Cornelius Nicolai) was one of the great booksellers of
the Republic, active in Amsterdam 1582-1609. His books appeared regularly
in the Frankfurt catalogues. In addition, he put out several stock catalogues to
advertise books in his Amsterdam shop; finally, after his death, Widow Claesz
published an auction catalogue for a sale on May 10, 1610. These catalogues
show that he carried a good stock of Latin books put out by Puritan authors;
generally he was not the publisher. I have used the five C. Claesz catalogues,
1608-10, at the Herzog August Bibliothek, Wolfenbüttel. Books of special
note are:

Broughton, Hugh, *Responsum ad epistolam Iudei* (1608 catalogue, *Librorvm, in
   Officina Cornelii Nicolai extantium catalogus*, sig. a3v).
   Comment: One of Broughton's books directed toward conversion of the
   Jews; probably printed by Theunisz; printed 1606. See Simoni B296.
Confessio fidei Anglorum quorundam in Belgio exulantium, 8.98 (Ibid., sig. b4r).
   Comment: This appears to be the Latin version of the Brownist confes-
   sion, a trans. of STC 18433.7; printed c. 1607 by Thorp. See Johnson,
   1951, p. 225; Simoni C153.
Ainsworth, Henry, *La communion des Saints*, translaté d'Anglois en Francois
   per Iean de l'Escluse, a Amsterdam, chez Cornille Nicolas, 8.1608 (*Livres
   de la theologie*, sig. A3r.).
   Comment: No copy of this 1608 version of the book is known; it is
   very uncertain that it actually appeared. A later French version, *chez Giles
   Thorp*, was published about 1617; see above for Thorp. The autumn
   1608 Frankfurt cat. advertised a Latin version, *Tractatus de communione...*
   Ambsterodami apud Cornelum Nicolai", sig. B1r; this trans., although
   promised, was not published.

LEIDEN PRINTERS AND BOOKSELLERS

A William Brewster and Thomas Brewer

The proprietors of the "Pilgrim Press" were active in printing 1617-19. The following list of their publications (21 books printed or published by them) is based on Harris and Jones, *The Pilgrim Press*, ed. R. Breugelmans (1987). Of the 21 books, several are severely questioned.

Ames, William, *Ad responsum Nic. Grevinchovii rescriptio contracta*, Prostant Lvg-dvni Batavorvm, Apud Guiljelmum Brewsterum In Vico Chorali, 1617.
   Lit.: Harris and Jones; Shaaber A298; Simoni A85.

An Abridgement of That Booke which the Ministers of Lincolne Diocesse Deliuered to His Maiestie, Reprinted, 1617, STC 15647.
   Lit.: Harris and Jones; *STC*; Simoni A5.

Whetenhall, Thomas, *A Discovrse of the Abuses Now in Question*, Reprinted, 1617, STC 25333.
   Lit.: Harris and Jones; *STC*; Simoni W75.

Dod, John and Robert Cleaver, *A Plaine and Familiar Exposition of the Tenne Commandements*, n.p., 1617, STC 6973.
   Lit.: Harris and Jones; *STC*; Simoni D66.

Dod, John and Robert Cleaver, *Een klare ende duydelijcke uytlegginghe over de thien gheboden des Heeren*, Tot Leyden, voor Guiliaem Brewster, Boeck-drucker, 1617.
   Lit.: Harris and Jones; Shaaber D86. Comment: Not printed by Brewster; this is another issue, with changed imprint, of an edition published by H. Laurensz of Amsterdam; the printer is unknown. See App. I, K on Laurensz.

Field, John and Thomas Wilcox, *An Admonition to the Parliament*, n.p., 1617, STC 10849.
   Lit.: Harris and Jones; *STC*; Simoni F13.

Travers, Walter, *A Fvll and Plaine Declaration of Ecclesiastical Discipline*, Reprinted, 1617, STC 24186.
   Lit.: Harris and Jones; *STC*; Simoni T137.

Johnson, Francis, *A Christian Plea Conteyning Three Treatises*, n.p., 1617, STC 14661.

Lit.: Harris and Jones; *STC*; Simoni J78. Comment: One of the most questioned books on the list. However, Paget, *Arrow*, p. 13, declared in 1618 that one part of a book that fits this description had been "imperfectly published" by "Mr. B."; Brewster is the most likely candidate for Mr. B..

Cartwright, Thomas, *Commentarii succincti & dilucidi in Proverbia Salomonis*, Lvgduni Batavorvm, apud Guiljelmum Brewsterum, in vico Chorali, 1617.

Lit.: Harris and Jones; Shaaber C132; Simoni B155.

De vera et genvina Iesv Christi religione, n.p., 1618.

Lit.: Harris and Jones. Comment: Authore Minist. Angl.

Calderwood, David, *De regimine ecclesiae Scoticanae brevis relatio*, n.p., 1618.

Lit.: Harris and Jones; Shaaber C11; Simoni C8.

A Trve, Modest, and Ivst Defence of the Petition for Reformation, n.p., 1618, STC 6469.

Lit.: Harris and Jones; *STC*; Simoni T167.

Dighton, Thomas, *Certain Reasons of a Private Christian against Conformitie to Kneeling*, n.p., 1618, STC 6876.

Lit.: Harris and Jones; *STC*.

Robinson, John, *The Peoples Plea for the Exercise of Prophesie*, n.p., 1618, STC 21115a.

Lit.: Harris and Jones; *STC*.

Harrison, Robert, *A Little Treatise vpon the First Verse of the 122. Psalme*, n.p., 1618, STC 12862.

Lit.: Harris and Jones; *STC*.

Chaderton, Laurence, *A Frvitfvll Sermon*, n.p., 1618, STC 4929.

Lit.: Harris and Jones; *STC*.

Cartwright, Thomas, *A Confvtation of the Rhemists Translation*, n.p., 1618, STC 4709.

Lit.: Harris and Jones; *STC*; Simoni C35.

Dighton, Thomas, *The Second Part of a Plain Discovrse in Refusing Conformity to Kneeling*, n.p., 1619, STC 6877.

Lit.: Harris and Jones; *STC*.

Euring, William, *An Answer to the Ten Covnter Demands Propovnded by T. Drakes*, n.p., 1619, STC 10567.

Lit.: Harris and Jones; *STC*.

Calderwood, David, *Perth Assembly*, n.p., 1619, STC 4360.

Lit.: Harris and Jones; *STC*; Simoni C9.

Robinson, John, *Apologia iusta, et necessaria qvorvndam Christianorum, dictorum Brownistarum sive Barrowistarum*, n.p., 1619.

Lit.: Harris and Jones; Shaaber R109; Simoni R73. Comment: A much questioned book on the Brewster list.

B *Willem Christiaensz van der Boxe*

In his early career he was known as Willem Christiaensz; later he added the surname Van der Boxe. He was an active printer with his own imprint 1631–58. His English printing mostly occurred in the early period up to 1640; this is the period emphasized in this appendix.

The Early 1630s (up to 1635)

Adams, Thomas, *Den witten duyvell*, trans. by Christiaensz, published by Z. Roman, Middelburg; colophon, "ghedruckt by Willem Christiaens, 1633".

> Lit.: Schoneveld no. 48. Translation of STC 131.

Adams, Thomas, *Den witten duyvell*, 2nd ed., published by Jan Jansen, Amsterdam, 1634; colophon, "ghedruckt by Willem Christiaens, 1633".

H., W., *The Trve Pictvre and Relation of Prince Henry*, Leiden: Printed by William Christian, 1634, STC 12581.

> Lit.: STC.

Rich, Barnaby, *De deegh'lijckheydt van onsen tiidt*, trans. by Christiaensz, published by Jan Janson, Amsterdam, 1634; colophon, printed by Christiaensz.

> Comment: Trans. of STC 20986.

1637

Bastwick, John, *The Answer of John Bastwick, to the Information of Sir Iohn Bancks*, n.p., 1637, STC 1568.

> Lit.: STC; Foster, *Notes*.

Bastwick, John, *The Letany of John Bastwick*, n.p., 1637, four parts, STC 1572, 1573, 1574, 1575.

> Lit.: STC; Foster, *Notes*. Comment: Four more parts were promised, but did not appear, plus "some of my Latine books". These five parts, *Answer* and *Letany*, were a collaborative project of Christiaensz and James Moxon of Rotterdam. Matthew Simmons reported that Moxon printed all five parts at Rotterdam; by November 1637 they "were then in the presse printed." Christiaensz was also involved, however, and in 1638 he was convicted and fined for printing the *Answer*, no. 1568. The other four parts, the *Letany*, must have been the work of Moxon. If so, *A Catalogue*, STC 4788, was also likely printed by Moxon because it has many similarities. The *Answer* has several ornaments and initials often used by Christiaensz.

Gillespie, George, *A Dispvte against the English-Popish Ceremonies, Obtrvded vpon the Chvrch of Scotland*, n.p., 1637, STC 11896.

> Lit.: STC. Comment: A collaborative project. Christiaensz and Canne were both convicted and fined for jointly printing the book; Christiaensz

did the larger part. Lilburne, *Come Out of Her*, 1639, p. 13, states that it was "printed at *Leyden*, in Holland, the last summer".

The Triall of the English Liturgie, n.p., 1637, STC 16452.
> Lit.: *STC*. Comment: Another ed., no. 16452.5 in 1638, was also by Christiaensz.

Prynne, William, *Hier, wat nieuws uyt Ipswich*, trans. by Christiaensz, n.p., 1637, Kn. 4473.
> Comment: Trans. of STC 20469; printed by Christiaensz. See Simmons, SP 16/387/79.

Scot, Reginald, *Ontdecking van tovery*, Leiden: Willem Christiaensz, 1637.
> Lit.: Schoneveld, no. 536, trans. of STC 21864.

1638

Bastwick, John, *A Briefe Relation of Certaine Speciall and Most Materiall Passages, and Speeches in the Starre-Chamber*, n.p., 1638, STC 1570.
> Lit.: *STC*. Comment: 10,000 copies were printed at Leiden, SP 84/ 155/6.

Bastwick, John, *Een cort ende bondich verhael, van seeckere bysondere ende voornaemste redenen en propoosten ghehouden in den Hoogen Raedt binnen London*, n.p., 1638, Kn. 4559.
> Lit.: Kn. Comment: Trans. of STC 1569, 1570; 3,000 copies printed in Dutch at Leiden, SP 84/155/6.

Hooker, Thomas, *The Sovles Preparation for Christ*, Printed (for the use and benefit of the English Churches) in the Netherlands, 1638, STC 13738.
> Lit.: Johnson, 1955; *STC*. Comment: Another issue, no. 13738.5, 1639, also by Christiaensz.

An Abridgement of That Booke which the Ministers of Lincoln Diocesse Delivered to His Majestie, n.p., 1638, STC 15648.
> Lit.: *STC*. Comment: Matthew Simmons, SP 16/387/79.

The Beast Is Wovnded or Information from Scotland, n.p., n.d., STC 22031.5.
> Lit.: Kn. 4559a; *STC*. Comment: 1638.

The Confession of Faith of the Kirk of Scotland, n.p., n.d., STC 22026.4.
> Lit.: *STC*. Comment: 1638.

De confessie des gheloofs vande Kerke van Schotlandt, trans. by Fredrick Willemsz Pennock, Amsterdammer, Gedruckt voor Thomas Craffort, 1638, Kn. 4561.
> Lit.: Kn. Comment: Trans. of STC 22026, 22026.4.

Lily's *Rules* and *Grammar*.
> Comment: According to Matthew Simmons [1637-38], Christiaensz printed the *Rules* and "bargained for to print" the *Grammar*, working with and for Mr. Tuthill of Rotterdam; SP 16/387/79.

Ames, William, *Conscience with the Power and Cases Thereof*, n.p., 1639, STC 552 (part I only).

Lit.: *STC*; Johnson, 1955. Comment: The role of Christiaensz is questionable; this may, in fact, be the work of Moxon; cf. STC 1572, 1573.

Gakels, Simon, *Oratie ter eeren...Prince, Bernhard*, Tot Leyden, Ghedruckt by Willem Christiaens, voor Thomas Crafford, woonende tot Amsterdam, 1639.
Lit.: Tiele 2663. Comment: Copy at UB Gent; see Appendix III, B.

Gods wonder-wercken nu onlangs voor-gevallen in Enghelandt, in de provincie van Devonshire, trans. and printed by Willem Christiaens, Kn. 4657.
Lit.: Kn.

Prynne, William, *Histrio-Mastix ofte schouw-spels treur-spel*, Leiden: Willem Christiaens, 1639.
Comment: Trans. and abridgment of STC 20464.

Young, Thomas, *Dies Dominica*, n.p., 1639, STC 226115.
Lit.: *STC*. Comment: Author of dedication is Theophilus Philokuriaces. It was promoted by a Brownist preacher of Rotterdam, according to SP 84/155/146.

A Guide unto Sion, printed for Thomas Crafford, 1639, STC 26126.
Lit.: Johnson, 1955; *STC*.

1640

Bibles: *The Bible: That Is, The Holy Scriptvres*, Amsterdam: Printed by Thomas Stafford, 1640. STC 2344.
Lit.: *STC*; Herbert, *Historical Catalogue*, no. 545. Comment: This Bible was begun at Leiden by Christiaensz; while in process of printing, Stafford moved the printing to Amsterdam to some other printing house. For the Christiaensz side of the story, see chap. 5.

A Part of the Lyturgy of the Reformed Chvrches in the Netherlands, trans. from Dutch into English. Leiden, 1640, STC 16560.5.
Lit.: *STC*; Meeter in *NAK*, 1990. Comment: c. 1640; it makes use of several initials and ornaments used by Christiaensz.

The Intentions of the Army of the Kingdome of Scotland, Edinburgh: Robert Bryson, 1640, STC 21919.5.
Lit.: *STC*, which ascribes it to Christiaensz.

The Lawfulnesse of Our Expedition into England Manifested, Edinburgh: Robert Bryson, 1640, STC 21923.5.
Lit.: *STC*, which ascribes it to Christiaensz.

A Remonstrance concerning the Present Troubles, n.p., 1640, STC 21927.7.
Lit.: *STC*, which ascribes it to Christiaensz.

1642-1643

Yrelandtsche Traenen, Amsterdam: Broer Jansz and Jan van Hilten, 1642; colophon, printed by Willem Christiaens, Kn. 4804.
Lit.: Schoneveld, no. 44; trans. of Wing C6824.

The Power of the Lawes of a Kingdome, Over the Will of a Mis-Led King, Leiden: William Christienne, 1643, Wing P3107.
    Lit.: Wing.

C   *Additional Puritan Books by Other Leiden Printers*

Ames, William, *Coronis ad collationem Hagiensem*, Leiden: Ex officina Elzeviriana, 1618.
    Lit.: Shaaber A273; Simoni A86.

Ames, William, *Rescriptio scholastica & brevis*, Editio altera, Leiden: Ex officina I. Livii, 1634.
    Lit.: Shaaber A300.

Bradshaw, William, *Dissertatio de iustificationis doctrina*, Leiden: Apud Ioannem Maire, 1618.
    Comment: See App. III, A.

Brightman, Thomas, *The Revelation of S. Iohn*, 3rd ed., Leiden: John Class, 1616; colophon: John Claesson van Dorpe, 1616, STC 3746.
    Lit.: *STC*; Simoni B273.

Jacob, Henry, *The Divine Beginning and Institution of Christs Church*, Leiden: H. Hastings, 1610, STC 14336.
    Lit.: *STC*; Simoni J28.

Parker, Robert, *De politeia ecclesiastica Christi, et hierarchica opposita, libri tres*, Prostant Francofvrti apud Godefridvm Basson, 1616.
    Lit.: Shaaber P17; Simoni P46. Comment: Has prefaces by William Ames and John Robinson; two title pages were printed, one with Basson's name, the other without.

EDITORS, PUBLISHERS, AND FINANCIAL BACKERS

Making on-the-spot arrangement for authors back in England or Scotland was the job of the "editor" or "publisher". The duties of this person involved seeing the book through the press and often finding the necessary financing. Sometimes they revised the book and wrote a preface. Many English and Scots of the Low Countries produced a body of books by taking care of the printing arrangements.

A William Ames

Ames lived in the Netherlands 1610-33 and had many contacts with printers. He facilitated and edited books for friends back in England.

Bradshaw, William, *Dissertatio de iustificationis doctrina*, Leiden: Apud Ioannem Maire, 1618.
Comment: Sent over by Bradshaw; Ames made the arrangements for printing. It was advertised in the autumn 1618 Frankfurt catalogue, also the autumn 1628 catalogue, STC 11331.
Bradshaw, William, *Puritanismus Anglicanus*, Francofurti: Prostat in Bibliopolio Aubriano, 1610.
Comment: Latin trans. of STC 3517; advertised in autumn 1611 Frankfurt catalogue, Leipzig ed.; preface by Ames. Although having a Frankfurt imprint, it was likely published in the Netherlands, where Ames lived from 1610 onward.
Bradshaw, William, *The Vnreasonablenesse of the Separation*, Dort: George Waters, 1614, STC 3532.
Comment: Preface by Ames; see 1640 ed., no. 3533, where Ames' name was printed.
Baynes, Paul, *The Diocesans Tryall*, n.p., 1621, STC 1640.
Lit.: *STC*, entry for 1640. Comment: printed by Thorp at Amsterdam; "published by Dr. William Amis", according to a later ed., still dated 1621, Wing B1546; preface by Ames.
Parker, Robert, *De politeia ecclesiastica Christi, et hierarchica opposita, libri tres*, Prostant Francofvrti apud Godefridvm Basson, 1616.

Comment: Preface, "Religioso lectori", by Ames; see Paget, *Defence*, p. 106).

Twisse, William, *Vindiciae gratiae*, Amsterdam: Apud Joannem Janssonium, 1632.

Comment: Preface by Ames.

B   Thomas Crafford

The Bible, That is, The Holy Scriptvres, STC 2309, New Testament title page: Imprinted at Amsterdam, for Thomas Crafoorth. By Iohn Fredericksz Stam, 1633.

Comment: The main title page has false imprint, London: By the Deputies of Christopher Barker, 1599.

De confessie des gheloofs vande Kerke van Schotlandt, Gedruckt voor Thomas Craffort, 1638, Kn. 4561.

Comment: Printed by Christiaensz at Leiden.

Een cort ende bondich verhael, van seeckere bysondere ende voornaemste redenen en propoosten ghehouden in den Hoogen Raedt binnen London, n.p., 1638, Kn. 4559.

Comment: Published and financed by Crafford; printed by Christiaensz; a trans. of STC 1569, 1570.

Gakels, Simon, *Oratie ter eeren den...Prince, Bernhard*, Tot Leyden, Ghedruckt by Willem Christiaens, voor Thomas Crafford, 1639, woonende tot Amsterdam.

Lit.: Tiele 2663. Comment: Copy at UB Gent.

Poynet, John, *A Short Treatise of Politike Power*, Printed in the year 1556 and now reprinted 1639, STC 20179.

Comment: Crafford arranged for Joost Broers to print this book.

A Guide unto Sion, printed for Thomas Crafford, 1639, STC 26126.

Comment: printed by Christiaensz.

C   Mr. T.L.

Mr. T.L. (perhaps Thomas Loof, an Amsterdam merchant) published at least three books. He lived on the Fluwelen Burgwal. He offered books for sale "at his chamber in Flowingburrow neare unto the English Church".

Hooker, Thomas, *The Poor Doubting Christian*, 4th ed., For T.L. for the benefit of our English nation, 1637, STC 13726.4.

Comment: Printed by Canne.

Hooker, Thomas, *The Sovles Hvmiliation*, Amsterdam: Printed for T. L. and
are to be sould at his Chamber in Flowingburrow, neare unto the
English Church, 1638, STC 13728.5.
    Comment: Printed by Canne.
Preston, John, *The Doctrine of the Saints Infirmities*, Amsterdam: Printed for
T.L. and are to be sould at his Chamber in Flowingburrow neare unto
the English Church, STC 20221.3.
    Comment: c. 1638; printed by Canne.

D Stephen Offwood

Offwood was first a Separatist, then a member of the English Reformed
Church. He edited, published, and financed a good number of books for the
Puritan cause; he also did translating from Dutch into English.

An Oration or Speech Appropriated vnto the Most Mightie and Illustrious Princes of
Christendom, ed. Stephen Offwood, n.p., 1624, STC 18837.
    Comment: Translation of Verheiden, *De jure belli Belgici*, Kn. 954 and
    Kn. 1490; trans. by Thomas Wood, printed by "Successors of Thorp".
    Offwood appended an essay of his own, *An Adioynder of Svndry Other*
    Particvlar Wicked Plots of the Spaniards, printed with the *Oration* but with
    its own title page; STC 18757.
Offwood, Stephen, ed., *A Relation of Sundry Particular Wicked Plots...of the*
Spanish, Gathered and trans. "by S. O.", n.p. 1624, STC 187576.
    Comment: A reprint of the essay STC 18757, first published as a part of
    Oration. STC proposes that this ed. was printed in London.
Scott, Thomas, *A Second Part of Spanish Practices. Or, a Relation of More*
Particular Wicked Plots, n.p. 1624, STC 22078.5.
    Comment: The *Adioynder* is attached; Offwood's role in publishing this
    Scott-Offwood work is not clear.
Casaubon, Isaac, *The Originall of Popish Idolatrie, or the Birth of Heresies*, "Pub-
lished by S. O.", n.p., 1630, STC 4748.
    Comment: Printed by the Successors of Thorp.
Ames, William, *A Fresh Svit against Human Ceremonies in God's Worship*, with
essay "Published by S. O.", n.p., 1633, STC 555.
    Comment: Printed by Staresmore.
Offwood, Stephen, *An Advertisement to Ihon Deleclvse, and Henry May the*
Elder, n.p., date uncertain, STC 18789.
    Comment: 1632 or 1633; this is Offwood's own story about church
    affairs in Amsterdam.

The Opinion, Judgement, and Determination of Two Reverend, Learned, and Conformable Divines of the Church of England, Concerning Bowing at the Name, or Naming of Jesus, n.p., 1634, STC 14555.
Comment: Commentary by S. O.; printed by Successors of Thorp.
Forbes, John, *Fovr Sermons*, "Published by S. O.", n.p., 1635, STC 11129.
Comment: Printed by Successors of Thorp.

E John Paget

Paget was pastor of the English Reformed Church at Amsterdam 1607-37, when he became emeritus. An avid anti-Separatist, he organized a campaign of books against the Separatists of Amsterdam, usually disguising his own role in the matter. In publication matters he had the assistance of Thomas Allen, the church's schoolmaster. The culmination of the campaign was Paget's own book, *An Arrow against the Separation of the Brownists* (Amsterdam: George Veseler, 1618). In addition, he aided the following:

Fowler, John, *A Shield of Defence against the Arrowes of Schisme*, Amsterdam: Henry Lawrenson, 1612, STC 11212.
Lawne, Christopher, *et al.*, *The Prophane Schisme of the Brownists or Separatists*, n.p., 1612, STC 15324.
Comment: Printed in London.
Lawne, Christopher, *Brownisme Tvrned the In-side Out-ward*, London, 1613, STC 15323.
Sh., Mr., *A Replye Answering a Defence of the Sermon, Preached at the Consecration of the Bishop of Bathe and Welles, by George Downhame*, n.p., 1613 (pt. 2, 1614), STC 20620.
Comment: Not by John Rainolds, as usually stated; a follow-up to no. 20605 of 1609; printed by Thorp. The author was a Mr. Sh. in England, who committed the manuscript to Paget "for the overseeing of the presse". Sh. also authorized Paget to "add, alter, or detract"; Paget, *Defence*, sig. ★★★★2.
Ames, William, *A Second Manvdvction, for Mr. Robinson*, n.p., 1615, STC 556.

F Thomas Stafford

Stafford was a long-time Amsterdam merchant, and he was Offwood's son-in-law. In religion Stafford was a Separatist.

Bibles: *The Bible: That Is, the Holy Scriptvres*, Amsterdam: Printed by Thomas Stafford: And are to be sold at his house, at the signe of the Flight of

Brabant, upon the Milk-market, over against the Deventer Wood-market, 1640, STC 2344.

Comment: printing was begun by Christiaensz but finished by another printer at Amsterdam; Other eds. in 1641 and 1644.

Ainsworth, Henry, *The Booke of Psalmes: Englished Both in Prose and Metre*, Amsterdam: Printed by Thomas Stafford; and are to be sold at his House at the signe of the Flight of Brabant, upon the Milke-market, over against the Deventer Wood-Market, 1644, Wing B2405.

Brightman, Thomas, *The Revelation of St. John…Together with a Most Comfortable Exposition of the Last Prophecy of Daniel*, Amsterdam: Printed by Thomas Stafford and are to be sold at his house…, 1644, Wing B4692.

APPENDIX IV

A SELECTED LIST OF ANONYMOUSLY PRINTED
PURITAN BOOKS

In addition to the books listed in the previous appendixes, a large number of
other books important to the Puritan cause, although most lack a Dutch
imprint, have the look and feel of Dutch printing. Many of these have not
been traced back to their printer or publisher; nevertheless, they should be
examined in connection with the topic of Puritan printing. Apart from
printing in Amsterdam and Leiden, much printing for Puritans was the work
of Richard Schilders of Middelburg, George Waters of Dort, James Moxon
of Delft and Rotterdam, and others; their printing, however, is beyond the
scope of the present study. What follows is a selected listing of books, many
anonymously authored and most without imprint, not covered in the previous appendixes. Many of these, one may surmise, were done at Amsterdam
and Leiden.

Ames, William, *A Second Manvdvction, for Mr. Robinson*, n.p., 1615, STC 556.
*Answeres to Certaine Novations Desired by Some To Be Embraced by the Reformed
    Church*, n.p., n.d., STC 664.7.
    Lit.: *STC*, c. 1638. Comment: Dutch title page ornament; cf. no.
    15591.5).
Certaine Argvments and Motives, of Speciall Moment, n.p., 1634, STC 739.
    Lit.: *STC*. Comment: A 2nd ed., no. 739.5, 1635.
Bastwick, John, *Flagellvm pontificis & episcoporum latialium*, 2nd ed., n.p., 1635.
    Comment: Matthew Simmons in 1637-38 reported that this book was
    available, and presumably recently printed, in the Netherlands; it was
    stored at Delft. SP 16/387/79.
Bayly, Lewis, *The Practise of Pietie*, Delf: Abraham Jacobs, for the good of
    Great Britaine, n.d., STC 1612.
    Lit.: *STC*. Comment: From the 1630s. This was one of the most printed
    books of the century; several of the 1630s had Dutch imprints. STC
    1612, 1616, and 1616.5 have the publisher/printer's name as Abraham
    Jacobs. STC 1614.5, "the last and most corrected edition", has the
    imprint "Printed at Amsterdam by Iacob Williams, for the good of
    Greate Britaine", n.d. This edition can be dated c. 1638. The autumn
    1638 Frankfurt cat. listed for sale the last and most corrected ed., from
    Jacob Williams of Amsterdam, sig. C1v. Who produced these Delft and

Amsterdam editions? The most likely person behind these dubious imprints was Johannes Janssonius of Amsterdam, reportedly in 1637 printing Bayly's book by the tens of thousands; see Appendix I, J.

Bradshaw, William, *The Unreasonablnes of the Separation*, n.p., 1640, STC 3533.
Lit.: *STC*; Sayle. Comment: Preface carries the name of Dr. Ames; first edition was printed by George Waters at Dort, no. 3532.

Brightman, Thomas, *A Revelation of the Reuelation That Is, the Revelation of St. John*, Imprinted at Amsterdam, 1615, STC 3755.
Lit.: *STC*; Simoni B27. Comment: 3 editions were produced in the Netherlands 1611-16.

Broughton, Hugh: He was one of the most prolific of Puritan writers, many of his books being printed at Amsterdam without imprint. His collected *Works* was published at London in 1662. For his publishing of Latin and Hebrew works, see chap. 4. Three English works deserve special mention:

Broughton, Hugh, *An Exposition vpon the Lords Prayer*, n.p., n.d., STC 3867.
Lit.: *STC*; Simoni B288. Comment: Posthumous work.

Broughton, Hugh, *The Familie of David*, Amsterdam: Zacharias Heyns, 1605, STC 3867.5.
Lit.: *STC*; Simoni B290. Comment: Another edition, Amsterdam: Ian Theunisz, 1606, STC 3867.7.

Broughton, Hugh, *Ovr Lordes Familie*, Amsterdam, 1608, STC 3875.
Lit.: *STC*; Simoni B291.

Busher, Leonard, *Religions Peace*, Amsterdam, 1614, STC 4189.
Lit.: *STC*.

Calderwood, David, *The Pastor and the Prelate, or Reformation and Conformitie Shortly Compared*, n.p., 1628, STC 4359.
Lit.: *STC*.

Calderwood, David, *Parasynagma Perthenese et ivramentvm ecclesiae Scoticanae*, n.p., 1620, STC 4361.
Lit.: *STC*; Simoni C10.

Clapham, Henoch, *Bibliotheca Theologica*, Amsterdam, 1597, STC 5331.
Lit.: *STC*.

Clapham, Henoch, *The Syn, against the Holy Ghoste*, Amsterdam, 1598. STC 5345.
Lit.: *STC*.

Clapham, Henoch, *Theologicall Axioms or Conclvsions*, n.p., 1597. STC 5346.
Lit.: *STC*.

Helwys, Thomas: All of his pre-1640 books were published outside of England without imprint, probably at Amsterdam.
Lit.: *STC*; Simoni.

Hieron, Samuel, *Aarons Bells A-Sovnding*, n.p., 1623, STC 13385.
Comment: Probably at Amsterdam; see Quick, "Icones", life of Hieron.

Hieron, Samuel, *A Defence of the Ministers Reasons*, n.p., 1607, STC 13395.
> Lit.: *STC*; Simoni H111. Comment: Pt. 2 is dated 1608; see Quick,
> "Icones", life of Hieron.

Jacob, Henry: All of his known works were published in the Netherlands,
many by Schilders at Middelburg.

Johnson, Francis. *An Answer to Maister H. Iacob His Defence*, n.p., 1600, STC
14658.
> Lit.: STC; Johnson, 1951. Comment: This appeared before the period of
> the Thorp press. All of Johnson's books prior to 1640 had to be printed
> abroad.

Johnson, Francis, *A Short Treatise Concerning the Exposition of Those Words of
Christ, Tell the Church*, n.p., 1611, STC 14663.
> Lit.: *STC*; Simoni J79. Comment: By this time, Johnson had broken
> with Ainsworth and Thorp, and he needed another printer.

Johnson, George, *A Discourse of Some Troubles and Excommunications in the
Banished English Church at Amsterdam*, Amsterdam, 1603, STC 14664.
> Lit.: *STC*; Moody, "Critical Edition", 1979.

Lightbody, George, *Against the Apple of the Left Eye of Antichrist, or the Masse
Book*, n.p., 1638, STC 15591.5.
> Lit.: *STC*. Comment: Has a Dutch ornament on the title page, the same
> as on no. 664.7.

P., J., *Christs Confession and Complaint, Concerning His Kingdom and Servants*,
n.p., 1629, STC 19069.
> Comment: Perhaps by Stam.

P., J., *Romes Rvin. Or a Treatise of the Certaine Destruction of Rome*, n.p., 1629,
STC 19072.
> Comment: Perhaps by Stam.

Parker, Robert, *A Scholasticall Discovrse against Symbolizing with Antichrist in
Ceremonies, especially in the Signe of the Crosse*, n.p., 1607, STC 19294.
> Lit.: *STC*, which ascribes to Schilders; Simoni P47.

Richards, John (publisher), *The Crowne of a Christian Martyr*, n.p., 1634, STC
21009.5.
> Lit.: *STC*, which ascribes it to J.P. Waelpots, Delft. Comment: Contem-
> porary reports about this book are in BP, I, 171 and SP 84/148/43-44.

Robinson, John, *Of Religious Commvnion Private, & Publique*, n.p., 1614, STC
21115.
> Lit.: *STC*; Simoni R76, which attributes it to Henrick van Haestens of
> Leiden.

Scott, Thomas, *The Workes of the Most Famous and Reverend Divine Mr.
Thomas Scot*, Utrick, 1624, STC 22064.
> Lit.: *STC*; S.L. Adams, "The Protestant Cause", App. III. Comment: A
> voluminous author on political and religious topics; a large part of his

books was printed in the Netherlands and collected into the *Workes*, with false imprints.

Smyth, John (the Se-Baptist): All of his Anabaptist books, after his immigration to Amsterdam, were produced in the Netherlands; several were printed by Schilders; see *STC* and Simoni. Because of his controversial views, the Thorp press was not available to him.

Tel-Troath, Tom, *Tom Tell Troath or a Free Discourse Touching the Manners of the Tyme*, n.p., n.d., STC 23868.

Lit.: *STC*. Comment: Discovered in the Netherlands in the 1620s; see Foster, *Notes*, p. 92. According to George Calvert, Lord Baltimore, it was printed in Holland; see his *The Answer to Tom-Tell-Troth*, p. 23.

INDEX OF PERSONS

INDEX OF SUBJECTS AND PLACES

BRILL'S STUDIES
IN
INTELLECTUAL HISTORY

1. POPKIN, R.H. *Isaac la Peyrère (1596-1676)*. His Life, Work and Influence. 1987. ISBN 90 04 08157 7
2. THOMSON, A. *Barbary and Enlightenment*. European Attitudes towards the Maghreb in the 18th Century. 1987. ISBN 90 04 08273 5
3. DUHEM, P. *Prémices Philosophiques*. With an Introduction in English by S.L. Jaki. 1987. ISBN 90 04 08117 8
4. OUDEMANS, TH.C.W. & A.P.M.H. LARDINOIS. *Tragic Ambiguity*. Anthropology, Philosophy and Sophocles' *Antigone*. 1987. ISBN 90 04 08417 7
5. FRIEDMAN, J.B. (ed.). *John de Foxton's Liber Cosmographiae (1408)*. An Edition and Codicological Study. 1988. ISBN 90 04 08528 9
6. AKKERMAN, F. & A. J. VANDERJAGT (eds.). *Rodolphus Agricola Phrisius, 1444-1485*. Proceedings of the International Conference at the University of Groningen, 28-30 October 1985. 1988. ISBN 90 04 08599 8
7. CRAIG, W.L. *The Problem of Divine Foreknowledge and Future Contingents from Aristotle to Suarez*. 1988. ISBN 90 04 08516 5
8. STROLL, M. *The Jewish Pope*. Ideology and Politics in the Papal Schism of 1130. 1987. ISBN 90 04 08590 4
9. STANESCO, M. *Jeux d'errance du chevalier médiéval*. Aspects ludiques de la fonction guerrière dans la littérature du Moyen Age flamboyant. 1988. ISBN 90 04 08684 6
10. KATZ, D. *Sabbath and Sectarianism in Seventeenth-Century England*. 1988. ISBN 90 04 08754 0
11. LERMOND, L. *The Form of Man*. Human Essence in Spinoza's *Ethic*. 1988. ISBN 90 04 08829 6
12. JONG, M. DE. *In Samuel's Image*. Early Medieval Child Oblation. (in preparation)
13. PYENSON, L. *Empire of Reason*. Exact Sciences in Indonesia, 1840-1940. 1989. ISBN 90 04 08984 5
14. CURLEY, E. & P.-F. MOREAU (eds.). *Spinoza. Issues and Directions*. The Proceedings of the Chicago Spinoza Conference. 1990. ISBN 90 04 09334 6
15. KAPLAN, Y., H. MÉCHOULAN & R.H. POPKIN (eds.). *Menasseh Ben Israel and His World*. 1989. ISBN 90 04 09114 9
16. BOS, A.P. *Cosmic and Meta-Cosmic Theology in Aristotle's Lost Dialogues*. 1989. ISBN 90 04 09155 6
17. KATZ, D.S. & J.I. ISRAEL (eds.). *Sceptics, Millenarians and Jews*. 1990. ISBN 90 04 09160 2
18. DALES, R.C. *Medieval Discussions of the Eternity of the World*. 1990. ISBN 90 04 09215 3
19. CRAIG, W.L. *Divine Foreknowledge and Human Freedom*. The Coherence of Theism: Omniscience. 1991. ISBN 90 04 09250 1
20. OTTEN, W. *The Anthropology of Johannes Scottus Eriugena*. 1991. ISBN 90 04 09302 8
21. ÅKERMAN, S. *Queen Christina of Sweden and Her Circle*. The Transformation of a Seventeenth-Century Philosophical Libertine. 1991. ISBN 90 04 09310 9
22. POPKIN, R.H. *The Third Force in Seventeenth-Century Thought*. 1992. ISBN 90 04 09324 9
23. DALES, R.C & O. ARGERAMI (eds.). *Medieval Latin Texts on the Eternity of the World*. 1990. ISBN 90 04 09376 1

24. STROLL, M. *Symbols as Power*. The Papacy Following the Investiture Contest. 1991. ISBN 90 04 09374 5

25. FARAGO, C.J. *Leonardo da Vinci's 'Paragone'*. A Critical Interpretation with a New Edition of the Text in the *Codex Urbinas*. 1992. ISBN 90 04 09415 6

26. JONES, R. *Learning Arabic in Renaissance Europe*. Forthcoming. ISBN 90 04 09451 2

27. DRIJVERS, J.W. *Helena Augusta*. The Mother of Constantine the Great and the Legend of Her Finding of the True Cross. 1992. ISBN 90 04 09435 0

28. BOUCHER, W.I. *Spinoza in English*. A Bibliography from the Seventeenth Century to the Present. 1991. ISBN 90 04 09499 7

29. McINTOSH, C. *The Rose Cross and the Age of Reason*. Eighteenth-Century Rosicrucianism in Central Europe and its Relationship to the Enlightenment. 1992. ISBN 90 04 09502 0

30. CRAVEN, K. *Jonathan Swift and the Millennium of Madness*. The Information Age in Swift's *A Tale of a Tub*. 1992. ISBN 90 04 09524 1

31. BERKVENS-STEVELINCK, C., H. BOTS, P.G. HOFTIJZER & O.S. LANK-HORST (eds.). *Le Magasin de l'Univers*. *The Dutch Republic as the Centre of the European Book Trade*. Papers Presented at the International Colloquium, held at Wassenaar, 5-7 July 1990. 1992. ISBN 90 04 09493 8

32. GRIFFIN, JR., M.I.J. *Latitudinarianism in the Seventeenth-Century Church of England*. Annoted by R.H. Popkin. Edited by L. Freedman. 1992. ISBN 90 04 09653 1

33. WES, M.A. *Classics in Russia 1700-1855*. Between two Bronze Horsemen. 1992. ISBN 90 04 09664 7

34. BULHOF, I.N. *The Language of Science*. A Study in the Relationship between Literature and Science in the Perspective of a Hermeneutical Ontology. With a Case Study in Darwin's *The Origin of Species*. 1992. ISBN 90 04 09644 2

35. LAURSEN, J.C. *The Politics of Skepticism in the Ancients, Montaigne, Hume and Kant*. 1992. ISBN 90 04 09459 8

36. COHEN, E. *The Crossroads of Justice*. Law and Culture in Late Medieval France. 1993. ISBN 90 04 09569 1

37. POPKIN, R.H. & A.J. VANDERJAGT (eds.). *Scepticism and Irreligion in the Seventeenth and Eighteenth Centuries*. 1993. ISBN 90 04 09596 9

38. MAZZOCCO, A. *Linguistic Theories in Dante and the Humanists*. Studies of Language and Intellectual History in Late Medieval and Early Renaissance Italy. 1993. ISBN 90 04 09702 3

39. KROOK, D. *John Sergeant and His Circle*. A Study of Three Seventeenth-Century English Aristotelians. Edited with an Introduction by B.C. Southgate. 1993. ISBN 90 04 09756 2

40. AKKERMAN, F., G.C. HUISMAN & A.J. VANDERJAGT (eds.). *Wessel Gansfort (1419-1489) and Northern Humanism*. 1993. ISBN 90 04 09857 7

41. COLISH, M.L. *Peter Lombard*. 2 volumes. 1994. ISBN 90 04 09859 3 (Vol. 1), ISBN 90 04 09860 7 (Vol. 2), ISBN 90 04 09861 5 (Set)

42. VAN STRIEN, C.D. *British Travellers in Holland During the Stuart Period*. Edward Browne and John Locke as Tourists in the United Provinces. 1993. ISBN 90 04 09482 2

43. MACK, P. *Renaissance Argument*. Valla and Agricola in the Traditions of Rhetoric and Dialectic. 1993. ISBN 90 04 09879 8

44. DA COSTA, U. *Examination of Pharisaic Traditions*. Supplemented by SEMUEL DA SILVA's *Treatise on the Immortality of the Soul*. Tratado da immortalidade da alma. Translation, Notes and Introduction by H.P. Salomon & I.S.D. Sassoon. 1993. ISBN 90 04 09923 9

45. MANNS, J.W. *Reid and His French Disciples*. Aesthetics and Metaphysics. 1994. ISBN 90 04 09942 5

46. SPRUNGER, K.L. *Trumpets from the Tower*. English Puritan Printing in the Netherlands, 1600-1640. 1994. ISBN 90 04 09935 2

47. RUSSELL, G.A. (ed.). *The 'Arabick' Interest of the Natural Philosophers in Seventeenth-Century England.* 1994. ISBN 90 04 09888 7
48. SPRUIT, L. Species intelligibilis: *From Perception to Knowledge.* Volume I: Classical Roots and Medieval Discussions. 1994. ISBN 90 04 09883 6
49. SPRUIT, L. Species intelligibilis: *From Perception to Knowledge.* Volume II. (in preparation)
50. HYATTE, R. *The Arts of Friendship.* The Literary Idealization of Friendship in Medieval and Early Renaissance Literature. 1994. ISBN 90 04 10018 0
51. CARRÉ, J. (ed.). *The Crisis of Courtesy.* Studies in the Conduct-Book in Britain, 1600-1900. 1994. ISBN 90 04 10005 9
52. BURMAN, T. *Spain's Arab-Christians and Islam, 1050-1200.* 1994. ISBN 90 04 09910 7
53. HORLICK, A.S. *Patricians, Professors, and Public Schools.* The Origins of Modern Educational Thought in America. 1994. ISBN 90 04 10054 7